les presses du réel new york series
Co-published with
The Cultural Services of the French Embassy in the United States

Collection directed by Sophie Claudel, Xavier Douroux, Franck Gautherot

Already published:
Catherine Perret, *Olivier Mosset: Painting, Even*, 2013

Contributions © the individual contributors,
Translations by Timothy Stroud, Patricia Chen, Simon Pleasance, and Helen Boulac
Les presses du réel, 2014

DANSE:
AN
ANTHOLOGY

Edited by Noémie Solomon

les presses du réel ✈ new york series

To Alain Buffard (1960-2013)

Sophie Claudel
Cultural Attaché & Head of the Arts Department

This anthology is the first step of *DANSE*, a project initiated by the Cultural Services of the French Embassy in New York in 2012. *DANSE*'s goal is to give an audible voice to contemporary dance, as an art form but also as a key player in our contemporary world. Drawing from common practices in contemporary art, *DANSE* has been conceived similarly to a museum exhibition: the project includes curatorial and critical tools and an editorial team led by the Québécois scholar Noémie Solomon.

The result of *DANSE* will be the publication of this anthology (February 2014), a 3 week-festival in New York in May 2014, and a catalogue describing what is at stake in contemporary dance to be published in Fall 2014.

DANSE: an anthology edited by Noémie Solomon draws on recent French choreographic creation to offer a reflection on the current international state of affairs of contemporary dance, its dialogue with other art forms, dance's historical position, and its perspectives with respect to contemporary issues affecting society at large.

DANSE's two books are co-published by Les presses du réel and the Cultural Services of the French Embassy and are part of the new collection entitled "Les presses du réel ✈ New York Series." This collection was created to offer perspectives on contemporary culture as a common good.

Contemporary dance offers a different viewpoint on the issues of our time. *DANSE: an anthology* attempts to prove this.

DANSE: an anthology
Edited by Noémie Solomon

INTRODUCTION
Noémie Solomon

> Forming concepts is one way of living, not of killing life;
> it is one way of living in complete mobility and not immobilizing life.
> —Michel Foucault

> When I dance, it means: this is what I am doing.
> —Merce Cunningham

Dance assemblages

DANSE: an anthology gathers key texts written in proximity to choreographic creation after 2000. It traces the ways in which dance has become the site for vital experiments on questions of the body, identity, and belonging; intensifying the historical and geographical conditions of movement in a globalized culture; enacting forceful interventions across regimes of perception and knowledge. Prompted by a series of influential works that have taken place on the French choreographic scene and at its peripheries, *DANSE* maps the numerous exchanges with U.S., European, and more broadly international contemporary dance fields, as they give rise to manifold creative practices and dynamic critical writings.

This volume constructs an anthology as assemblage for dance: a partial and temporary collection of living, mobile bodies in relation to discourse. Here, the Greek roots of "anthology"—from "anthos" referring to flower and "logos" to discourse—as a flower-gathering remind us of the paradoxical dynamics entailed by such a project, as it selects and dissembles life around thresholds of signification and visibility. This is an operation that is never exhaustive or definitive, but calls for shifting relations between the material that is given to be seen and the knowledge it delineates. As Michel Foucault suggests

9

in relation to the formation of concepts, such critical articulations do not stand in opposition to life, or movement, but rather offer "one way of living in complete mobility and not immobilizing life."[1] *DANSE* seeks to move past a tenacious resistance to theorizing dance on the one hand—an idea of dance that runs beside systems of knowledge and power—while at the same time formalizing a series of critical tools implemented by its practices.[2]

This folding together of dance and discourse is instrumental in the choreographic practices examined throughout the anthology. In a letter addressed to the dancer and choreographer Xavier Le Roy in 2002, Myriam Van Imschoot proposes that what distinguishes the practices of some French and European choreographers working from the late 1990s onward from a more "traditional choreographic model" is how they "incorporate critical discourse into [their] practice, thus blurring the boundary between art and its critique."[3] Seen as a forceful instance of what Beatriz Preciado has called a "productive contraband"[4] between experimental practices and critical theory, fostering wide-ranging encounters across artistic and epistemological fields, this mobilization of discourse by dance makers has met fierce resistance on the part of dance institutions. A well-known instance in France can be seen in Dominique Frétard's much-discussed article published in *Le Monde* in May 2003: "The end of the non-dance is announced."[5] Inscribed in bold letters across a full page of the French daily newspaper, this title labels the work of a certain group of dancers and choreographers, while declaring the coming undone of the content they have put forward on the contemporary stage. The article begins with an unequivocal position:

> THEY SHOT at anything that dances, and still are shooting. At the inevitable, repeated figures, the *belle danse*, the effects, the clichés, the déjà-vu, the schools, the techniques,

while trying to build conceptual works where it was primarily about showing a thought in motion. These choreographic artists [...] are neo-existential with a nihilist tendency, sometimes even jokers. But also sermonizers, navel-gazers, quick to exclude.[6]

Frétard's strident statement encapsulates a series of paradoxes in experimental choreography's relations to the discursive apparatus and dance institutions. First, by naming a choreographic movement "non-dance"—as dance's antithesis; that which fails to dance; the absence thereof—the article proposes through its clear oppositions a distinct ontological ground for dance: for what dance *is* and what it should look like. Frétard notes the exhaustion of this symptomatic "refusal to dance" on the choreographic stage, but perhaps most importantly foresees a return of the *"beau mouvement"* as that which is opposed to "showing a thought in motion." Moreover, while declaring the existence of a *non*-movement, the critique nevertheless alludes to its forms as emerging from and belonging to a "self-proclaimed community." This autonomy is seen in a negative light, as that which arises from the use of discourse, while pointing to the ways in which the immanent forms of this "collective" are defined from within, rather than from outside or above. Here, there is a palpable anxiety regarding a community unaccredited by dance institutions: the creative work of its members is seen as an intimacy that troubles the security of stratified identities, through critical experiments that shift relations of power and knowledge across the dance field.

And yet, if what has been described as a "non-dance" poses a threat to dance's integrity, one could argue it is not so much because of the absence of the dance supposedly at stake, but rather because of what these experiments *do* to dance. And indeed, as the texts gathered in this anthology make clear, recent choreographic works have profoundly transformed the scene of theatrical dance by challenging our experience and understanding of movement, embodiment, and time. In particular, one can look at the work by a string of dance artists across the French cultural landscape such as Jérôme Bel, Alain Buffard, Boris Charmatz, Alice Chauchat, Latifa Laâbissi, Xavier Le Roy, Myriam Gourfink, Emmanuelle Huyhn, Jennifer Lacey, Rachid Ouramdane, Claudia Triozzi, Loïc Touzé, to name but a few, to see how they have generated debates around the artistic, methodological, and conceptual nature of dance; its disciplinary borders and epistemological status. By putting forth a range of new forms and contents on the dance stage, by experimenting with alternative modes of composition and address, by creating new articulations with other art forms, as well as with the discursive, social, and political spheres, these works ask us to thoroughly reconsider the role and function of the dancing subject across culture. These projects operate at dance's thresholds, and yet they *do not* fall outside of the dance discipline: rather, through a range of groundbreaking creative and critical practices, they address the very disciplinary mechanisms that have shaped dance—its codes, conventions, vocabularies, logics of representation—while experimenting with new orders, organizations, and assemblages. Here, in retaining the French word *danse* as its title, and through its specific articulation in the English language, the anthology points toward a hybrid enunciation, a certain altering of the discipline of dance itself, as prompted by a series of groundbreaking works.

Scores for the contemporary

The first part of the anthology examines questions of temporality and technique across the surface of the score. In this, dance emerges as a practice of contemporaneity: its experiments at once intensify the present while making persistent articulations toward past and future gestures. The work of the Quatuor Knust is instrumental in this regard. Initiating a series of dance recreations throughout the 1990s, the collective of dancers experimented with the choreographic score as tool, method, question, and perceptive horizon, resolutely addressing dance's heterogeneous time, and reactivating "lines of intensity from the choreographers of an unfinished modernity."[7] Of particular importance were the redoings of Steve Paxton's *Satisfying Lover* (1967) and Yvonne Rainer's *Continuous Project – Altered Daily* (1970) with several contemporary dancers and choreographers as it opened rich perspectives for the field in relation to questions of history and futurity. Here, the score allows dancing bodies to access and experiment with other temporalities, and other narratives, which go beyond the here and now of dance. As the late José Esteban Muñoz argued, there is an actual danger in confining performance to the present since it may structure and lock the experience of minoritarian subjects: to exist only in the present means to have no access to history or futurity. What Muñoz names the "burden of liveness" shadows and relegates subjects to the live event and may "evacuate such personages from history."[8] In this light, one can see the Quatuor Knust's notational practices figuring a political urgency on the French dance scene and beyond, enacting an affective call for experimentation that "looks into the past to critique the present and helps imagine the future."[9]

If the appellation of "contemporary dance" intensifies the experience of the moment, it does so "using that moment to reveal a different history," as Bojana Kunst reminds us.[10] In France, specifically, one can locate the emergence of the broad category of contemporary dance at the beginning of the 1980s, when a vast program for the promotion and regulation of dance creation was launched.[11] Throughout the following decade, dance underwent a period of significant expansion, both through the proliferation and dissemination of its forms. Indeed, via a major process of decentralization, a number of institutional structures, the Centres chorégraphiques nationaux, were established throughout the territory, each directed by a given choreographer in charge of creating, presenting, and transmitting movement practices. As dance gained considerable visibility across the French cultural landscape, it unfolded in diverse aesthetics. Contemporary dance throughout the eighties was characterized by multiple and deeply singular languages developed by a range of choreographers. Coined *nouvelle danse française* or *danse d'auteur*, these practices call attention to the preponderant role of the choreographer as an author of the dance work, while putting emphasis on stylistic and formal issues. If the poetic potential of the dancing body constitutes a recurrent motif of this work, the abundant gestures displayed on stage can be mapped as expressions of an individual, interior body intimately guided by the choreographer.[12] The prosperous *danse d'auteur* therefore figured an authorial and institutional ground for contemporary dance in France, promoting dance as an autonomous art form, delimited by a series of self-reflexive gestures.

If contemporary dance's early developments in France can be seen as carving out new artistic territories for dance creation at the dusk of the twentieth century, moving away from the conventional codes and vocabularies proper to classical dance, this institutionalization rapidly lead to new forms of normalization. Those effects can be seen in the standardization of a range of aspects across the choreographic field: the performances' format and scheduled touring; the internal organization of the companies; the training methods and the growing imperative to produce highly skilled, versatile dancers—a new form of contemporary virtuosity; and the hierarchies between the different actors of the field. In reaction to this homogenization, a range of artists, many of whom worked as dancers in major French companies during the eighties, responded with a series of critical gestures that emphasized the work of the dancer in relation to diverse aspects of contemporary society, thus challenging the self-reflective nature of the newly established form and its constitutive power relations. The work discussed throughout the anthology describes a field which simultaneously articulates dance with a broader set of current artistic, social, and political concerns, while calling attention to the labor of the dancing body as temporal matter—as that which paces, sustains, repeats, dilates, interrupts, and alters the dance work. It is precisely this examination of the definition and imperatives of "a work," its recasting within the conditions of labor and cultural production in late capitalist societies, that comes to pre-occupy contemporary dance. Dance stands simultaneously as emblematic of and resistant to "perverse capitalism," in Boyan Manchev's words, through its experimental praxis of transformation of the body.[13]

From this perspective, the works approached in this anthology might be seen as exemplary of the second wave of contemporary dance practices that surfaced from the mid-nineteen-nineties onward. By exploring the margins of institutional structures; creating disruptive intersections between the role of the choreographer, the dancer, and the spectator; experimenting with the dancing body in close relation with issues of history, modernity, and contemporaneity, these practices weave a consistent, open, and active field for dance experimentations.[14] Extensive collaborative energies are characteristic of the contemporary dance scene. Drawing from a series of affective exchanges between artists, research objects, methodologies, and discourses, this anthology traces the movement of contemporary dance beyond French borders as it engages with artistic creation throughout the European territory. Sharing similarities and differences, artists have gathered in collectives in order to create multiple performance projects, claim better working conditions, or foster discursive and critical lines of activity.[15] Describing these nomadic phenomena across the European field,

Christophe Wavelet speaks of the imperative of "temporary coalitions."[16] As phenomena that resist categorization, any single identity that would "fix that which precisely devotes itself to restlessness," these practices form fluid, and ever shifting assemblages: provisional encounters that map incessant re-combinations of movements, ideas, practices, and thoughts.[17] In this light *DANSE* develops a critical evaluation of contemporary dance not only as it pertains to a specific time period and a geographical territory, but also in the ways in which it establishes connections and linkages across different times and spaces through their singularities—defined by Gilles Deleuze as "that which can be extended close to another, so as to obtain a connection."[18] One might understand the "contemporary" then as a structure of time that draws connections with other choreographic acts and maps the particularities of movement dynamics and their ethos. In this regard, the very appellation of French contemporary dance requires examination through its diasporic gestures, in which the many exchanges with an American scene have been determining, through the aesthetic influences of Modern and postmodern dance, to Cunningham's work and recent experimentations. The anthology thus traces a genealogy—a history made of ruptures and discontinuities—of the works of contemporary French choreographers across the European stage and toward an U.S. and international scene, while refiguring the contours of such a category of "contemporary dance." The contemporary therefore emerges in Roland Barthes' words as that which is necessarily "untimely": a time that adheres to yet shifts the unfolding of the present; it is at once consistent with our time while being inherently anachronistic.[19] Different choreographic experiments examined in this anthology expose the concept of the contemporary, and yet draw disconnections with the present: as they perform a series of temporal gaps, overlaps, and disjunctions to unwork normative structures, nominations, and experiences of our times.

Writing the choreographic

The second part of *DANSE* explores the relation between dancing and writing, meaning and affect, gathering texts by critics, scholars, curators, and artists that address the complex, shifting ways in which the dancing body intersects with sense. As Yvane Chapuis suggests, "there seems to be a very widespread idea at work whereby dance is considered inexpressible—some would say it cannot be recounted—and yet, paradoxically, gives rise to words."[20] This tension between dance's unspeakable gestures on the one hand and its ability to invent languages on the other opens up a space to re-imagine the potentials of and relations between regimes of perception and knowledge. What are the words—and the worlds—figured by contemporary dance? What do they look and feel like? How do they point toward heterogeneous gestures and prompt shifting meanings? Here, writing the choreographic maps affective encounters, as words meet a string of gestures, images, sensations, memories. In this respect, Jenn Joy describes the choreographic as a "sensual address": "it is a mode of working against linguistic signification and virtuosic representation; it is work about contact that touches even across distances."[21] The singular modality of relation thus entailed by the choreographic outlines a different, renewed ethics for writing and dancing bodies. In his manifesto imagining "the perfect dance critic," Miguel Gutierrez reminds us of the stakes in writing on and with contemporary dance, a practice that must engage with the language of dance and its materiality, and "speculate as to what the choices of movement vocabulary mean in relation to [...] the larger vision that the dance artist offers."[22]

Discussing semiotics, translation, and performativity, the texts outline the dancing body as abstraction and complexity, without attempting to connect its gestures to a narrative or psychological content: they apprehend the choreographic field as it builds an incorporeal plane for meaning. As Brian Massumi writes in *Parables for the Virtual*, "The problem with dominant models [...] is not that they are too abstract to grasp the concreteness of the real. The problem is that they are not *abstract enough* to grasp the real incorporeality of the concrete."[23] As an alternative to dominant models of subjectivity, what choreographic writing proposes within contemporary culture is to dwell on the moving body that exposes the real, material, yet abstract complexity of the world. In this way, the writings in the anthology move resolutely beyond an opposition between movement and language: it is here a matter of renewing our attention to the multiple ways in which dancing bodies press upon and fold meanings. If, as Maurice Merleau-Ponty teaches us, the moving and sensing body is always already linguistic, one cannot grasp a gesture by isolating it from the ways in which it relates to meaning: "the meaning of a gesture thus 'understood' is not behind it, it is intermingled with the structure of the world outlined by the gesture."[24] Dance is not that which is unaccountable for, nor is it that which has the potential to stand for everything and everyone. Hence, to speak of choreographic writing is not to say the dancer functions as a metaphor for reality—or for thought. The dancing body that emerges is autonomous, simultaneously shaped by languages while pushing against the boundaries and structures of meaning.

Across the work of translation—moving back and forth from dance to writing, French to English languages—a few words require our attention. "*Dispositif*" appears throughout the anthology to refer to the conditions set up by choreographic works as well as the heterogeneous assemblages they perform. Here, the use the word "*dispositif*" over its common English translation "apparatus" is instrumental: not only does "apparatus" seem to underscore the mechanical and totalizing aspect of the term at the expense of that which is proper to a "disposition"—both as arrangement and tendency—but it also emphasizes the initial, firm conditions set up by a machinery—the Latin etymology of "apparatus" indeed refers to "preparation," "to make ready for"—thus somewhat overlooking the agency or possible trajectories of its many constituents.[25] The term *dispositif* might be described after Foucault as a "thoroughly heterogeneous ensemble" composed of a range of elements such as institutions, scientific statements, administrative measures, philosophical propositions, moral conducts.[26] As a coordinated assemblage of diverse functions and processes, Foucault argues, "the *dispositif* itself *is* the system of relations that can be established between these elements."[27] What is at stake in the concept of *dispositif* is thus a mobile, transversal thought that accounts for many singular choreographic acts and their potential for building heterogeneous, modular assemblages. "Écriture chorégraphique" is another expression often used in the French dance literature to designate processes of composition while alluding to the writing metaphor. This of course evokes the score, and further the activity of reading as integral to the making and perceiving of a dance performance. Furthermore, the dancer is traditionally referred to as *interprète*—the one who interprets the choreographer's score. In the anthology, the word performer has been used, especially when referring to experimental practices, where the dancer emerges as a powerful agent who not only embodies the dance work, but moves from a muted position to create words and discourses.[28] Finally, the word "performance" has been used from the late 1990s onward to describe the experimental practices taking place on the choreographic scene and at its limits. Not exclusively connected to "performance art," nor as broadly indeterminate as "the performing arts," performance can here be read as a genre in itself that keeps gesturing toward other aesthetic traditions. Laurent Goumarre uses "perfo-dance" to render explicit this hybrid gesture.[29] In a similar vein, the question of "the performative" appears in French literature, sometimes to echo performativity (with reference to Judith Butler's theories as in Chapuis' and Alexandra Baudelot's texts). But it also emerges as an adjective to describe these new experimentations: as a quality of their affects and of the materiality of their languages.

Practices of exteriority

The third and final section of the anthology maps the movement of dance toward its outside. In this motion, dance gestures *away from* disciplinary formations, unraveling a series of objectified bodies, meanings, artworks, and histories; and moves *toward* broad areas of life, engaging in mobile articulations with artistic, political, and epistemological fields. One might follow these unruly interdisciplinary acts as they venture through various spaces, and assemble ideas, bodies, and things in order to assess and reinvent the roles and functions of the dancing body across contemporary cultures. In a text from 2001, Chantal Pontbriand proposes that "contemporary dance is dance that stretches outward, that has expanded."[30] The work of Boris Charmatz is emblematic in this regard: through the many trajectories enacted by *Le Musée de la danse*, their distinctive critical velocities and incorporeal virtuosities, the dance artist invents the conditions for "getting rid" of choreographic borders—see for instance his manifesto that prompts the removal of the words "center," "choreographic," and "national"—and meets foreign practices, thoughts, methodologies. Here, the dancing museum is outlined through and as the actions of the performing body; such a structure is as far-reaching as it is immediate, it "exists as soon as the first gesture is performed."[31] And indeed, for Charmatz, "dance should be a practice of investment in all that a body can touch,"[32] spanning everyday and minor gestures to broad interdisciplinary and political actions.

As witnessed recently, one space dance has ventured toward is that of the museum, functioning in turn as the newest desirable art object, or engaging in practices that re-imagine how things and bodies are assessed around thresholds of visibility and knowledge in such institutions. And yet, despite keen interest and increased visibility, "dance will always be on the outside," as Ralph Lemon suggests.[33] Remaining on the outside, at the threshold, dance's practices of exposition can address diverse issues. This engagement can be seen through the notion of *en-dehors* as an ontological and ethical impulse, an outward, immanent motion which entails a constant negotiation and redefinition of a body's borders. As a constitutive technology of the choreographic discipline that shapes the dancing body and its conditions of visibility, the *en-dehors* can expose—as Jean-Luc Nancy reminds us, "pose in exteriority"[34]—the work of the dancing body in a generative proximity with its outside. *DANSE* maps the ways in which these experimentations turn the tightly defined choreographic discipline inside out (a discipline that has traditionally be confined to a triangulation between the body, the studio, and the stage). Here, the affective force of dance resides in its enfolding of intensive choreographic gestures that always point to a series of "foreign" elements, outlining an experimental praxis that is based upon propositions for differences, variations, and metamorphoses. As the danced gesture reaches toward its surrounding and folds it upon itself, simultaneously incorporating the world while stretching its contours inside out, it expressively shapes an intensive outside and thus delineates new possibilities of existing through dance acts. Or, as Burrows says: "It is about what happens when the score fails, when the structure implodes, when the idea gets lost in its own dead-ends, as all scores, structures and ideas must, and then the limit is reached and the world expands."[35]

[1] Michel Foucault, "Introduction" to *The Normal and the Pathological*, by Georges Canguilhem (New York: Zone Books, [1966] 1989), 21.

[2] This articulation of text and movement in the anthology might be seen in relation to the seminal *Chorégraphie* (1700), which arguably marks the birth of the western disciplinary project of dance. Responding to the royal demand of codifying dance, Raoul-Augé Feuillet coins the term "choreography" as the binding of writing and dance in light of the Baroque's propensity to motion. Choreographic bodies thus emerge through the affective and energetic encounters between techniques of moving and writing, grounding dancing acts in their discursive materiality. Another genealogy might be traced back in the experimental work of Fluxus, or in that of the American poet Jackson Mac Low, which experiments with the creative potential of the anthology—a collection of lists, poems, syllables, images, calling for readings, saying, movements. In other words, the anthology emerges as a score to be performed. See Raoul-Augé Feuillet, *Chorégraphie ou L'Art de Décrire la Danse par Caracteres, Figures et Signes Desmonstratifs, Avec lesquels on apprend facilement soy même toutes sortes de Dances* (Paris, 1700); La Monte Young and Jackson Mac Low eds., *An Anthology of Chance Operations* (New York, 1963); or Jackson Mac Low's 1978 performance *An Anthology*, http://vimeo.com/21575024

[3] Myriam Van Imschoot, "Lettres sur la collaboration," in *Être Ensemble. Figures de la communautée en danse depuis le XXᵉ siècle* (Pantin: Centre national de la danse, 2003), 362.

[4] Beatriz Preciado, *Manifeste contra-sexuel* (Paris: Balland, 2000).

[5] Dominique Frétard, "La fin annoncée de la non-danse," *Le Monde*, May 6, 2003.

[6] Dominique Frétard, "La fin annoncée de la non-danse."

[7] Dominique Brun, "Le Quatuor Albrecht Knust," *DANSE: an anthology*, 29.

[8] José Esteban Muñoz, *Disidentifications: Queers of Color and the Performance of Politics* (Minneapolis: University of Minnesota Press, 1999), 198.

[9] Muñoz, *Disidentifications*, 25.

[10] Bojana Kunst, "Subversion of the Dancing Body: Autonomy on Display," *DANSE: an anthology*, 61.

[11] It should be noted that modern dance was not significantly established in France, in contrast with the scenes in Germany and the U.S. The sudden and extensive institution of contemporary dance at the beginning of the eighties thus bridged a century of aesthetic developments. For more on the singularity of French dance history and its relation to modernity, see Michelle Marcel and Isabelle Ginot, *La Danse au XXᵉ siècle* (Paris: Bordas, 1995); Agnès Izrine, *La danse dans tous ses états* (Paris: L'Arche, 2002); and Denise Luccioni's "Avant-Propos" in her translation of Sally Banes' opus, *Terspichore en baskets, post-modern dance* (Paris: Chiron and Centre national de la danse, 2002).

[12] One might read the appellation of *danse d'auteur* in relation to the well-known French *cinéma d'auteur*, which also emphasizes introspection and interiority, foregrounding the author of the work, through the subtly controlled play of its actors.

[13] Boyan Manchev, "Dance, the Metamorphosis of the Body," *DANSE: an anthology*, 128.

[14] Many of these works draw from various traditions of dance, breaking with the recent aesthetics and methodologies constitutive of French dance in the nineteen-eighties. As such, one could trace diverse influences such as the choreographer Merce Cunningham; the actors of the American Postmodern dance, including Yvonne Rainer, Trisha Brown, and Steve Paxton; the *Tanztheater* of Pina Bausch; and the Japanese Butoh dance.

[15] See for instance the collective of Les Signataires du XX août, which first gathered in 1997. For

more on this group, see Coralie Bougier, "Le regroupement et l'engagement politique des artistes chorégraphiques: une nécessité?" *Funambule. Revue de danse* 4 (June 2002): 47-60.

[16] Christophe Wavelet, "Ici et maintenant, coalitions temporaires," *Mouvement* 2 (September-November 1998): 18-21.

[17] Wavelet, "Ici et maintenant, coalitions temporaires."

[18] Gilles Deleuze, "A philosophical concept," in *Who Comes After the Subject?* ed. Eduardo Cadava, Peter Connor, and Jean-Luc Nancy (New York; London: Routledge, 1991), 94.

[19] "Le contemporain est l'inactuel." The author further argues: "History is repressive, History forbids us to be untimely." See Roland Barthes, *Œuvres Complètes* (Paris: Seuil, 2002). Barthes draws on Friedrich Nietzsche's *Untimely Meditations*, trans. R.J. Hollingdale (Cambridge, UK: Cambridge University Press, [1876] 1997).

[20] Yvane Chapuis, "Toward a Critical Reading of Contemporary Dance," *DANSE: an anthology*, 139.

[21] Jenn Joy, *The Choreographic* (Cambridge: MIT Press, forthcoming).

[22] Miguel Gutierrez, "The Perfect Dance Critic," *DANSE: an anthology*, 173.

[23] Brian Massumi, *Parables for the Virtual: Movement, Affect, Sensation* (Durham: Duke University Press, 2002), 5.

[24] Maurice Merleau-Ponty, *Phenomenology of Perception*, trans. Colin Smith (London; New York: Routledge, [1945] 2002), 216.

[25] Here the distinction between the terms *dispositif* and *appareil* in film and cinema studies might be particularly enlightening. Jean-Louis Baudry has defined the *appareil de départ* as the sum of equipments and operations necessary to the production of a movie and its screening, whereas the *dispositif* concerns the screening and thus involves the subject to which the screening is addressed. See Jean-Louis Baudry, *L'effet Cinéma* (Paris: Albatros, 1978), 31.

[26] Foucault, "The Confession of the Flesh," in *Power/Knowledge: Selected Interviews and Other Writings 1972-1977*, ed. Colin Gordon (London: Harvester, [1977] 1980), 194.

[27] Foucault, "The Confession of the Flesh," 194.

[28] For a singular account on the creation of a narrative for the contemporary dancer, see Énora Rivière, *Ob.scène. Récit fictif d'une vie de danseur* (Pantin: Centre national de la danse, 2013).

[29] Laurent Goumarre, "Disobedience and DIY," *DANSE: an anthology*, 279.

[30] Chantal Pontbriand, "Expanded Dance," *DANSE: an anthology*, 286.

[31] Boris Charmatz, "Manifesto for a Dancing Museum," *DANSE: an anthology*, 239.

[32] Boris Charmatz, with Alexandra Baudelot, "Des formes ouvertes et malléables," *Mouvement* 16 (Avril–Juin 2002): 57. "La danse devrait être une pratique d'investissement de tout ce à quoi le corps peut toucher."

[33] Ralph Lemon, quoted in Mark Franko, "Boris Charmatz at MoMA," http://www.jampole.com/OpEdgy/?p=231

[34] Jean-Luc Nancy, *The Inoperative Community*, trans. Peter Connor and al. (Minneapolis: University of Minnesota Press, [1982] 1991); xxxvii.

[35] Jonathan Burrows, "Rebelling Against Limit," *DANSE: an anthology*, 86.

I.

TIMES
SCORES
TECHNIQUES

LE QUATUOR ALBRECHT KNUST[1]

Dominique Brun, Anne Collod, Simon Hecquet, Christophe Wavelet

After an interview with Yvane Chapuis

Simon Hecquet: The birth of the Quatuor is linked to an experiment in recreating a duo by Kurt Jooss, entitled *Märtzlied*, undertaken by Anne and I as part of our final exam for Laban cinetography in Jacqueline Challet-Hass' class at the conservatoire of La Villette in Paris. We invited Christophe Wavelet and Dominique Brun to join us for this project. No film exists of Kurt Jooss's duet; no trace other than Knust's score, written the same year as the duet was created. We had to reinvent this dance in another time, another space, in other bodies, knowing that none of us had been through the school in Essen where the piece was created in 1953. The pleasure that we gained from performing this work and our interest in the questions the use of the score raised made us want to continue further.

Christophe Wavelet: At once an inscriptive and prescriptive device, each choreographic score is above all a text that requires the work of reading. As we moved further in our practice, we had to problematize, specify, and complexify the modalities of this work, which involves behaviors that are jointly kinaesthetic, cognitive, and discursive. We were proposing to open up a space of questioning that seemed at first rather simple: what constitutes the process of transcribing movement and danced gestures? To which project and to which form of necessity does it answer? What are its conditions of possibility? What does it presuppose or imply? What does it allow and what does it exclude? Even though the transcription of choreography within a system of notation will do justice to all of its constitutive features, it will nevertheless fail to bring back what relates to the subjective investment of each dancer, without which no dance can happen. Each score thus restores the choreographic dimension of a work, but not its conditions of emergence or the dance itself (which is the act and its actuality). And yet, our project aimed less toward the score as an object of analysis than as a vector of experiences and spawning of possibilities.

Anne Collod: As a contemporary dancer, trained late and mainly in the Cunningham technique, I had been through a number of diverse experiences with movement. They were influential for me and formed the basis for this new experience to unfold: experiences that involved interpreting/performing choreographic scores, in collaboration with other dancers coming from various backgrounds. Interpreting choreographic scores, in other words recreating movement from dance texts, considerably changed my previous perspective: it was no longer a question of trying to find a personal movement at the service of a choreographer's project, but on the contrary it was about looking for a way to give birth to a new danced movement from a completely different position that escaped the traditional relationship between dancer and choreographer. From that moment, a field of freedom and of questioning opened up with regards to my status as a performer. For even if the text defines a certain number of constraints, they are no longer played out in terms of a relation of subjection by another person, a relationship that is always difficult to problematize. Faced with a score, along with other dancers, in what way was I—were we— to become the performers? What was to become of the role usually played by the "choreographer"? So many questions that allowed me to think the issue of interpretation in dance anew, away from biased terms and hierarchies. As a result, this enabled the generic names of "choreographer" and "performer" to be problematized in fruitful ways.

CW: The relational mode we adopted from our first meeting enabled us to put forward and enact an equal relationship; in other words, a co-responsibility for our artistic choices in the dynamics of a conversation made up of dialogues and debates that shaped our common experience. A politics of friendship was therefore created, which spread to other artists who joined us on different projects: Boris Charmatz, Eve Couturier, Matthieu Doze, Yves Godin, Emmanuelle Huynh, Jennifer Lacey, Laurence Louppe, Martha Moore, Pascal Quéneau, Laurence Rondoni, Jean-Jacques Palix, Jean-Christophe Paré, Cécile Proust, Loïc Touzé, and a few others. Retrospectively, I would say that it is precisely thanks to this exercise of equality, and sometimes thanks to its ordeal—let's avoid useless optimism—that the experience undertaken by the Quatuor over these eight years was so enlivening and fruitful in my eyes.

AC: I began to understand how important it was for my dance practice to reactivate pieces that we would never have been confronted with otherwise.

Dominique Brun: The work of the Quatuor consisted of numerous, intense intellectual discussions, part of the physical and psychical work that we called "the lines of intensity from the choreographers of an unfinished modernity," of which we felt we were "both the trustees and the heirs."

CW: We had the feeling that we were part of a generation of amnesic dancers for whom the relationship with history (artistic practices or projects), as well as the relationship with memory and transmission, was not sufficiently problematized. On the one hand, there was this "ideal sky" in which some names floated to fetishize (Graham, Wigman, Humphrey, Limon, Nikolaïs, Cunningham, Bausch, …) according to a teleological conception of history. On the other hand, its consequence: a denial of the questions bequeathed by the activities and projects of those same names. History should no longer remain a dead continent whose object is seen to exist in a state of eternal renewal or as an eternal native state. We shared this necessity to confront ourselves with history, without really knowing what that meant, but to confront it in a concrete way. In other words to confront ourselves with works through a choreographic act, which, like all human activity in general and artistic activity more particularly, prompts questions and thoughts. We wanted to put an end to this hierarchization of discourse and gestures from which we, as so many others, had suffered for so long. We were not heaven sent and knew that we had, as had everyone, been through different processes of institutionalized learning—family, school, artistic learning, etc. Among other things, it was with regard to these "learned experiences" that we wanted to engage a critical work by re-examining different assumptions linked to what constitutes us as subjects, as "dancers." That is what we set about doing, and most of the time with a great deal of joy...

SH: We decided to take on different choreographic projects that we considered important in view of what could be described as contemporary dance's specific conditions of emergence. So we began with notational elements, in other words, documents of a particular kind and status, unusual in dance, which, unlike the musical field, is a field lacking a written tradition. A score is a vector of transmission that articulates the testimony of an event and a protocol of action that must be *interpreted* and not *applied*. But to which events do the scores attest? Even when the authors themselves make them, as was the case for the *Faune* written by Nijinski in 1915, the question still remains. For a map is not the territory, and writing is not the thing itself. In other words, the abstract representation offered by notation does not in any way deliver a reality that could be fantasized like the work itself. What it offers, quite precisely, are the conditions of possibility for a version of the work; for a translation that it realizes by recreating it. The notation therefore emphasizes (and in a way this mobilizes thinking in dance in a forceful way) the dimension of interpretation. Furthermore, we were concerned, as much as possible, with understanding the context of the emergence of the pieces we were attached to in order to detect how they had caused a rupture. These are questions that were and still are an open field for us.

DB: We engaged in numerous experiences with the dance score, which often seems to involve an act of "diving." Reading a notation always promises to be like an upside down horizon. We do not read to levitate toward dance's aerial spheres but rather to sink, to perish in the sea of signs. We have to face the obvious, whether we are turning to or returning to the score. The signs do not always make a sign to us even if something appears to be held within their path. This presence that stands there in an "uncanny" way acts as a "closed certainty."[2] It distracts our apprehension of the sign—in both senses of the word "apprehension": the act of taking as well as the notion of anxiety—avoiding, through this feeling of uncanny familiarity, an overly painful confrontation with the *emptiness* that the signs evoke. However, this *emptiness* insistently takes the form of a polymorphic question, whispered and locked within its form. This question could be asked in the following way: if the notation's signs act as a guarantee for the fullness of a shape—the obvious susceptibility to volume that they hold—do they not just as much summon up *emptiness* like the clay vase turning in the potter's hands around *nothing*? Admittedly the signs are an injunction to see, a promise of dance. But they also show themselves in scores as "emptied" of the presence of movement. They indicate movement's absence. If movement has indeed taken place, by seeing the sign we know that it is no longer there. The only remaining trace is this mark on the whiteness of the paper that deposits the movements in a "lost and found," sometimes even like bodies in a morgue. By denying this tomb-like dimension of the sign, the reader that I am lets herself be enticed into idealizing them. She gives in to a sort of fascination with the numbered and checked space-times that the movements were encoded with at the time they were registered, before being read. The reader attempts, in a crazy, fantastical way, to extract a faultless movement from them. By staring at the score, the reader only sees doubt. She *doubts,* time and again faced with the permanency of the sign, faced with its coldness, its discoloration, its silent opacity.

And yet, a few moments appear when the "closed certainties" of the signs stop outbidding their existence with the test of doubt. Dance allows itself to be glimpsed through the great escape of the body. And the reader—unwillingly—closes the score to go and look outside. So she abandons the tautological injunction of the sign in order to build on the incomplete accounts of memory that she has and that drive her by default. Like the signs, "the stories have no function besides that of suggesting materials for doubt"; they work like "fragments of memory, to be dissolved."[3] So the one who starts moving, even if she loses her place as a reader, wins the echo of her memory, which tells her where it happens, how it happens, how it sings within her and "it"— in other words, the occurrence of the sign's immediate memory adjoins to her deep memory as a subject—allows her to stir the air, to produce nothingness. Sometimes, after what seems to be a sterile exercise, something surreptitiously erupts and becomes a kinesthetic sensation. We don't quite know how it happened and yet we think that the movement is, or rather was, there. Because we felt something, we understand that we have freed ourselves from the grip of the sign, and we can then turn back to it as we would to a place of grief, but also of rest. This is how the mark of writing down movement asserts itself—as if prompting someone who doesn't know how to answer the question— at the risk, for the one who starts dancing, of making a mistake.

AC: Yvonne Rainer's project *Continuous Project – Altered Daily* (1969-70) was decisive. That experience forced us to consider our work with recreation differently, in particular because the choreographic materials used in the piece had taken on a very special and very new status in the dance field. The score we were facing did not outline a work with defined contours, but rather a precise but minimal protocol of actions and tasks to be put to work. The "work" therefore appeared to be the more or less random result of a set of rules. The combination of materials was not defined once and for all and could be drawn randomly. In fact we began by trying to elaborate coherent "*grids*" in order to combine these different materials in the best way possible, and then we ended up deriving their order of appearance at the beginning of each performance. This of course committed, in radical terms, each performer's presence and responsibility. Because the impossibility to anticipate requires one's maximum availability in the face of whatever happens. It also relied on the re-initiating character of every event of alteration, entrusted, as they were through this method, to the hazards of surprise. The material of *CP – AD* are extremely varied by nature. There are simple actions, such as manipulating objects (cushions, a screen) and also manipulating the body of another (the body itself becoming an object). The dancers could also import materials from experiences with other choreographers. Likewise there was the possibility of inventing choreographic fragments on site and passing them on, which meant rehearsing a rough sequence in public, in other words to be doing the work of rehearsal such as we know it as dancers in the studio. Here the will to question the limits of the spectacular form, such as it was conceived at the time, was at work. It is a way to conjure up what is "off-stage" and to call into question the instituted hierarchy of the choreographic piece, according to which only a completely controlled object can be presented publicly. What about the status and the value of the generally concealed work that is left in a hidden space? These questions take on their full meaning from the moment that it is not so much the finished product but the process at work that is questioned. Thus the materials of *CP – AD* constitute different strata of sensory experiences dedicated to questioning the dancer's practices. The body of the work also asks usually forgotten questions about the interactions and interrelations between participants in a project, in other words all the exchanges outside of movement, taking verbal or some other form. For example, Yvonne Rainer made an inventory of a group of letters that she sent to her dancers, which are, for her, as much materials of the work as the rest. Such practices generate a crisis for the status of authority, for the place of the choreographer. In other words, who contributes to developing the work? To what extent does the presence of the participants modify the instructions prompted by, in this instance, the choreographer? The complex game of human relations that takes place in any project, in any choreographic work, was displayed here in an explicit way.

SH: There are also some texts among the original material of *CP – AD*. Laurence Louppe, who was until recently the reader in the work, questioned the function of these texts through her way of making them heard in a surprising dialogue with Eve Couturier, or with Jean-Jacques Palix, who mixes on turntables the musical material that we introduce into our version of *CP – AD*. These texts—which are heard like musical materials but in a slightly different way, since sound materials purposefully belong to a shared musical field (the Beatles for example)—are not without relation to what is seen. And yet they are not commentaries. They are often texts linked to cinema, texts from Buster Keaton or Louise Brooks, that dismantle the effects produced by the cinematographic machine. What makes an emotion for example? Very precise things, like the positioning of the camera in relation to the actor. During the last iteration of *CP – AD*, Sabine Prokhoris, who took over for Laurence as the reader, again brought the status of the texts into question. Yvonne Rainer indicates that they should intervene by being read like quotes, which implies that the name of the author should be mentioned. However these are not quotes in the academic sense, affording an element of legitimacy to the work. Our discussions with Sabine allowed us to underline the special status of the quote, in other words to introduce a heterogeneous element into the movement of the work's production. Yvonne Rainer says that this (textual) material does not work, and yet she is nevertheless attached to it. Is this not precisely because it does not work, in other words that it works as a vector of alteration, or that it takes on a function of disruption?

AC: And as with all quotes, the disruption created by these texts is formed by the intrusion of a space, a time, a thought other than the one made at that moment in a given place.

SH: In the work of recreating *CP – AD*, we have used other texts, in particular Beckett or texts linked to the current events of the time. It's a story that has not stopped moving. Beside, the project as it was conceived by Yvonne Rainer included this dimension of alteration. It can constantly be reconfigured and the effects it bears remain active far beyond the time when it first existed. In fact, the recreation by Quatuor is one of the unpredictable figures of this alteration.

CW: The relation we have undertaken with history has not stopped changing. We could not have presented *"… d'un faune" (éclats)*— Quatuor's third and ultimate project—if we had not understood that all historical material is liable to interpretation, and that every artistic project, past or present, is in itself already the result of an interpretation. Our preliminary research freed us from the ideological fantasy of the origin or original that animates conservative and legacy discourses on "reconstruction" in dance. And the extraordinary practice of freedom made possible by the collective experience resulting from Yvonne Rainer's *CP – AD* forced us, by using different methods, to continue exploring the questions and ways of doing that it had initiated. In this sense, taking an interest in *L'Après-midi d'un faune* was taking an interest initially in a heterogeneous and polyphonic space. We decided to work with three versions of the faune: Mallarmé's poem, as well as Debussy's and Nijinski's scores. We also closely examined their respective geneses and the stories around their receptions.

SH: By comparing certain remarks from Nijinski, related by the press of the time, with indications given in his sister Bronislava's memoirs, we noticed, for example, that Nijinski shifted the shared boundary between choreographic writing and interpretation. At the beginning of the 20th century in Russia, the only choreographic elements that dancers had to respect were paths and intentions, as was already the case in classical ballet. So dancers at that time worked on their interpretations by themselves. In contrast, Nijinski detailed each gesture, modifying the notion of movement's orchestration. Drawing a parallel with the musical field, he specifies that at no one moment can a musician allow himself to change a note on the grounds that it would sound better to the public. Thus Nijinski reconfigures the field of the choreographer's intervention and at the same time the possibilities for the dancer. However the score gives us no information about these specifications.

CW: Nijinski is one of the names through which modernity in dance found itself spawned. The world's imagination found itself modified. We see a critical tradition emerge in art where the work problematizes its own conditions of possibility. How could we argue this aesthetic choice? By entrusting dancers, with a diverse and slightly different kinaesthetic culture from so-called "ballet" dancers, with the duty of performing this dance, and each time presenting not one but three quite distinct and successive versions, we were already opting for an explicitly critical work of gaps and differences. It was also an opportunity to offer this dance a different poetic intensity. It should be remembered that when "great repertory companies" program so-called "historical" pieces in their calendar every year, the implicit discourse underlying these initiatives aims above all to validate certain types of ideology. Under the cover of "tradition," history is held to this ideology, not as a question, but, in a fantastical way, as a response: a magical and unalterable source into which we can simply dip. That is forgetting a little too quickly that the historicity of practices and techniques, in dance and elsewhere, is incompatible with such a fixed ideal and that if there is any artistic tradition, it can only be discontinuous. As Benjamin reminds us, "every image of the past that is not recognized by the present as one of its own concerns threatens to disappear irretrievably."[4] Relating to history as a question therefore consisted of first considering it as a concatenation of narrative regimes and ways of doing, an assemblage of statements and actions, concepts and affects, processes of mutation, transformation or rupture, that could only be considered from a present. And if *l'Après-midi d'un faune* was indeed the name of a triple event of artistic modernity, it was appropriate not to lose sight of what an event is: less homogenous than heterogeneous, less order than disorder, of which the structure, as Arlette Farge reminds us, "in itself already forges relations": "it is not given, and its way of being seen, spoken, communicated, differed, projected, imagined, is part of its essence, by disseminating around it an infinity of meanings." This dissemination and its effects were our starting point.

AC: Referring to dance history, the discourse is always developed from the outside and rarely from the dancer's experience of movement. We thought it important to be able to talk from the position of someone who dances. The relation to history thus becomes tangible, not fixed. Moreover, we were confronted with very lively reactions from those active in the dance world. Dancers, pedagogues, and theoreticians accused us of seizing a legacy without having a direct relationship to the work. Dance is an experience of the process of permanent modification. What takes place will never take place again in the same way. The way we think is also the way we perceive, and dance is an experience of the importance of the phenomena of perception. The work of the dancer consists in opening up his fields of perception as much as possible. From the moment the movement is initiated, all the information that comes to us, with all its complexity, requires that we can no longer think without the process of movement. It is the same thing for the spectator. Vision is already a physical commitment to the phenomena of perception, even if it is more discreet. Beside, these questions, informed by the philosophy of Merleau-Ponty, are summarized in the title of Yvonne Rainer's text from 1966, *Mind Is A Muscle*. At the same time, they were also at work in the field of visual arts and they partially formed minimalism's history. The texts written in Labanotation, like all texts, only have meaning once they have been read, interpreted. The reading here is a reading in movement(s), and it is from that work that our interrogations formed. Our questions gradually developed as the danced experimentation progressed. If we had worked from films, the work method would no doubt have been somewhat different.

SH: When images of the pieces we were working on existed, we first wanted to be free of them in order to allow the largest range of possible interpretations to emerge. A film of the *Faune* with Nijinski would obviously have reduced and short-circuited our reading of the score. How to infiltrate this writing? When we see an image, we cannot separate the writing from the interpretation. When we see a dancer on stage, the writing is interpreted—performed. This separation is only possible theoretically. On stage or in a picture, both are intimately linked. The second step was to measure the gap that separated our reading today from the original images of such or such a project. We tried to avoid the fantasy of reproducing sameness. In dance, there is an idea that the original work exists. But where does this "origin" lie in time and in space? Is it the day of the first performance of the project? Today in dance, the "premiere" still retains a privileged or even superior status in comparison to other performances. Yet each interpretation is one of the possibilities of the work, not designed as a consistent whole that could or could not be grasped one day, but as a potential of dynamic actualization.

[1] The Quatuor Albrecht Knust is a collective of dancers who engaged in manifold projects of dance recreation through the use and questioning of the choreographic score from 1993 to 2002. *Les danses de papier* (1994) offered a new visibility to relatively unknown works of Doris Humphrey and Kurt Jooss; in 1996 they staged *Continuous Project – Altered Daily* and *Satisfying Lover* from Yvonne Rainer and Steve Paxton, respectively, drawing a series of new articulations between American Postmodern dance and contemporary dance; *D'un faune... (éclats)* (2000) engaged with Vaslav Nijinsky's seminal work to extend a critical exploration of the relation between a dancer and its histories. The Quatuor met while studying Labanotation in Paris. Albrecht Knust is the name of a German dancer and pedagogue who spent a vast part of his life developing Rudolf Laban's movement notation system, including compiling a dictionary. What follows is an assemblage: the words from Collod, Hecquet, and Wavelet were collected by Yvane Chapuis between March and May 2002 and first published in Médium: Danse, *Art Press* 23 (2002): 16-23; Brun's words are excerpted from her "Le trait et le retrait," published in *Quant à la danse* 3 (February 2006): 34.
[2] Brun is here referring to Sigmund Freud and Georges Didi-Huberman's notions, respectively.
[3] Alain Badiou, *Handbook of Inaesthetics*, trans. Alberto Toscano (Stanford: Stanford University Press, [1998] 2005), 125.
[4] Walter Benjamin, "Theses on the Philosophy of History," in *Illuminations* (New York: Schocken Books, [1940] 1969), 255.

RESTS IN PIECES:
ON SCORES, NOTATIONS, AND THE TRACE IN DANCE[1]
Myriam Van Imschoot

First part

> Archè, we recall, names at once the commencement and the commandment. This
> name apparently coordinates two principles in one: the principle according to
> nature or history, there where things commence—physical, historical, or
> ontological principle—but also the principle according to the law, there where
> men and gods command, there where authority, social order are exercised, in
> this place from which order is given—nomological principle.
> —Jacques Derrida, *Archive Fever*[2]

In her essay "Archives. Performance Remains," performance theorist
Rebecca Schneider thoroughly questions the archival logic that operates
in western culture.[3] According to her, the archive is inscribed in our
habits insofar as we understand ourselves in relation to the remains
that we accumulate. The archive is "a utopian 'operational field of
projected total knowledge'" on the basis of which the law derives its
authority to "command."[4] The archive is not only the guardian of
professed "origins", but also the guard who polices: its practice of
conservation is also a matter of patriarchal conservatism. Its protective
embrace of storing and housing is simultaneously a normative gesture
of restoration with the force of an imperative.

In his 1995 book *Archive Fever: A Freudian Impression*, Jacques
Derrida points at this dual structure, when he refers to the etymological
roots of the archive, the "archè," which can relate both to
commencement and commandment. Derrida's book has taken an
important foothold in performance theory, because of its implications
for performance. Seen through the lens of archival logic, performance
is that which does *not* remain and therefore appears as a "loss." This
deeply rooted perception explains the somewhat problematic status

performance has within western culture, a reputation it shares with oral culture at large. In that sense, we could complete the string of Derrida's dual structure of commencement-commandment with a third value: the condemnation. As Leonardo da Vinci said about music, which he believed inferior to painting, *"Infortunée musique," "qui périt aussitôt créée"* ("unfortunate music," "which is consumed in the very act of its birth").[5] Because visual art takes the form of a tangible object with permanence and durability, it was thought to be more "advanced" than music, and for that matter all art whose medium is unstable (sound, gesture, etc.) and which must rely on "interpretation" (or "performance", the English term) to exist, was considered to be *"une activité toujours à périr et toujours à recommencer"* (a constantly vanishing activity that has to be constantly restarted).

It is in the light of this long tradition of condemnation that the performing arts have been looking for salvation. Music could overcome its "misfortune" and obtain respectability in so far as it succeeded to obtain a certain "graspability" in the confines of the musical object: the score. Its refined system of notation, developed over 2000 years and nearly universally applied, could secure a stability in very much the same way as the archive functions: it consecrated an "origin," the composition, which would then become the "commandment" for all the interpretations to come. From the site of "writing," the score would regulate and prescribe the action. Even long after the composer had died, he could therefore spectrally haunt the afterlife of his creation by way of the score, a bare-boned skeleton in search of new flesh,[6] Rebecca Schneider draws attention to this polarity of bones and flesh, when she equates the archive with the bones. The archive is fixated on the bones, which are the leftovers once the flesh has decomposed. It depreciates the soft matter, the malleable stuff where the laws of entropy are more clearly visible. Every archive is therefore also a mausoleum, a tomb that guards the remaining pieces, i.e. the bones and *not* the flesh.

It was for a long time believed that if dance could take on the model of music and extend itself into a "written object," it would as well be able to survive its short lifespan and build a more solid foundation for its history. Maybe the performances themselves would still perish, but thanks to the "cryptic" symbols of notation dance pieces could nevertheless be reanimated in a perpetual series of resurrection. From the seventeenth century onwards, quite advanced dance notation systems like those developed by Pierre Beauchamps (1636-1705) and Raoul-Auger Feuillet (1675-1710) and, later in the twentieth century, the one developed by Rudolf von Laban, have circulated widely and had a more or less committed following.[7]

In retrospect, however, one can now see that none of the systems could establish a lasting or pervasive foothold. When looking for an overview on the notational endeavors of choreographers and dance makers in the last centuries, what one sees is more a sort of "babelisation" of idiosyncratic instructions than a commonly and widely applied overarching language. To some, the dream of making dance visible and thus indelible has therefore proven to be an illusion. Unable to furnish the bones, dance would linger outside, on the threshold of the archive. Its practitioners could not practice the necrophilic archival love of the remainder (the caress of the relict or bones), but would compensate by recalling. Their pathology was not fetishism—replacing the lost object (which has never been an object in the first place); they would rather be enthralled in the *"Trauerarbeit"* (mourning labor) of the melancholic.[8] The reason why so much dance discourse has an elegiac overtone is this melancholic undercurrent.

Peggy Phelan, one of the best known and perhaps the melancholic performance theorist par excellence, wrote an apologetic text on the incapacity of performance to become an "object" in her seminal 1993 book, *Unmarked: The Politics of Performance*.[9] Her argument differs not so much in her analysis of performance, which she argues is ontologically unique, ephemeral and pervaded by loss, but in the positive value she attaches to this evanescence. Rather than deploring its impermanence, its lack of durability, she celebrates it, claiming that it constitutes performance's political resistance. Because it cannot become an object and cannot be reproduced, performance resists commodification and hence capitalist exploitative regime, Phelan argues.[10] This position must be cherished, Phelan states. To dwell on the threshold of the archive and, *in extenso*, of the market, makes performance wander, migrate as a "vagrant." Its movement is not the circulation within the networks of product exchange but the swirls and dwindles of disappearance, of leakage, of spilling.

The problem with Phelan's view of performance as disappearance, however, is that it stays within the frame of the archival logic it precisely seeks to thwart.[11] For it is only within that logic that performance is perceived as a loss. Ironically enough for an instance that professes to "safeguarding," the archive *produces* loss where it condemns all cultural production that does not solidify into the tangibility of the object, and where it dismisses performance from the field of relevance to the point of annihilation and myopic negation.

In her essay—*Archives. Performance Remains*—Schneider unravels more in depth these intricate relations between the archive and performance, which (as the title clearly suggests) has remains too, that is, if one is willing to see its traces. Whereas Phelan prioritizes performance as disappearance, since it happens once and only once before it enters the mnemonic field of memory, Schneider speaks of performance *as* memory. And rather than underscoring uniqueness, she points at body-to-body transmissions and to the way they are deeply characterized by a practice of repetition. In doing so, Schneider does not so much want to escape the archive; rather, she seeks to expand its scope, so as to emphasize the value not only of the bones, but also of the *flesh*. Flesh—not as a passive matter, but as a physicalized relational field of interaction, intensities, techniques, histories, traces, and relicts of experienced information. Flesh—with its own history and genealogy.

One could take up Schneider's thread of thought and see its relevance for dance as one of the performative fields in which the practice of "incorporation" and "excorporation" of physical templates through imitation and repetition is still very strong, since it is not only perpetuated in the training of dancers, but also constitutive of many creation processes where dancers learn by copying the generated material, often using video as a tool. These disciplinary processes require both technologies of "image reading" and of writing, for the dancer "reads" the body of the *master*, the tone of the muscles, the dynamics of the pulsations, etc., in order to shape (inscribe) her or his own physicality through repetition and rehearsal.[12] It is precisely on this unstable terrain of perpetual reenactment and mimetic desire that we find an opening to think of other types of archives, far beyond the direct concerns of reproduction. Besides the archives that consolidate in the architectonics of the House or Law as a sedentary depository, one could think of performers as mobile body-archives. They are not merely domiciled containers, but metabolic ecologies that compose the living traces of experience. Such mobile architectures of sedimentation would not align with the fetishising culture of dead bones but keep a sympathetic link with the processes of gasses, fermentations, as they are aggregated in the body.

Second part

Effective democratization can always be measured by this essential criterion: the participation in and the access to the archive, its constitution, and its interpretation.
—Jacques Derrida, *Archive Fever*[13]

What does it mean to collect and publish dance scores against the background of the debate on the ontology of performance, as it has just been sketched out here? Over the past months, the visual artist

Ludovic Burel and I have met up with a number of artists working in the field of dance to discuss their use of scores.[14] What vision is implied in this project? What sorts of archives did we have in mind, assuming beforehand that they might exist; what kind of archives have we found or produced? What fictions were we pursuing?

One of the first artists that Ludovic and I met in Paris was Vincent Dunoyer, who has been working as an independent choreographer since the late 1990s. For *Solos for Others* (2003), he made a photo-score of 99 photos, which were "copied" by himself and then by the young dancer Etienne Guilloteau. In the first round Guilloteau was sitting and showing the photos to Dunoyer, by holding them up in the air one after the other in random order, before throwing them onto the ground, where they would clutter on the floor, visible to the audience. The executioner, Dunoyer, would glimpse at the photos and reproduce the poses on the spot. The stage was arranged so as to create an allusion to the photographic set-up of photo-shoots (with a backdrop and strong light). Overall, the presence of the *photographic* was strongly marked, as if Dunoyer wished to point out that self-representation would never be the same once the photographic paradigm entered our culture in the nineteenth century, having rearticulated our *self-image*.

When we met Dunoyer in person (*en chair et en os*), we could take a closer look at the photo-score, which he had brought to our appointment in a brown envelope. It was a pile of cardboard pictures, which visibly showed the traces of having been frequently used over time. On all of them he was naked to his underwear, reenacting "moments" from his own performance history: one could recognize the curving, spiraling spine of a Steve Paxton, from whom Dunoyer copied an improvisation-solo (in *Carbon*); relicts from dances by Anne Teresa De Keersmaeker, with whom he danced for a long time; or fragments from a piece he performed in, by the Wooster Group.[15] In most of these "source-performances" Dunoyer copied the movements of dancers or choreographers other than himself. "My body is my work," he told us, and for a moment he looked like an exquisite assimilation machine which, plugged into the motor of mimetic desire, "incorporates" other bodies.

Following Schneider's vision, one might say that Vincent Dunoyer is a mobile archive that samples the living relicts from his physical memory. Yet, one has to be careful not to reduce this living stock— gestures, actions, sounds and images—to the level of sheer flesh. That would precisely deny the fact that this body is never "pure" flesh, but is always already extending into an elaborate circuitry of technologies of all sorts. The flesh is never a safe "home" of departure or arrival, nor is it an interiorized history one "owns"; rather, it constantly functions in a loop with other modes of mediation. Just as in the photographic self-portraits, the poseur must leave himself and "be with" the camera in order to present himself as himself (a dislocation to locate oneself as oneself), Dunoyer has been oscillating among a series of mimetic apparatuses for more than a decade—video, photos, the gaze of the spectator, other bodies, etc. The remains of his performance history were physical, indeed, but a physicality that was always mediated and remediated as it was pervaded by the existence of other objects, relations, agencies—human and nonhuman.

Later, as Ludovic and I would pay visit to other artists at their homes, studios, or rehearsal spaces, we would get an opportunity to deepen this more complex understanding of dance-related performance practices and their remains. Performance practice is restricted to none of the sides: the oral or the written, the bones or the flesh, objects or physical traces. What characterizes performance is a perpetual enmeshing all of these planes of emergence, thwarting any binary opposition.

The homes themselves bore witness to this; performance objects merged there with the habitual surroundings of ordinary life. A flight case, so common in theaters, would serve as a coffee table in the domestic setting, or a former prop could transform back into a couch or an object for everyday use. Videos and dossiers were piled on shelves, flyers and notes were stacked away in folders, receipts and bills were lingering around as reminders of the expenses that the performances entailed. The homes were not dormant mausoleums, designed for commemoration, but practical households where lives and careers were interlocked. During the talks we frequently tapped into our memories to recall the performances we had seen, or we used our imagination to fill the blanks of what we had not seen. Quite naturally, choreographers would enter their body archives and demonstrate certain gestures, or hum the melodies that helped them memorize movements (neenneeNaaaaHUPsakeenee; tatatatatata; dumdumWAITWAITdumdum). But we would also consult computers, watch DVDs, browse through notebooks, or listen to recordings on minidisk. All these sources of information were already integrated into a process of mediation, quotation, recycling, often shifting from one mode to the other. The written would be talked about, and the talking would be written down, while bodies reenacted gestures, handled objects, entered circuits of information, activating formerly lived experience and further imaginations thereof, etc. To look for "scores" in this context was a particular challenge. Contrary to the music tradition, dance practice has never strictly reserved the word "score" for a specific object, encoded in notation on a piece of paper, indicating a body of work that can then be instantiated with great rigor in performance. Likewise, it has never depended on copyright laws and distribution networks to publish and sell these scores. Up to date there is only one known example in contemporary dance, of such an autonomously and officially published dance score in the form of a marketable book: *Schreibstück* (2002), by the German choreographer Thomas Lehmen. But for the rest, most scores in dance do not aspire to "autonomy" or "self-sufficiency"; they are heteronomous working tools, whose use is ad hoc, local and mostly in tandem with verbally or physically communicated agreements.

Moreover, the English word "score", so it became clear in many conversations, covers a far larger range of applications than the French word "partition" allows. The French choreographer Mark Tompkins stretched this to its widest sense by defining the score, in his improvisational practice, as "the determination of one or more parameters for decision-making in action."[16] Much in the same way, when Lisa Nelson speaks of her *Tuning Scores*, she does not refer to a written score at all, but to a set of shared agreements and tools that together constitute "a communication and feedback system for an ensemble of players." The dancers make use of "calls" (*stop, go, replace, reverse, repeat, end*, etc), which function as editing tools and enable them to choreograph the performance activities on the spot. To a certain extent, following a score in this case resembles more a process of learning and enacting the "rules" of a game than following a unilateral and linear set of directions.

This is not to say that dance scores cannot circulate outside their original biotopes of labor; obviously some do. In Europe and the United States, for example, there are study groups of dancers who continue to work with Lisa Nelson's *Tuning Scores*. In 1996, William Forsythe used a book of preparatory drawings by Italian Baroque painter Tiepolo as the basis of a score for Daniel Larrieu and the Centre Chorégraphique de Tours. He had scribbled lines, arrows, and numbers on the book's reproductions of the drawings, which together formed an enigmatic riddle that Larrieu and his dancers were free to interpret. In the meantime, Forsythe would remain in dialogue with the group through fax. The choreography-at-a-distance that resulted from this, *Hypothetical Stream*, later resulted as well in other versions by the Ballett Frankfurt and by the students at the dance school Parts, in coordination with the ex-Ballett Frankfurt dancer Elizabeth Corbett.

In a similar vein, the score that Antonia Baehr made for *Holding Hands* (2001), the first piece of a trilogy of research on emotion, has also been used by other artists, notably by Sophia New and Petra

Sabish[17]. After *Schreibstück*, Thomas Lehmen developed parameter-based systems (*autopoietic* in nature, in analogy to the systems theory of Niklas Luhmann), which he collected in a box, *Funktionen* (2004); these can serve as a toolkit for anyone who feels inspired to make use of it. Yet, when moving outside the sphere of the immediate proximity of the choreographer, these scores enter a whole range of possible implementations, ranging from attempts to stay as close to the practice from which they emerge, to free applications, and even bolder pirate versions. In most cases, however, scores are fundamentally characterized by the contiguity and metonymy of tools and aids: they are a trace *of* and a reroute back to a praxis, whether directly or indirectly, mimickingly or mockingly, revered or reversed. Metaphorically, linking us back to the body and its modes of enactment, one could say that they are neurological centers of determinacy in a larger synaptic network where information fires.

Scores can proliferate in yet another way: through their *emergence* in the public arena of the performance itself. Indeed, what characterizes many contemporary uses of scores is that they let the score telescope into the order of the performance. As a result, the score is not a hidden recipe, the "obscure" blueprint that secretly steers and determines once and for all the "thing"—a Wizard of Oz, behind the curtains. Rather, in many of these recent works, the performers show their interactions with the score and point at the specific conditions of emergence of their actions, instead of sustaining an illusion that movement comes solely from a deep interior source. Sometimes this happens in quite subtle ways, as when the score is present as an *index* that *suggests* a wider set of arrangements. For example, in performances by Myriam Gourfink, such as in *Contraindre* (1993), the scores are integrated in the scenography on computer screens; and in certain dance pieces by Anne Teresa De Keersmaeker the dancers follow floor patterns, furnished by her composerfriend Thierry De Mey, which are marked on the floor. In *Après-Midi* (2003), a proposal by Antonia Baehr, William Wheeler and Henry Wilt, four untrained female performers are invited to perform in drag and follow the instructions that they hear through the headphones of a mini-disk.[18] At certain times during the performance the audience hears flashes of these instructions aloud and can observe the interrelation between the "instruction" and the actual performance activity. For *Both Sitting Duet* (2002), the performers Jonathan Burrows (an English choreographer) and Matteo Fargion (an English composer) decided to bring the score into the spectacular frame. They perform the dance with their books in front of them very much like musicians in concert use their scores as a memory aid.

In other cases scores move beyond this subtle indexicality and become fully accessible and comprehensible sources, so that spectators and performers share the same information. In *The Show Must Go On 2* (2004) Jérôme Bel reveals the script behind his piece. He rearranges the letters of the title of the piece as if participating in a game of Scrabble, and with every new word that shows up (for example, "s t u n t m a n," "s h o w m e n") the dancer Frédéric Seguette performs a matching action. Interestingly, Seguette never jumps into action right away, but allows the word that was just composed to resonate for a while. In doing so, he makes the spectator a co-actor who can also follow the script and imagine an action. The script becomes then a score for audience and performers alike.

Thomas Lehmen too, wants the audience to have full access to the score, which they can hold in their hands while watching the performance of *Schreibstück*[19]. According to Lisa Nelson, such a democratic "sharing" of the tools will help the audience enhance their observation: "When the intelligence of the system appears it can be very fun". Ultimately, the aim, she says, is not the score itself (its execution) but what it produces and facilitates. Scores are not systems to cultivate as such, but a "generatrix" for more complex interactions to happen and to observe.

Some of the scores that Ludovic and I have come across during these generous meetings with the artists were published in the section "Icônes" of the French journal *Multitudes* (2005, nr. 21). For this publication, a small selection was opted for, and perhaps that is just fine. There is always something tricky about publishing such materials, for although many of these scores and notations have an aesthetic appeal, the aim is not to mystify them and have "documents (...) transformed into monuments,"[20] "exiled from practice (...), by carving them out of their sphere of use."[21] It is, quite on the contrary, to add further possibilities of extension, (re)emergence and access to these performance documents, as they drift in and out of context(s) and echo their multiple existences.

[1] This essay was first published in *Multitudes* 21 (Spring 2005) as an introduction to a portfolio assembled by Ludovic Burel and Myriam Van Imschoot. It is published alongside visual documentation of the scores and other research material on www.oralsite.be.

[2] Jacques Derrida, *Archive Fever. A Freudian Impression*, trans. Eric Prenowitz (Baltimore: Johns Hopkins University Press, 1995), 1.

[3] Rebecca Schneider, "Archives. Performance Remains," *Performance Research* 6.2 (2001): 100-108.

[4] Rebecca Schneider cites here Richard Thomas, *The Imperial Archive: Knowledge and the Fantasy of Empire* (New York: Verso, 1993), 11.

[5] Antoine Hennion, "Infortunée musique, qui périt aussitôt créée...," *Marsyas* 34 (June 1995): 13. Hennion quotes here from *Paragone ou parallèle des arts*, republished in the André Chastel edition *Traité de peinture* (Paris: Berger-Levrault, 1987), 96.

[6] In *The Rational and Social Foundations of Music* (Carbondale: Southern Illinois University Press, 1958), the German sociologist Max Weber relates this development in music to an overarching process of rationalization in Western culture. The development of notational systems (amongst others) would standardize and homogenize musical practice until it culminated into the dictatorship of the score in the nineteenth century. As composers overthrew the reign of musical performers, improvisation would disappear from performance and the formerly fluid boundaries between composition and interpretation hardened.

[7] The earliest known manuscript of dance notation was found in the municipal archives of Cervera, Spain, and dates back to the second half of the fifteenth century. Louis XIV took a firm interest in the development of a notational system for dance, which spurred several ballet masters to come up with a model from the late seventeenth century onwards. This historical link between notation and state control confirms Weber's thesis of rationalization and, for that matter, bureaucratization. For an insightful overview of notations in dance see Laurence

Louppe, *Danses tracées. Dessins et notations des chorégraphes* (Paris: Dis voir, 1991) and Ann Hutchinson Guest, "Notation," in *International Encyclopedia of Dance*, vol. 4 (Oxford, New York: Oxford University Press, 1998).

[8] For a seminal text on melancholy, see Sigmund Freud, "Mourning and Melancholia," in *Collected Papers*, ed. and trans. Joan Riviere, vol. 4 (New York: Basic Books, 1959 [1917]).

[9] See Peggy Phelan, "The Ontology of Performance. Representation without Reproduction," in *Unmarked. The Politics of Performance* (London, New York: Routledge, 1993), 146: "Performance's only life is in the present. Performance cannot be saved, recorded, documented, or otherwise participate in the circulation of representations *of* representations: once it does so, it becomes something other than performance. To the degree that performance attempts to enter the economy of reproduction it betrays and lessens the promise of its own ontology. Performance's being, like the ontology of subjectivity proposed here, becomes itself through disappearance."

[10] "Performance refuses this system of exchange and resists the circulatory economy fundamental to it" Phelan, "The Ontology of Performance. Representation without Reproduction" 149.

[11] Another problem, I would like to argue, is that it underestimates the perversion of late capitalism, which can just as well commodify the "ephemeral" by wrapping it up in a promotional machine, formulas and formats that precisely sell the event as a "unique event."

[12] I play here on the double meaning of "master" as in the authoritative figure (one could certainly problematize the lingering dangers that exist in body-to-body transmission with its mythic idolization of the "master's paradigm") as well as in the "master copy", the first "take", that determines further renditions of it. For an insightful neo-materialist theory of repetition as a shaping of identities from a feminist perspective, see Judith Butler, *Bodies that Matter. On the Discursive Limits of 'Sex'* (London, New York: Routledge, 1993).

[13] Jacques Derrida, *Archive Fever*, 4.

[14] Encounters took place with Myriam Gourfink (5 February 2005), Mark Tompkins (6 February 2006), Christophe Wavelet (6 February 2005), Vincent Dunoyer (6 February 2005), Thomas Lehmen (12 March 2005), Antonia Baehr (12 March 2005), Kattrin Deufert & Tom Plischke (13 March 2005), Susanne Beggren (16 March 2005), Thierry De Mey (28 March 2005), Heike Langsdorf (28 March 2005), Elizabeth Corbett (29 March 2005), Lisa Nelson (29 March 2005), Matteo Fargion (10 April 2005) and Jonathan Burrows (14 April 2005). Any quotes or cited ideas below were taken from these interviews/encounters.

[15] In 1997, Dunoyer performed *3 Solos for Vincent Dunoyer*, choreographed for him by Elizabeth Lecompte of The Wooster Group (*Dances with TV&Mic*), Steve Paxton (*Carbon*) and Anne Teresa De Keersmaeker (*Solo for Vincent*). He has already reused fractions of this movement material in the photo-based installation *Etudes #31* (1999), in collaboration with Mirjam Devriendt, on music by Conlon Nancarrow.

[16] The description was given during a talk in Paris, on February 6th, 2005.

[17] This was in the frame of *hors-séries* in Montpellier, December 2004. In an email of April 26th, 2005, Antonia Baehr writes: "Since the structure of *Holding Hands* is an apprentorship (sic), I wanted to try to teach it to others, and also perceive it from outside for once. As a result it was very nice to see that this score can have a live on its own, and can exist without its mama or papa."

[18] The letter of invitation to the performers addresses in fact their "desire": "You should have the desire to dress up and pass as a man. Preferably, you should be an experienced Drag King, but

you can also be one to be born. In which case Drag King Werner Hirsch (alias Antonia Baehr) will be happy to give you birthhelp. (...) You should have the desire to get told during 32 minutes of your life what to do, since the piece is not rehearsed but the interpreters hear the instructions over headphones."

[19] In that sense, the first sentence of the book *Schreibstück* is very telling: "This is a work book for choreographers, dancers, presenters, and at the same time it is a book for everybody's own imagined version of Schreibstück."

[20] Michel Foucault, *The Archeology of Knowledge and the Discourse on Language*, trans. A. M. Sheridan Smith (New York: Pantheon Books, 1972), 7.

[21] Michel de Certeau, *The Writing of History*, trans. Tom Conley (New York: Columbia University Press, 1988), 73.

SUBVERSION OF THE DANCING BODY:
AUTONOMY ON DISPLAY[1]
Bojana Kunst

Introduction

The inspiration for the following essay sparkled my interest quite
some time ago, but I become aware of its immense importance
whenever I attempt to discuss the dancing body and the potentiality
of its subversion. It was a performance conceived by Conrad
Drzewiecki, the well-known doyen of Polish dance; it was his work
Waiting for that struck me, at the International Contemporary Dance
Conference and Performance Festival in Bytom a few years ago
(1999). Despite not being featured in the official part of the program,
and somewhat bashfully presented by the organizers themselves,
Waiting for turned out to be one of the highlights of the festival. This
surprise did not occur due to a relief of chancing upon something
"contemporary." It had nothing to do with the heavy search
interventions of "western" producers for "different" performances,
which could be successfully presented at the stage market, fitting the
"acquired taste" of dance audiences. Nor was it a result of
paternalistic approval in the sense of "well done, but we have seen
this already," which, of course, is not the guarantee to sell, but at least
a polite and respectful way of admitting someone's quality.

Drzewiecki's performance—an excellent short solo by a dancer
wearing a wealthy gold costume, and whose movement and gestures
were bent on decorating his body—clearly evoked the Central
European dance of the thirties. Nonetheless, Drzewiecki's "past" was
not that of the long gone historical traditions, now vaguely present
only as a recognition of the former dancing articulation that remains
in western scholarship knowledge and the categorizing of dance
history. Nor was it a past reflecting the impossibility of

development—the still innocent state of the dancing body, which, because of its specific historical situation, could not become aware of all the contradictions and aesthetic deconstructions of its bodyscapes. It was somewhere in-between: a utilization of the past to stay in the present. It revealed our eternal confrontation with different ways of being present. For me, the surprise lay in the manner the performance disclosed our disillusioned idea of the exclusiveness of the present—of the exclusive and hegemonistic ways of forming our present presence, which are inscribed in the articulation modes of the dancing body. All in all, what was this "Waiting for"? It was a pure display of autonomy, of a deep belief in the autonomy of the body. An autonomy, which was not out of time, an articulation of the past— but about the time. Its content had been discreetly embroidered already in its title: fixation and openness, distance and closeness, decoration and subversion, all at the same time. It opened the possibility to disclose a variety of histories.

1. Autonomy: Inauguration of Present Body

Drzewiecki's case brings us to the kernel of bodily autonomy—one of the basic aesthetic utopias of early contemporary dance. It helps us detect the complexity of the concept, which not only obsessed dance innovators and creators, but also became one of the main philosophical and poetic metaphors of the body in the contemporary thought and artistic innovations of the 20th century.

As we well know, the "fleshiness" that characterized the beginnings of contemporary philosophy was very often connected with the dancing body. For example, Friedrich Nietzsche associates the dancing body with the state before intellect emerged. Dance is thus given the privilege of describing thought, and thought the privilege of being like dance. A thought that is like dance does not know the spirit of weight, says Nietzsche, and it is crucial to relax the benumbed body by means of dance.[2] Dance can thus be defined as a "self-rotating wheel," or, as Alain Badiou states in his interpretation of Nietzsche's thoughts on dance, "dance is like a circle in space, but a circle that is its own principle, a circle that is not drawn from the outside, but rather that draws itself."[3] The body of dance is the original body, which is cleared of intellect, separated from discourses, a metaphor for existing in a Dionysian world. Its rotations and movement mirror its original existence. It is autonomous and yet evasive, never fixed, non-repetitive, never beheld in its entirety. The longing for the autonomous yet evasive was also quite strongly present in the poetic writings on dance by Valéry and Mallarmé. We find it in Mallarmé's statement that the body of dance can never be a body of someone, but always an empty emblem. A dancing body does not depict some other body or person, and is not conditioned by anything outside it. "The dancer is not a woman who dances for, the juxtaposed reasons that she is not a woman but a metaphor."[4] Valéry's views, stated in his essay *Philosophie de la danse*, are similar to those of Mallarmé. He, too, is fascinated by the female dancer, comparing the state of dancing to that of sleep; the dancing body is preoccupied with itself, and nothing exists outside the system formed by the dancer's actions. This is therefore a state where everything moves, but there is no reason or intention to supplement anything; there is no exterior reference, and nothing exists outside the system or movement. Dancing is described as *"artificially created lunacy (...)*, a specific manner of inner life that gives this psychological term a new meaning within which physiology is dominant."[5] These statements on different aspects of autonomy of the dancing body clearly correspond to Isadora Duncan's famous opening of the 20th century: "1900. For hours I would stand quite still, my two hands folded between my breasts, covering the solar plexus... I was seeking and finally discovered the central spring of all movement."[6] As an underlying philosophical utopia, these statements go along with the *Körperkulturbewegung* and other dance innovations in the beginning of the 20th century, and finally, with the aesthetic interventions in movement which John Martin, one of the first American dance critics, defined as *metakinesis* in 1933.[7] The common denominator of all these articulations is a strong awareness of bodily autonomy. This autonomy could be described as one of the main strategies employed by the body to enter the stage of modernity and disclose its own contemporary flow: it is autonomous yet evasive, self-disclosing yet artificial, an eternally wanted but never touched self-rotating wheel. Not only does this point of bodily departure to modernity reveal itself as a specific aesthetic strategy, but as much more: it is a philosophical, aesthetic, social and ideological utopia; a new possibility of articulating the subjective embodiment; a reaction to and an upgrade of modern rationalization; an employment of artificial tactics, and at the same time, a return to nature. To sum up: bodily autonomy could be described as a disclosure of the modern obsession with presence and being in the present at the same time.

Throughout the history of contemporary dance, we can follow different articulations of bodily autonomy. In its return to movement and an autonomous expressive flow, in its modernist transformations of hierarchical relations in the new ideal of the democratic body and minimalist dispersion of structures, in its postmodernist flirting with the narrative, the body of contemporary dance more or less corresponds to the initial image of the self-rotating wheel. It could be argued that this perspective is too narrow, but we do not understand this image in a formal and essentialist way. What is important is the complex utopian moment, which underlines the representation of modern dancing bodies throughout history, and causes the argumentation on the autonomy to return in different disguises. It is interesting, for example, to study the arguments of American postmodernist dance in its reaction to early modern bodily autonomy. One of the well-known debates arouse with Sally Banes, who states that modernism was not present in American modern dance before

1960 because, till then, we can not really talk about absolute dance, with no reference to the outside world. Thus, the real autonomy of the body lies in the modernist deconstruction and minimalist dispersion of hierarchical body relations, and not in the still connection to the outside (as advocated by emotionalism and essentialism), which could be found in the beginnings of the contemporary dance (e.g. by Martha Graham). Interestingly, with the staging of the everyday, democratic body (Trisha Brown, Judson Church etc.), autonomy became a specific privilege. It was not viewed as an utopian tension anymore (a feature strongly present at the beginning, when it was still possible to observe the variety of links with the outside), but as a political, even educational strategy of the dancing body. The "self-rotating wheel" enters the field of technique and thus that of universality. The problem of autonomy returns as an underlying utopian moment in the 1980s and '90s dance articulation, but with a completely different perspective. In its reaction to the universality and disclosure of different ways of (artistic) subjectivity, bodily autonomy discloses itself as the way of performing the particular; it embodies various subjectivities, individuality, personality, stories, gender, illness, constructions of contemporary identities, etc. Even then, the image of the "self-rotating wheel" remains, but as if rotating in a different way, with its course shifted not only from aesthetic to political strategies, but from a universal course to a complex geography of routes.

2. Paradoxes of "Self-Rotating Wheel"

The brief historical overview that follows is intended as an illustration of the concept discussed. It is not possible for me to go into the interesting particularities of historical relations to bodily autonomy and its dance articulation. My objective is but to reveal the complexity of this bodily utopia, and disclose a possible subversion of the body in this scope. Many authors approached the possibility of subversiveness by discussing various characteristics of the autonomous body. Not only was bodily subversion associated with disclosing the authentic, original, natural substance of the body, but also with the techniques and strategies of the artificial, especially in the first half of the century. It was present in the de-hierarchization of the body, a result of minimalist dispersion (Michel Bernard), as well as in the abstraction of movement. It is also very strongly connected with the ideal of the democratic body and its everyday movement. The possibility to embody and perform various subjectivities was one of the main subversive bodily modes in the European postmodernist dance approaches. All these approaches could be linked to the complex utopia of autonomy, to the images of the "self-rotating wheel" and "artificially created lunacy," dealt with at the beginning of my essay. This link is somewhat contradictory: it opens the possibility of subversion and, at the same time, it is also located at the very border, attracted to self-rotating exclusiveness and isolation. In other words, there is something tricky in this display of bodily autonomy, which could also be defined as a strong belief in the possibilities of different ways and subversions of representation.

On one side, bodily autonomy can be understood as a philosophical metaphor that reveals the unstable relation between the object and the subject; it seems that, within this relation, the body regains its original (forgotten) power. The dancing body does not serve as a metaphor to philosophers and poets just because the contact with the essence would shine through it, but because its autonomous streak reveals a different (perhaps imaginary, artificial) *history*, covered in hierarchical systems of the rational, language, and accepted representative webs. A history of evasiveness and instability, where representation is inefficient due to a freedom lurking in stitches and cracks; a place where the body is allowed to glitter without form, freely generating a playful tension between its presence and disappearance. It is not a history of representation anymore, of taking the place of the other; it is an artificial, playful field of performing, where different potentialities of embodiments are disclosed. The bodies will indeed perform in relation to the present; however, it is not about being in a certain moment, but about using that moment to reveal a different history. It is not about the exclusiveness of the moment, but about different possibilities of presence and being in the present. Only by means of presence and being in the present, the history of forgotten, overlooked and forbidden bodies can come to light. The self-rotating wheel is not so much about the rotation to self-sufficiency, but has been put onto the stage of modern bodies primarily as an image of disappearance, absence, negativity, hysteria, simulation, decadence, womanliness. Its course is governed by the self—a disoriented, evasive, fragile, connected but not organized, opened and deeply dubious. The "self-rotating wheel" has another dimension of subversion, which was beautifully described by Valery as "artificially created lunacy": it is a form of self-reflection, a tactic of intervening "lunatic" embodiments. It is a performed embodiment, opening the possibility of in-betweens; in this sense, it could also be defined as a specific way of acting.

On the other side, the liberating and democratic impulse arising from the concept of the autonomous body is not so obvious as it may seem. We could say that the autonomous body is extremely fragile, and that the disclosure of its colorful history is forever threatened by power, exclusiveness, institutionalization, organization, by privileges of style, form—and finally, those of norm. We could say that the autonomy could quickly become trapped in its own enthusiasm over self-sufficiency, which basically regards the autonomous body as transparent, predictable and exclusive. The autonomizing can quickly result in the achievement of a perfectly manipulated, predictable and controlled body. We could observe that fact by example in the complex relationship between the libertarian and nationalist concepts of the body in the '30s, with the body's autonomy transformed into a style of authenticity, privileging the presence in the name of one history. Autonomy became a privilege of style in American dance, especially with its expansion (together with action painting) to other parts of the world (Europe, Russia etc.); dance became an important export product of contemporary, free American culture. Carefully planned by the NEA and the American government, contemporary dance was presented abroad as a democratic and cultural body of capitalism.

It is especially interesting to observe the autonomy issue from a local perspective. Coming from Slovenia, where contemporary dance emerged practically in the middle of the '80s, and knowing the situation in other former eastern countries, it is particularly useful for me to observe and compare two different histories of bodily articulation. On the one side, bodily articulation has been acknowledged by institutions and academic history for quite a few decades, developing institutional, educational and production networks. On the other side, it has been forced to the margin for decades, condemned to non-existence or fighting to survive, without a basic structure that would assure its development, with no dialogue with institutions and critique, rising only in the last decade to fight for basic infrastructure. At first sight, the opening of the East to the West and vice versa could be understood as a somehow natural need for professionalism and institutionalization, for exchanging models and knowledge, or as an urgent need of overcoming the differences. It is interesting, however, to observe that the institutional difference discloses the privilege of western contemporary dance. In its institutional form, contemporary dance paradoxically became a token of contemporaneity, urbanity, modernity, freedom, and democracy. By means of educational and other more or less developed infrastructural production networks, the western body is trained and exploited to the maximum; there is a number of techniques at its disposal, always disclosing its physicality, which is somehow "in-time," present. The representation of the body of the West / East reunion reveals a variety of embodiments: that of the western dancing body, completely equipped for the present—and on the other side, that of the other, unarticulated body with a dark, closed and incomprehensible attraction to the past; if articulated, the latter cannot communicate with the western gaze without having a strong political, or even better, local meaning. We could say that the development of western contemporary dance has somehow turned the autonomy of the body into a specific and exclusive privilege.

The problem is that, due to the ruthless dictation of the present, we feel uncomfortable whenever we are faced with something different, a "subversion of the other." Western gaze is still hesitant when bodily autonomy and potentiality should be bestowed upon the other; it would rather perceive the other as unarticulated, 'still not there', confused, clumsy, too bodily / romantic / narrative, as an attempted or a delayed physicality, always reduced to a special context (political, traditional, ethnical, local, etc.). Western contemporary dance somehow institutionalized an exclusive right to contemporaneity, urbanity, autonomy. The contemporary dance which is not part of the western institutionalization of autonomy, is not recognized as a legitimate quest for modes in-between, for the potentiality and presence of the body, with its own privileged view of contemporaneity and universality. Instead, it is perceived as reduced to the past, otherness, the other. According to André Lepecki, it is viewed as something "not being of the moment," "doubtly late"—culturally, aesthetically, technologically.[8] As Lepecki very well observed, the West behaved as if synchronicity were the exclusive matter of western dramaturgy, and chronology the exclusive matter of geography.[9] Western contemporary dance has twisted the potentiality and autonomy of the body, as well as the discovery of the body in-between—making it a specific and exclusive privilege. The problem is that, due to the ruthless dictation of the present, we feel uncomfortable whenever we are faced with a difference. We could even say that, somehow perversely, the West perceived in the other its own autonomous beginnings and articulation of the present body.

Of course, we could say that this kind of attitude is the result of the inability of the East to introduce an articulation other than that established or prescribed for decades: any attempt toward a different history, autonomy, representation was ostracized in advance. Where an original democratic impulse was nipped in the bud, where there was no possibility of discovering another, hidden history, with everybody having to bear the weight of its official version, contemporary dance could not develop. The metaphor of a dancing body as a self- rotating wheel (Nietzsche) bears witness to an existential legitimacy that can be placed within a body and its existence (which, in the former socialist societies, was inevitably blurred and replaced by the legitimacy of the system). This confirms the fact that there is a coexistence of different ways to articulate the autonomy and disclose the potentiality of its subversion; the yardstick by judging these ways should not be a hierarchical time line, or geographical ideals by the expansion of universality. Instead, we should open different possibilities of presence and being in the present, as this is the only way that the history of forgotten, ignored and forbidden bodies will shine through.

The problematic fragility of the autonomy concept could be further explained by means of political philosophy; it is namely quite aware of the paradox inherent in this concept. The oscillation between aesthetics and politics will always be present, due to a very important common denominator: the issue of representation. Autonomy is deeply intertwined with the representation process; we could even say autonomy is the way of performing the modern subject. Interestingly, autonomy is constructed as a constant paradox, discussed as early as by Hegel in his mediating concept of self-actualization. The subject always possesses a process or capacity to let himself go, to deliver himself to that what is not himself, to remain by himself only into the relation to otherness. Accordingly, autonomy is not a static essentialist concept, and has nothing to do with originality, but is more of an artificial process where representation and necessity links to the modern subject can be disclosed. The biggest problem of the representation process is that, paradoxically, autonomy is also a self- rotating process: the otherness is there represented only in the way that the self could be autonomously performed. To say it differently: the otherness is always perceived in its negativity, so that the self could step into the moment. Even the great theorist specializing in the disillusion of the modern rational concepts, Adorno, doesn't have an answer to this paradox. He concludes that our talking about the autonomy and place of the other, is ultimately a mere aesthetic experience, and not a social one: the non-responsive autonomy is ultimately not a moral and political problem, but an aesthetic one—the self-rotating process of modern representation procedures. But in this self-rotating trajectory, a hierarchical shift has been inscribed: the outside is a necessary link for the self to be represented, but when the representation does take place, otherness will inevitably be performed as negativity.[10]

3. "If I Can Not Dance, I Will Not Be a Part of Your Revolution."

How can we then articulate the introductory image of the dancing body, the "self-rotating wheel," and connect it with the "waiting for a different history"? What kind of subversion is at work with the body entering the concept of autonomy and its entire range of evasiveness, tricks, mimicry, movements, and fluids?

A well-known interview with Derrida will come to mind, one dealing with dance and various aspects of feminism. The interview begins with the sentence by Emma Goldmann, a 19th century feminist castaway, with which she refused the invitation to join her fellow suffragettes: "If I can not dance, I will not take part in your revolution."[11] This sentence, of course, echoes the democratic impulse entailed in the autonomous body of dance. Unlike the established and recognizable history of the body (e.g. as shown by the figurative-rhetorical context of ballet), the autonomous dancing body introduces a "history of paradoxical laws and non-dialectical discontinuities, a history of absolutely heterogeneous pockets, irreducible particularities, of unheard of and incalculable sexual differences..."[12] But even Derrida himself hastens to add that, perhaps, he is only speculating on what Emma Goldmann really wants to say. Thus, the initial "power" of the autonomous dancing body reveals itself as fragile, oscillating between the beliefs and the actual tactics of acting and performing. To dance otherwise, said Derrida, is presented just in a form of most unforeseeable and most innocent of chances, "the most innocent of dances would thwart the *assignation a residence*, escape those residencies under surveillance; the dance changes place and above all changes places. In its wake they can no longer be recognized." It is thus important to understand that this as a result of the "artificially created lunacy," this madness of dance (Derrida), is a strategy to avoid organized, patient, laborious struggles and every exclusiveness (even certain subversive feminist struggles in Goldman's case), and enter another impossible and necessary compromise: "an incessant, daily negotiation—individual or not—sometimes microscopic, sometimes punctuated by a poker—like gamble, always deprived of insurance, whether it be in private life or within institutions."[13]

This is not only a question of atopia, a question of non-place, as Derrida said, but also a dystopian question of time, of not being *in the moment* but of connecting and disclosing different ways of presence and being in the present. At a certain point, the dilemma of the autonomous body comes close to the internal paradox governing the autonomy of the subject. If its performing has become a strategy of exclusiveness—a disintegration of authority where a different authority has been reproduced—the body loses its sensibility of time, and its autonomy becomes that of the moment. But this being in the moment is a privilege of decoration and style—with differences perceived through respect and polite affection. Thus, the real question which has to be asked in the connection with the body's potential for subversion, is the following: how can we come out of the exclusiveness of our moment, how can we risk and disclose the networks through which the moment is given to us? Are we able to accept the radical disconnecting tactic of the other, and still allow the possibility of catching the glimpse (*entre-voir*) in-between?

[1] This essay was first published in *Performance Research* 8:2 (2003): 61-68, in the Bodiescapes issue edited by Peter M. Boenisch and Ric Allsopp.

[2] Friedrich Nietzsche, *Die Geburt Der Tragödie. Unzeitgemäße Betrachtungen I–IV, Nachgelassene Schriften 1870–1873* (Munich: Deutscher Taschenbuch Verlag, 1988), 234.

[3] Alain Badiou, "Dance as a Metaphor for Thought," in *Handbook of Inaesthetics*, trans. Alberto Toscano (Stanford: Stanford University Press, [1998] 2005), 58.

[4] Stephane Mallarmé, "Ballets," cited in Sandra Kemp, "Conflicting Choreographies, Derrida And Dance," *New Formations* 16 (1992): 34-45.

[5] Paul Valéry, "Philosophie de la danse" (1936), in *Oeuvres I* (Paris: Éditions Gallimard, 1995), 44.

[6] Isadora Duncan, *My Life* (New York: Liveright, 1927), 75.

[7] John Martin, *The Modern Dance* (New York: A.S. Barnes, 1933).

[8] André Lepecki, "The Body in Difference," *Fama* 1 (2000); see http://sarma.be/docs/608/.

[9] Lepecki, "The Body in Difference."

[10] Slavoj Žižek, *Tarrying with the Negative* (Durham: Duke University Press, 1993).

[11] Jacques Derrida and Christie McDonald, "Choreographies," *Diacritics* 12:2 (Summer 1982): 66-76.

[12] Derrida, "Choreographies," 68.

[13] Derrida, "Choreographies," 68.

ON THE USE OF THE CONCEPT OF MODERNITY
AND ITS PERVERSE EFFECTS IN DANCE[1]
Michel Bernard

To illustrate the prevalence of the moment over all temporal considerations, Montaigne has this expression, which though banal and tautological, is oh so fitting and meaningful in my eyes: "When I dance, I dance; when I sleep, I sleep."[2] Actually, this reference to dance is not, for me, a coincidence: it aims, on the contrary, to show that this art of movement cannot be understood or *a fortiori* appreciated with the prospect of a succession that would carry us away toward a better future. As François Jullien writes, "The tautology signifies that I am careful not to anticipate. I do not go beyond the scope of the moment, neither by desire nor in thought. I coincide: when I dance, I dance, I am not doing anything other than what I am doing. I embrace this fact of dancing. Or, to say it in Montaigne's terms: I do not 'froth' this moment up, I don't 'sound' it out or 'bend my reason to obtain it.' I don't 'pin myself down' with it or 'grovel' in it, but I 'apply' myself, I 'sample the delights' of it, I 'insist' on it."[3] In other words, the act of dancing is a singular moment that is not determined by its beginning and end, as interval and lapse of time; it distinguishes itself exclusively through its quality, which is how it is like the seasons, as the Chinese say. Therefore, why do we have the desire to judge it according to and with the aid of the normative model of Occidental temporality, as a uni-linear, extensive, progressive, and serial process? Isn't this model, for that matter, starting to disintegrate and implode of its own accord in the very flow of our everyday life as the Italian novelist Antonio Tabucchi demonstrates? Whole pieces of ourselves are condemned to jetlag for life. "Time ages quickly," say the pre-Socratics,[4] which is why it seems that artistic activity must not be comprehended and evaluated except as a qualitative experience, intensive and heterogeneous, and not as a so-called "progression" relative to the irreversible succession of the temporal arrow.

But if we are now no longer obliged to situate art and, in particular, dance in the framework of a progressive transition, it is advisable *a fortiori* to challenge the category of modernity and its different avatars that pretend to designate, characterize, and evaluate art and dance, and instead resort to another form of enunciation that emphasizes and reconstitutes this fundamentally qualitative experience of the artistic process itself. This process is, to my eyes, that of sensorial scanning, that is to say, the play immanent to the twofold mechanism of disjunction/conjunction carried out by the artist on the materialized and hybrid specter of the generalized chiasm of all our heterogeneous sensations. To do so, this new enunciation should restore a new way of playing with each of the seven principal modes of scanning that constitute the seven fundamental *sensorial tonalities:* picturality, plasticity, fragrance, taste, musicality, theatricality, and orchesality.[5] Dance must be linked with the orchesality that underlies and drives it, and not solely with the history to which it belongs, even if this history weighs heavily in what it makes visible. This orchesality implies temporality of course. However the temporality of dance is not the one defined by the transitional and successive process mentioned above, but rather through the play of sensorial chiasms that are ceaselessly woven and unwoven by the fortuitous shifts in motor functions required by situational changes. In other words, each moment offers and models a distinct corporeity. This transformation or mutation of the corporal moments is carried out in dance (as I have repeated many times) according to four major characteristics: an undefined dynamic of metamorphosis, the random play of temporality's weaving and unweaving that was just mentioned, the more or less uneasy dialogue with gravitational force, and the unpredictable effects of the auto-affective impulse or, if you like, the irrepressible desire of corporeity to fold over onto itself or coincide with itself. Consequently, if I want to specify and designate a dance that I perceive, I cannot be satisfied with just bringing it back to the formal classification of *a priori* norms of modernity and post-modernity or *a fortiori* of premodernity, antimodernity, hypermodernity, or contemporaneity. We have to find a modality of enunciation that enables us to translate all at once these kinetic metamorphoses, temporal ruptures, gravitational variations, and auto-affective fantasies.

This is a difficult and, some will say, impossible task, since the use of these parameters is relative to the nature and length of artistic training received, which we traditionally call the transmission of techniques and styles. We already know that this training is not the same in the East as it is in the West—where teaching methods diverge according to nation and era. In France itself, the training is far from being homogeneous and Hubert Godard is certainly right to say that we will never understand anything about dance as long as we have not attempted to reconstitute a history of the learning of this art in our country. But a characterization of the taught and learned techniques using the single category of modernity and its derivatives does not enable us to shed light any better on the act of dancing such as is it given to us *hic et nunc*, including, first and foremost, the technique that most assumed, claimed, and made accessible the qualification "modern" in dance, that of Martha Graham.[6] "One of the characteristics of this style," Jacqueline Robinson rightly observes, is the breaking down of movement according to the contraction-release factor: the torso absorbs the passage from one pole to another. A "percussive" attack of the movement produces an intense vitality. Daily training includes a section on the floor, either lying, sitting, or kneeling, in order to give the torso more freedom and concentrated sensitivity, and to enable the spine to "blossom out of the pelvis and hips." The second portion of the class is the barre, in which ballet exercises are executed with many variations. The third portion of the class is movement in space, meaning infinite sequences of all possible and imaginable movements. "Some technique details seem to be worth keeping: in the balance work, an extraordinary feeling of security is given, not only by the highly considered play of counterbalance and complementary tensions, but also by a pressure of the wrists, heels, even the top of the head, which seem to be pushing against and supported by the space."[7]

It is undeniable that such technical training marks the bodies of the dancers who subject themselves to it, shaping them and predisposing them to certain motor configurations. Nevertheless, it does not suffice to characterize the act of dancing such as it is presented to us on a stage: it gives us, in fact, only an easy way to find our bearings, a rapid and superficial label of recognition. Dance cannot be summed up by only calling up its conditions and modalities of learning. The type of designation that I want to promote, as an alternative, would instead consist of liberating the eyes of the spectator from the requirements of identification commanded by the cultural, social, and institutional demand that, in my opinion, denatures the singular and unique process of the act of dancing *hic et nunc* while overlooking the sensorial work that gives rise to it and which it presupposes.

In fact, wanting to define an audience community based on what is seen, using the category of modernity and all of its avatars, may possibly have only one pedagogical virtue and even then merely a didactic one: it is a matter of each time relating one's viewing experience to another through the misleading mechanism of recognition of supposed similarities. However, the work of artistic creation actually consists of shying away from living up to such expectations and, even more, of perturbing them by ingeniously and ironically playing on unpredictable conjunctions/disjunctions; in short, by using an unusual sensorial scanning. Mainstream discourses on the arts and its categorizations were proposed by journalistic critics anxious above all to render the arts accessible to a public eager to reduce or write off the confusion, embarrassment, or even unease caused by this unusual or strange dimension of the perceived work (the famous "*décept*" that Anne Cauquelin talks about in her *Petit traité d'art contemporain*)[8] and thus referred them back to previous experiences. Of course, most artists demonstrate an extreme reserve, or even an incontestable aversion, with regard to this sort of reaction and judgment: *a priori* they don't much like classification and, sometimes, are wary of all conceptualization that they consider to be denaturizing or a violation of the creative process. Nevertheless, they themselves often cannot help but have recourse to these forms of media categorization when they hear proclamations, like prophesies, of the originality of their process or their artistic work in "manifestos" or collective declarations. In other words, the power of critical discourse is much more insidious and virulent than we generally believe it to be: the best artistic intentions can in this way become trapped and disfigured in their very enunciation.

To avoid this pitfall, it seems to me necessary and urgent to, on the one hand, evacuate the formatted vocabulary of institutionalized and trivialized classification that uses the category of modernity and its derivatives, and, on the other hand, to stay focused on the sensorimotor work in the production of the dancing act. In other words, it is advisable, as Paul Valéry invites us to do, to rediscover the specificity of the artistic process: "The artist," he writes, "is he whose sensations develop, or rather who is sensitive to harmonics, to secondary consequences, to the developments of sensation. He who, on this path, will go back, reconstitute the spheres that exist, that link the raw sensation to the idea, to intelligence, and finally to the reconstructive action, is the one who is an artist but even more than that."[9] Without a doubt, the way I see it, this is less an idea or an intelligence that must be revealed than the random fictionary projection that commands the innovative scanning; yet my approach belongs to the same direction: that of rediscovering the sensorial process in creation.

Now, this return to felt sensation is applicable above all to dance: it is done there on the stage *hic et nunc,* and imposes its presence to my gaze independent of any reference to a prerequisite knowledge that situates it in a history reconfigured according to the categories of modernity, postmodernity, hypermodernity, or even contemporaneity. If, in fact, as Giorgio Agamben rightly notes, the latter marks "a singular relation with one's own time, which adheres to it and, at the same time, keeps a distance from it"—in other words "through a disjunction and an anachronism," it enables one to "recognize the obscurity of the present" and break its "vertebrae"[10]—it is no less true that this subversion by "the contemporary" accomplishes itself in the act of sensing that is put into play by the artist, and that this category is therefore not enough to reveal the work in its strange dimension. In fact, most of the time commentators and historians content themselves with emphasizing, with the help of this category, the rupture produced by the artist's work rather than its radical specificity. This is what Jean-Yves Jouannais does, for example, when he turns to the concept of "idiocy" to signify the idea that so-called "contemporary" creation expresses itself as a resistance to conventional forms, to hallowed norms: it imposes its *idios,* the inalienable character of its singularity.[11] However, in doing so, he defines only the negativity of the contemporary, and not the positivity of its veritable and profound driving force. For example, one can say that Boris Charmatz, Jérôme Bel, Xavier Le Roy, and many others have been hailed as "contemporary choreographers" because they don't want to conform to a compositional and representative system accredited by and inherited from the dance tradition. But this qualification of "contemporary" in no way sheds light on the sensorial process that moves these choreographers and drives them to this refusal.

In reality, the fundamental error that underlies the characterization of dance by the so-called historical categories that constitute modernity—its different substitutes and its latest offshoot, that of "contemporaneity"—resides in the confusion with the simultaneous and hidden requirement of increased value and, through it, a secret hierarchization. As I have attempted to show, this demand dwells in and innervates all of our desires insofar as it determines our choices and, consequently, proposes value. The generic category of value circumscribes the function of desire at every given moment, in every given situation with regard to all of the preceding events, all of the exterior conditions (economic, social, political, and ideological) and, more radically, with the fictionary dynamic of my sensations. Hence the difficulty of its use in the appreciation of an artistic work and *a fortiori* the sterility and inanity of the approach that pretends to be able to reduce that work to the sole criterion of its relation to a supposed modernity. Thus we recall the fundamental philosophical question: to what extent is it necessary and legitimate to want to assign a value to a production that calls itself "artistic?" In fact, usually such a question is eluded or judged to be superfluous and absurd by arguing that, to be precise, this type of production belongs to a history that obliges us to confront or compare it to others so that a public in search of reassuring bearings can understand it; in short, that increasing prestige is a necessary and legitimate way of putting works in relation. But doesn't this forget the production process itself, the one that engendered them? In other words, before even giving oneself over to this little adventitious game of comparing, isn't it advisable to interrogate ourselves about the way in which each work reveals its own process of increasing the value that is immanent and absolutely irreducible to it—as I have tried to establish above in outlining a genealogy of artistic judgment? The moment I attend, for example, a choreographic performance that captures my attention, it takes on value *in and of itself for me.* It interests me, in the etymological sense of the Latin verb *inter-esse*; that is, to insert itself in the immanent and singular dynamic of a twofold corporal historicity: that of my own corporeity with its ups and downs and its unique and inalienable affective trajectory, and that of the artist's corporeity and of the sensorial scanning enacted by his work. Thus, the stated value means nothing other than the concordance, or even just the connection, between the conditions of my perception and the artist's creative sensorial process. It does not therefore refer to any universal norm that would supposedly be "beautiful," nor *a fortiori* to the requirements of a modernity to which the artistic work must necessarily be subjected, but rather exposes only the relativity, contingency, and complexity of an encounter between two modalities of perceptive management and, more exactly, of fictionary projection. In other words, what defines and justifies the aesthetic value of a particular work in a given place and at a given moment are the conditions under which one system of sensorial production is linked to another system of sensorial production and, consequently, the possibility of their concordance even if this latter is, almost ironically, nothing but a misunderstanding—as is demonstrated by the untimely emotional reactions and the intellectual interpretations of spectators that are completely antinomic to the intentions announced by the creator of the piece.

Nowadays, the dimension of the spectacle evidently occupies a prominent place in all of the arts (and in life in general!) to the point of overwhelming or masking the aesthetic specificity of the work presented. And yet, the very modalities of this spectacularity are far from being identical: as Jean-Luc Nancy notes in a letter to Mathilde Monnier, the relationship of dance to the stage is not the same as that of the theater, although it is more often than not the same stage. In fact, although theater started with the stage, dance has distinct and autonomous origins.[12] This is why we can interrogate the nature of the relationship of dance to the spectacle. Already in *De la création chorégraphique*,[13] I strived to argue, on the one hand, that the stage derealized not only the corporeities that it was supposed to exhibit, but also the corporeity of the spectator who pretends to perceive them; and, on the other hand, that this very perception constitutes a permanent mechanism of fictionary projection that assimilates and appropriates the fictions proposed by the piece, even if it means to transform or amplify them. In other words, when a spectator goes to a performance, he or she is given a fictive reality to see, or more generally to feel, that stimulates his or her own fictionary power. The performance ends up enlarging, enriching, multiplying, or shattering this inherent power that we each have and, in the same movement, alters itself. There is thus in a way an immanence of the spectacular function within each corporeity that moreover reverberates and has repercussions both on its entire surface and in all of its acts: it constantly gives itself up to performing itself for itself, from one anatomical region to another, from one movement to another. But, of course, stage representation, through its socio-cultural finality, if not formats, at least formalizes, arranges, and reconfigures this immanent fictionary dynamic in order to better captivate the attention of the audience and arouse its emotion. It is still true, nevertheless, that the truly choreographic performance, unlike all the others, exhibits animate corporeities through a quasi-uninterrupted motor impulse that metamorphoses into an infinite diversity of shifts, movements, physiognomic expressions; in other words, into an incessant flow of more or less disorderly hybrid figures and evanescences, what I believed I should call "phantasmagorias," which fictionalize them even more. In this way, the choreographic performance—because of its random and paradoxical action of construction and destruction, its disconcerting process of weaving and unweaving a temporality that pulverizes corporeity into a savage and unrestrained succession of instants (Merce Cunningham's famous *events*)—not only renders any control over the duration of the performance impossible, but also reinforces the ontological derealization carried out by the stage dispositif, the dissolution of its form and its identity as produced by its imagistic mutation and, conjointly, the temporal disintegration of its apparent unity. From which, to my eyes, comes the vanity and occasional absurdity of the numerous current attempts to, out of a desire for embellishment or originality and because of the conventional submission to the demands of a supposed modernity, overload choreographic performances with a profusion of artifices and sophisticated technical means. This scenographic saturation certainly seduces the eyes and ears of the audience who give in to facile and entertaining effects of lighting magic, colors, pictorial or video images, sound or musical orchestrations, and *a fortiori* alluring, indulgent, or provocative scenes, but it masks or glosses over the specific, veritable, and underground character of the sensorial and fictionary work of choreographic creation.

To sum up, as I have tried to demonstrate through this analysis, today dance seems to me to be suffering more than it is benefitting from its desire to bend itself to the normative and ambiguous criteria of the category of modernity and its multiple subterfuges. Much to the contrary of popular belief, the rediscovery of the random sensorimotor and fictionary process that engenders dance in a plurality of instants springing from the performances of dancers emphasizes the qualitative and fundamentally rebellious autonomy of this artistic experience. This is what Merce Cunningham seems to have understood and wanted to give voice to, in his own way, when he said: "In my performances, there is no symbolic, no psyche: everything that is seen has its meaning in the moment itself and the performance is nothing other then what one can see. The subject of dance, is dance itself."[14]

[1] This is an excerpt of the chapter by the same title in Michel Bernard, *Généalogie du jugement artistique. suivi de Considérations intempestives sur les dérives actuelle de quelques arts* (Paris: Beauchesne, 2011). In this chapter, Bernard argues that "the concept of 'modernity' entirely occupies, runs through, and guides, inexorably it seems, the history of western thought." Through an epistemological analysis, the philosopher seeks to elucidate and denunciate modernity's "belief" and the "values it promotes." The present text constitutes the second half of the chapter and focuses on dance's singular relation to time, and its resistance to and reinvention of the category of modernity.

[2] Michel de Montaigne, *Essais* (Paris: Gallimard, 1950), 1246.

[3] François Jullien, *Du temps. Éléments d'une philosophie de vivre* (Paris: Grasset, 2001), 153 and 115; Michel de Montaigne, *Essais,* 1251.

[4] Antonio Tabucchi, *Le temps vieillit vite* (Paris, Gallimard, 2009).

[5] For more on the philosopher's definition of these different aesthetics and sensorial tonalities, see Bernard, *De la création chorégraphique* (Pantin: Centre national de la danse, 2001).

[6] In this regard, the American critic John Martin has been instrumental in the sacralization and popularization of "modern dance." See John Martin, *The Modern Dance* (New York: A. S. Barnes, 1933).

[7] Jacqueline Robinson, *Une certaine idée de la danse. Réflexions au fil des jours* (Paris, Chiron, 1997), 33.

[8] See chapter 1, in Anne Cauquelin, *Petit traité de l'art contemporain* (Paris: Seuil, 1996).

[9] Paul Valéry, *Cahiers*, vol. 2 (Paris: Gallimard, 1980), 948.

[10] Giorgio Agamben, "What is the Contemporary?" in *What is an Apparatus and other essays* (Stanford: Stanford University Press, 2009), 41, 47, 52.

[11] Jean-Yves Jouannais, *L'Idiotie, Art, vie, politique-méthode* (Paris: Beaux Arts Editions, 2003).

[12] Letter of September 22, 2000, in Mathilde Monnier and Jean-Luc Nancy, *Dehors la danse* (Lyon: Droz, 2001).

[13] Michel Bernard, *De la création chorégraphique* (Pantin: Centre national de la danse, 2001).

[14] Merce Cunningham, interview reproduced in *Libération*, July 18 2009, 3.

REBELLING AGAINST LIMIT[1]
Jonathan Burrows

> He delighted to tread upon the brink of meaning.
> —Samuel Johnson, writing in the 18th century on fellow poet John Dryden[2]

Right from the very start the person watching a performance is looking for clues as to what might be happening, grasping lightly at straws and seeing rules where there may perhaps be none. Our lazily pleasurable efforts to figure out what's happening are clouded by the residual shape of other films, musical phrases, patterns of words, rhythms, sounds, half-forgotten dances and the detritus of bits and pieces of broken images and logic that flood by accident into what we're watching. And always the echo of performance—other performances and tones of voice and atmospheres that take the mind to some other thing seen in some other place. These traces of buried form sing, speak, dance, think, feel and act alongside every performance we watch, whether we want them there or not, manifesting themselves within our own physical memory to direct, re-order and anticipate at sensory-level the flow of what we're seeing. The effort required brings us equal pleasure and irritation, which experiences we store half-heartedly up for our final verdict. And even our mistaken readings stand in for the order and meaning we were looking for, doing their job as well as any other more deliberate shape and whether want them to or not.

And there are other unavoidable structures which give us handholds as we climb. That set of glances, in-breaths, hesitations, unisons and interruptions which are the moment by moment agreement between performers to coordinate and clarify what we're watching, opens another set of parameters by which we might read the game. This live working-out of the conditions under which the performers are operating appears softer than the rules, drawing us in and inviting us at skin-level to empathize and feel equal with what is unfolding in front of us.

And present above all, our habitual marking out of time with seconds, minutes and hours, which is a constant and inescapable measurement against which all other times and pulses are read.

In this crowded space of jostling forms it becomes absurd perhaps to talk of anything but relative freedom to choose our pathway between beginning and end. We seek to liberate ourselves from the mystery we are required to solve, which freedom and solution remain always imminent and always impossible.

I fill the performance I am watching also with all the residues in my body of other text, film, dance, song, music, touch, motor-pattern, speech-pattern, blockage, delusion, pre-occupation and desire that have passed through me. What the body remembers.

Such embodiment meets, shapes and affects what can happen. The performance sings through the spectator, whose own bodily response gives permission for the performers to draw the logic forward towards what might imminently be revealed. This embodiment beyond the form of the piece can manifest itself as visceral, tangible force, or as a whisper. And it is not about something more authentic than the form, since it does not exclude the superficial, the absurd, the ironic, the cynical or the daft as a brush. This embodiment, unconcerned with form, becomes anyway its own form.

The body is also sometimes called a score, being that repository of memory and possibility at cellular level which holds within itself a map of where you've been and might yet go: the body as an archive of trace elements, configuring and re-configuring themselves on the border between the private and that which is communicated. The subject of this talk is how in the hands of an artist who has practiced such things, the organizational part gives way eventually to this sensory realm. For some, formal scores and structures are a device to over-control this fruitful place of shifting perception. On the other hand one might see the score or structure as holder and provoker of the conditions under which we might experience perceptual shift, and from which otherwise we can sometimes too easily escape into our own habitual comfort zone.

When I choose to work in ways which measure and direct what I'm doing in ways I cannot always control, I ask must ask myself am I the agent of the score or have I become subject to it? At which point could I re-assert control without having to force a too solid structure into shapes which it resists? How might I find a working practice which embodies within it the room I need also to play? And when I play, how do I know when to trust my intuitive delight or when to be cautious of my too easy self-satisfaction? When intuition and play bring delight in rehearsal I must ask myself always, "But I am doing enough?," and when the same delight arises in performances I must ask, "But am I doing too much?" Between these two uncomfortable positions I catch glimpses of my own score, and all it embodies.

> When a rhyme surprises and extends the fixed relations between words, that in itself protests against necessity. When language does more than enough, as it does in all achieved poetry, it opts for the condition of over life and rebels at limit.
> —Poet Seamus Heaney, quoted by Colm Tóibín, *The Guardian London*, 2010[3]

Modern dance, as André Lepecki has pointed out, was once associated with the idea of bodily expression as a metaphor for universal emotions and experiences, an expressiveness which has largely fallen out of fashion. By reconnecting familiar images or language in new and startling ways however, one arrives at a different kind of metaphor, forged by rapid exchange and transformation of ideas, provoking and opening our minds to new perspectives. This transformative shift is common to music, poetry and dance, all of which share a familiar response from those who bear witness to them, that the spectator has followed what is happening but cannot necessarily understand how, and that is exactly the point. In these gaps between one thing and the next, time is momentarily sensitized, held still or erased, and a performative shift occurs.

I must write always towards the meanings which will imminently reveal themselves, through the gaps between one possible thread of unfolding connection and the next, in which momentary emptiness I am most myself and most lost. The decisions I make in each tiny void have repercussions for future possible events, but also for damage, subversion, de-railing, flattening or loss of what I have already made. Any decision I make at this stage could affect the sense of what happened before, and my previous decisions have the capacity to transform what might happen in the future, between which my only job is to notice in which way things are changing and what has been made manifest by that change. I am wrestling with the traces of meanings I wished for but can no longer control. The decisions I make in this tiny void between one idea and the next can only be intuitive and will never be enough, and I must submit to my lostness beyond any possible structure or lack of structure.

But to speak of a singular decision is to reduce the work to its simplest and luckiest moments. In reality each fragmentary place of intuition is beset by competing and overlapping layers and levels of decision which I am required to tackle simultaneously, each one fraught with change. The tensions between these simultaneous demands is the fuel which drives the sense of imminence forwards, each gap revealing a flash of competing possibilities by which the spectator might compose their own journey of anticipation and desire.

This falling out, subverting or extending of connections between disparate images leads also to absurdity, which arises in the mind of the spectator when the leap demanded between events is too great. The absurdity belongs not to the individual material but to the layers of perceived continuity with which the spectator knits their sense of the unfolding piece. This is where the work happens for all participants or witnesses in that thing we call a performance. The moments of too great a leap teeter on a knife edge between sudden understanding or liberation, and the snapping shut of that string of consequent thought, image or emotion we've been following. As Tim Etchells has said, "the leaps of absurdity must remain within the bounds of the possible," or else we stop believing that an answer might be imminent.

> I like to hear the sound of form, and I like to hear the sound of it breaking.
> —Frederick Seidel, *The Paris Review*, 2009

Sometimes you go in to work in the morning and the score you're trying to grapple with seems like a deadening chore. You project your imagination ahead to the empty space not yet filled and wonder what could possibly be gained by filling it, and the more pleased you are with the little you've done so far, the less feasible it seems to go on. And it's impossible to tell whether the dramaturgy or logic has simply collapsed, or whether your own view is so clouded by desire for what might happen that you can neither see nor believe in what is happening. Your patience for the job is exhausted while your head bursts with frustration, and in response you work too fast, too desperately, layering idea upon idea in a frantic attempt to solve the problem, and by the time you come grinding to a halt you have no idea where you are and at the same time realize you can never get back to where you were, even if you wanted to. It's in this place of disorientation that you catch sight for a moment of the way structure sometimes sustains but also easily empties your piece of meaning, and how intuition followed religiously cannot necessarily save you. You end up somehow stuck between the two, feeling slightly ashamed of your lack of faith in either, and yet it is perhaps in this place that the real work begins.

I like to hear the sound of form, and I like to hear the sound of it breaking.

The performance which chooses to accept a pact with those two unavoidable structural bullies, the beginning and the end, has already set in motion an unstoppable force, whether the middle is structured or not. It goes without saying then that the performance which subverts, extends, ignores, massages, sidesteps or leaves the theatre to avoid those two structural bullies, the beginning and the end, has invited them into the room by its very awareness of their absence. This awareness of the logics of familiar conventions shapes and alters our making and viewing, engendering a sense of release, a tiny void within which we catch sight of our own giddy absences. It is in the endurance of these gaps that the inner, sensory world of the performer rises to the fore and the performance occurs, whether the middle is structured or not.

Our tendency is to want to call everything score. This is good if we recognize also that score is nothing. There is an amount of change without which the dancing or moving body seems only to be searching for itself, and it is to avoid this searching that one sometimes turns to a score or structure. Or perhaps it is to avoid this searching that one mostly avoids scores or structures like the plague, or buries them as deep. This talk is about what happens when the score fails, when the structure implodes, when the idea gets lost in its own dead-ends, as all scores, structures and ideas must, and then the limit is reached and the world expands. For this most immaterial and impermanent of art forms in an increasingly disposable global art market, no structure, score, improvisation, material, image, movement or idea can ever matter enough to argue. In this we begin and end with the image of a human being walking onstage to endure, resist or confront an audience, whose discomfort reveals something to us about our own uncertainty and bloody-mindedness in the world. And that is enough for me, whether or not the piece has a beginning or an end, and regardless of whether the middle is structured or not.

[1] This text was written as part of the Misery of Form symposium, conceived by Susanne Foellmer and Thomas Plischke for Tanzkongress in Düsseldorf in 2013.

[2] Samuel Johnson, *Lives of the English Poets* (Oxford, New York: Oxford University Press, 2009), 201.

[3] Poet Seamus Heaney quoted in Colm Tóibín, "Review of *Human Chain* by Seamus Heaney," *The Guardian*, August 21, 2010.

ON NOTATION[1]

Laurence Louppe

> What becomings pass through us today, which sink back into history but do
> not arise from it, or rather that arise from it only to leave it?
> —Gilles Deleuze and Félix Guattari, *What is Philosophy?*[2]

Today dance notations, used as tools of analysis and reflection, raise a lot of interest. The remarkable work of the Quatuor Knust and the very advanced research of Myriam Gourfink on technological dispositifs are indicative of a concern that is already at large not simply in the field of choreography but in contemporary art in general.

The use and the teaching of notations in dance, long marginalized in France, have over the last decade blazed completely new paths in creation and reflection. The significant work of the Quatuor Knust has contributed a great deal to this new direction: thanks to Labanotation, this group, often working as part of a larger team, has succeeded in reviving emblematic works of modernity, and in so doing has highlighted and problematized the identity of and an interest in the score. That is to say, in the words of Jean-Christophe Royoux, "the elaboration of a process of anamnesis that restores to the surface a buried event, something initially forgotten, predisposed to make re-emerge, always and again, modes of appropriation of the modernity to come."[3] This amounts to re-injecting a new attitude in dance's modes of production: that of extracting the work from the domination of an original state (often fetishized in the choreographic community), and accepting its unstable "allographic" status, in the terminology of Nelson Goodman,[4] in other words the plurality of occurrences and infinite potentialities of its "re-workings." The word "workings" is not used here by chance, as it opens up the semantic field of labor. Revival in dance is always linked to the involvement of a subject in an action.

The production of a gesture is always accomplished through an "expense." (Re-production, not in the sense of duplicating but of producing again, whatever the registers of this re-production might be.) The body is at work, and one of the options of the revival will have to do with the contents of the work itself. In notation practices, the body at work in the re-production simultaneously reveals the modes of this re-production.

Rudolf Laban's project from the 1920s (the construction of a choreographic field for the 20th century on the basis of a notation system that would be a useful tool for the practices of archiving and analysis) here reveals its impact and power of premonition. Notation—sensitive to "modus operandi," deployment, and trajectories—does not create a concrete materiality (i.e., Goodman's concept of the "autographic," which was taken up by Gérard Genette under the term "immanence"). Therefore, it frees the dancer from the peremptory emphasis of a gesture that, without recognizing its processes of production, keeps the circumstances of its own advent hidden. But, above all, it allows dance to take part in this discourse that, since Benjamin, have affected contemporary art as a whole: the reproducibility of works, and the critical questions pertaining to an object whose identity (and authenticity) could only be gauged from its inalterable immutability. In this way, dance opens a dialogue with other artistic procedures developing today. Better: Dance has become a model, in the sense that a choreographic score (more so than a traditional musical score) sets a program of activities, or "scripts" that in turn generate "scenes" that multiply in time and space. But this program of activities, whether captured live or as a recording, remakes or re-configures differently each time and projects the shadow cast by the score into numerous contemporary practices (variously legible or asserted).

First, let's note the irreversible dynamics brought about by the revalorization of choreographic notations. An example is given by the important artistic and theoretical research carried out by Myriam Gourfink, and the way she uses the score in computer-assisted dance composition. By superposing different notation practices, with her partners (Laurence Marthouret, dancer-choreographer and a transcriber in Labanotation, and Frédéric Voisin, programmer-musician, co-author with the choreographer of the LOL software), Myriam Gourfink opens a surprising creative path. The point here is not to analyze at length Gourfink's aesthetic choices or artistic practices. Her discourse and her approach are extremely subtle, and her research on new parameters that question the elements of movements that have already been referenced in modern dance seems very promising. Her shows involve multiple, shifting internal journeys charged with a slow-burning intensity and an extreme concentration that gathers around the apparent continuity of micro-orientations, requiring sustained attention from the spectator.[5] In her very enlightening and sharp analysis of the current choreographic scene, Geisha Fontaine writes: "Each of this choreographer's shows contains an infinity of events and movements, but they are often barely perceptible, or only become apparent with the passing of time [...] It is a question of presenting all the almost microscopic alterations in the body, not in terms of decomposition but of transition."[6] Now, our purpose is not to demonstrate the capacity of the score to develop a compositional logic, however pertinent and vibrant, but rather to observe notation practices as a means to alter the modes of production, to make the choreographic project, and (perhaps) art in general, operate differently.

Testing limits

The natures of systems of notation are multiple. The Labanotation mentioned above proposes a literally coded and structured system of signs. But other methods can also provide scoring functions. Two pieces reconstructed by the Quatuor Knust—*Continuous Project –*

91

Altered Daily (1969) by Yvonne Rainer, after the title of a work by Robert Morris, and *Satisfyin' Lover* by Steve Paxton (1967)—are archived using oral descriptions, recapitulations, notes, and grids not so different from the "tasks" elaborated by Ann Halprin at the end of the 1950s. Tasks had two aims: first, that of de-subjectivizing the source of the movement, and second, that of ridding it of stylistic or ornamental concerns. Robert Morris, who attended Halprin's workshops, reaffirms her idea, saying "A fair degree of complexity of these rules and cues effectively blocked the dancer's performing 'set' and reduced him to frantically attempting to respond to cues—reduced him from performance to action."[7] In proposing banal activities such as "sweeping" or "climbing repeatedly up a ladder," a task defends against the arrogant aesthetics of the spectacle and returns to tension-free practices, whose peaceful rhythm inspires a new quality of presence. The drafting of "charts" (both grids and instruction manuals) allows the body to be revisited without being subjected to sequences of organic determinism and to invent new "undetermined" scores (not far from John Cage's "indeterminacy"), in which the line of thought, linked to improvisation, leads the subject to work outside the normal set of possibilities. The list of movements to be performed, linked to elementary (generic) functions of the body (rotation, flexion, extension, etc.), is determined by a random process. This produced unexpected results, things that the corporeal subject did not know about himself. The value of this experimentation is significant. "Then," says Ann Halprin, "I tried to do it. I got into the wildest combination of movements, things I never could have conceived of. All of a sudden, my body began to experience new ways of moving."[8] In fact the score, a word that keeps coming back in the dance field until today, reveals ways of testing limits. Its purpose is to subvert the usual references. But also, as we shall see several times, to create artistic communities around an objective project in which no individual power or narcissistic command could take control of its regulations.

What we call the "program of activities" involves no stylistic preference related to the qualitative decisions of a single person. "As the teacher or director of the group, I never told anybody why a movement should be or how it should look. In that sense, too, they had to build their own technique. Even now in our company there is no unified look; there's a unified approach but everybody is different in movement."[9] Thus the rules of the game are open to interpretation, but the process to be followed remains, since neither the theoretical foundation nor the operating modalities of the project are concealed. These words, written forty years ago, still resonate powerfully in dancers' consciousness. Notational practices emerge as a means (an opportunity?) to create a non-Oedipal framework in which adhesion to a model of the body would no longer be necessary, nor would the transmission of established values or, above all, beliefs.

The score can also lie within the space of the performance: Simone Forti's "dance constructions" at the Reuben Gallery in 1960 presented material dispositifs (platforms in *Platforms*, boxes on wheels in *Rollers*, a balancing beam in *Seesaw*, etc.[10]). In this case, the score is built up from variously constraining and heterogeneous materials: instructions and objects, space, sound, the presence of spectators, etc. This provides the basis for the prescription of the desired, or the possible, activities that the material framework can in turn trigger or inhibit. For *Rollers*, non-dancers in simply made small boxes on wheels were pulled about by performers: the physical restrictions of the space and the unplanned circulation of the carts transformed the setting into a bumper-car ring. The score not only plans the chaotic and unpredictable paths of the carts and their collisions, but also the frightened cries of their occupants. Following this example, numerous works by the Judson Dance Theater used objects as scores to determine routes to follow. It is possible to see, as Sally Banes did in her famous *Terpsichore in Sneakers* first published in 1980, an approach to the mediating object as the supreme factor to remove "the drama from the dance performance, substituting a purposive, directed concentration,"[11] and therefore a tool of stylistic transformation. Later, looking back on this mythical group of artists from a distance that corresponds to our own today, she altered her analysis, considering the object as a constructive element of dance, specifically taking Robert Morris's "Notes on Dance" (mentioned above) as a basis: "For Morris, objects were superior to tasks as a means to solve problems and thus create a structure for the dance." Then she draws up a list of the "problems" in question, which are no different from those involved in a compositional score, such as "setting up relationships among movement, space, and duration, or shifting focus between the 'egocentric and the exocentric'."[12] Even if the conditions of the relationship with the object are not specifically prescribed, the score as an object contains within it all the movements that can be used to manipulate it: today the "reading" of objects or environmental elements is sometimes used as a score in Simone Forti's workshops.

Between presences

In the (generally sterile) debate about dance notation, a common reproach is that a score defines, assigns, and formalizes territories. However, it should not be thought that a score is limited on one hand to a form of pre-organization for the choreographic work, or, on the other, to a mapping of traces—that is to say a linear vision of what was before and will be after. This reproach is made invalid by the connections that have constantly been woven between the score and improvisation up into the present day. In the same way as a biodegradable sculpture created by Robert Morris, Yvonne Rainer's *Continuous Project – Altered Daily* proposes that the work "be altered," in other words reinvented, daily. The score is recreated in the very arising of events, starting from determined modules reorganized at each performance, and in the unexpected corporeal events it triggers as a result of their encounter or their succession.

For Lisa Nelson, the score in improvisation is presented as a "montage" in which verbal instructions as well as corporeal images in time and space converge.[13] In her essentially improvisational work, the Brussels-based choreographer Patricia Kuypers (who has long been familiar with the work of Steve Paxton and Lisa Nelson) deals with "the interactive aspect of group improvisation, where invention occurs in what emerges between individuals and their environment, in a space that avoids the isolated thought of an individual person." The score gives legibility to the moment and "what happens through the relationship between several intelligences in movement."[14] This concept of the score is very far from Goodman's, who sees it as in stasis, as a guardian of the identity of the work between two performances. Here, the score is developed between presences; it is a component of the actions that brought it into being. Or rather, it is destined to experience constant transformation. It undergoes mutation, and consequently is unable to guarantee any permanence. Furthermore, the notion of an improvisational score heightens the associated quality of the gestural choice with a result yet to be seen, blurring the moment of invention with that of its being written and read.

It is not irrelevant that improvisation as a notational reading practice ("improvisation has the possibility of making process visible," said Ann Halprin[15]), putting interpretations or grids simultaneously into action, originated in the 1970s at the very moment technological dispositifs of reflection (in every sense of the word) on the lapse of time—the awareness of the instant as already recorded, already represented—were being developed. This is the case in Bruce Nauman's *Corridor* (1970) and Dan Graham's *Present Continuous Past* (1974). In these two works, we find two specific characteristics of notational practices: 1) the setting of a subject in movement within a spatial script that entails a certain itinerary; 2) the persistence of a transient movement by means of a recording process that is part of the moment of its occurrence, and beyond. This is how the revolving door in Graham's *Altered Two-Way Mirror Revolving Door and Chamber with Sliding Door* (1987) operates. The gesture to push the door is captured by the glass surface as it occurs. As the door rotates, it multiplies and diffracts the gesture onto the different surfaces. The passage of a subject through the images of his own gesture, which he allows to vanish behind him. Action-reflection, mirror-reflection, trace-reflection. In other words, to use Pierce's vocabulary, index and icon at once. The linear vector of time explodes with the shattering of chronological categories. The score operates at length here: it exists prior to movement and establishes the modalities of the movement's trajectory. At (almost) the same time, it delivers its tenuous and fleeting recording. It provokes a crisis in the time of the gesture, which escapes from a single moment to a multiple "present." Lastly, it offers an experience (here of sensorial confusion) to an acting subject.

Body mapping

Let's consider the body as a score. Or rather the score as a constant reference to a body in action, to a body-subject circulating and not enclosed in the transcendent and unequivocal definition of a Self. At the end of the 1950s, the grids designed by Ann Halprin reorganized the body by fragmenting it into parts (head, shoulder, torso, etc.), allowing the anatomy to become a map in itself, a "plan" of gestural production according to the part of body selected.[16] For Sally Banes, *Trio A* (1966) by Yvonne Rainer creates a "catalogue" of all the movements of the human body.[17] Today, along the lines followed by choreographer Alain Buffard, it is possible to speak of dance as "body mapping." This notion exists on several levels: first, the still vivid memory of body art with the designation of places on the body, and sometimes their function (either undifferentiated or erogenous sexual zones, with the interplay of possible displacements and exchanges). The body, as a site, can be the very stage where movement unfolds (cartography-scenography). Vito Acconci, *Using the Body as a Place* (1972): The artist, naked and standing, moves his hand in front of his torso. The landscape-body becomes a background that hosts the movement of this object-limb as something almost alien to its owner.[18] Another example is Contact Improvisation (which emerged in the same period) in which touching and sharing weight with another body permits the identification of areas of anchoring, contact, and sliding. This observation is reinforced by tactile information that extends the prism of perception through inter-corporeal trajectories (i.e., the body of the other as a score for my own movement). *More et Encore* (1999) by Alain Buffard offered a remake of a somewhat altered performance by Acconci (a remake of a remake if we recall *Fresh Acconci* by Mike Kelley and Paul McCarthy. Memories, revivals, variations. The body as a palimpsest, etc.). A performer wearing a blindfold touches a part of somebody else's body and names it (with all the possible mistakes). Corporeal geography as a place of exploration; touching as transmission, rather than speech. Steve Paxton says: "I tried to simplify the issues of the body for transmission to another body. I moved the mind of my mouth into my body, located issues, and reported the issues speaking (I assumed) directly to another body."[19] Naming, but also touching, folding, fiddling with parts of the body, describing the nature of the tissues (smooth, hairy), can be used, as was done by Jérôme Bel, to take away the sacred aura of the gesture and make it a simple means of self-reading in the context of an extreme intimacy with oneself, as well as to escape the traditional codes of representation (though genre painting in the past knew how to make visible the search for lice or fleas on a background of skin or hair). However, touching also offers a body to be "read." In *Jérôme Bel* (1995) by Jérôme Bel, two dancers stand in the foreground and very frontally present their naked bodies to the audience. Immobile bodies with no particular attributes labor with their own neutrality. These bodies do not communicate any information, except what is explored on their own surfaces: (touching, indicating, writing with lipstick) as if they had become a blank page on which their own history can be deciphered, including the cultural and identity codes that they reveal in a process of elimination.[20] In so doing, each body is itself led to its reification, and consents to being explored—externally, as soon as the manipulation or demonstration comes into contact with the body and skin, and internally, like the view of a visceral landscape, as Mona Hatoum presents in *Corps étranger* (1995) (a video work that presents itself to the viewer by diving through a screen in the form of a body orifice, realized by a camera inside the entrails of the artist). In both cases, external and internal, it is about questioning the visibility of the body—that which can appear (in Bel, within the framework of spectacular conventions). This reading of the body from an essentially anatomic standpoint (partial or global) can also be achieved through a sensorial approach. Floor exercises, as in Steve Paxton's *Helix*,[21] make it possible to study the configuration of the body through supports, sensations, and exchanges of tensions (*Helix* meaning the volumetric helical sculpture of the human body). It shows a series of rolls on the floor that revisit metaphorically, we might say by transcription, the essential elements of human locomotion. The surface of the floor becomes a receptor/reader of the corporeal landscape in contact with the skin/score. In this respect, the choreographic field is certainly the place where the distance between (and overlap of) the "optic" and the "haptic" is demonstrated most poignantly. Touching is an active component that, through a sensorial wave triggered in the spectator, enhances her vision. The "cartographic eye" described by Christine Buci-Glucksman, and which reads the cartography of the body, "establishes the visual as on a skin."[22] At the same time, this synesthesia questions itself and draws a dialectics.

Game rules to be interpreted

The journey of the notation through various topographies extends to other critical spaces. In 1995, at the time of the "revival" of the *Saut de l'ange* (1986), a work created by Dominique Bagouet and Christian Boltanski, the latter made a parallel between the transmission of a choreographic work (which automatically raises the question of notation) and the future of all contemporary creation after the death of its author. Just as a choreographic score is transmitted through new "interpretations," a work of art is constituted by "game rules to be interpreted" (the rules and tasks are all notation models). Taking his clothes "stacks" as an example, the detailed reality of which is irrelevant in comparison with the process, Boltanski imagines a museum filled with scores, "a museum with a number of game rules and plans that would have to be re-played every time."[23] The idea of "interpreting," and therefore of submitting any work of visual creation to a totally allographic regime, can also be found in the work of Pierre Huyghe, in particular in *Traffic* (Bordeaux, 1996) and the film *Dubbing*. The artist appropriated the urban or cinematographic heritage to "replay" it in another time-space, "dubbing" replaces the "original version" using new "interpreters." Therefore the score-film unfolds without images, which, in the case of dance notations, is analogous to a statement in signs of non-actualized gestures. With reference to this film, Pascale Cassagnau talks of "the score appropriated by an interpreter to reactivate it."[24] The notion of an "interpreter" of an already-made film relates to the reading of a score written by both the filmmaker and the actor of the original version.

Concerning the essential importance of notation practices (positioning oneself more in the diegetic than in the mimetic), Jean-Christophe Royoux had this to say about another work of Pierre Huyghe's, rightly entitled *Remake* (1995), a rereading of Hitchcock's *Rear Window*: "Rather than stick to or imitate a character, the performer [*interprète*] seems, though unostentatiously, to be quoting him or her." A role in every sense of the word falling to the person Pierre Huyghe calls the "doubler" (*Dubbing*, doubling as a new representation of the "double"?). So any score, whatever practice is concerned, performs a role crucial to modernity: "to evidence the work of representation in progress."[25]

This catalogue of unnamed scores seeping into contemporary art could be continued indefinitely. But let's go back to dance, to what is developing in this field today, to what the body and its presence are able to question and reactivate, to bring to life and survive (in the sense of Warburg's term *Nachleben*). Far from establishing itself as a tool of museum conservation, the score, says Pascale Cassagnau quoting Nietzsche, authorizes a "process that offers an escape from the tyranny of time and the resentment that accompanies it."[26] The different notational figures, whether in the instantaneous or the reconstruction, have to deal with time: time as a material to be managed in the performative act, but above all time as an aspect of History in which the corporeal event does not cease to recreate its own scene.

[1] This essay was first published as "Du partitionnel," in *Médium Danse*, *Art Press* 23 (2002): 32-39.

[2] Gilles Deleuze and Félix Guattari, *What is Philosophy?* trans. Graham Burchell and Hugh Tomlinson (New York: Columbia University Press, [1991] 1994), 113

[3] Jean-Christophe Royoux, "Remaking cinema: les nouvelles stratégies du remake et l'invention du cinéma d'exposition," in *Reproducibilité et irreproducibilité de l'œuvre d'art* (Brussels: La Lettre volée, 2001), 216.

[4] In *Languages of Art*, Nelson Goodman distinguishes between "autographic" works, whose material nature corresponds with its identity, and "allographic" works, which are "interpreted" from a score or text. See Nelson Goodman, *Languages of Art* (Indianapolis: Hackett Publishing Company, 1976).

[5] See Gourfink-Marthouret-Voisin, "LOL–un environnement expérimental de composition chorégraphique," in *EC/arts* 2 (2001).

[6] Geisha Fontaine, *Les danses du temps. Recherche sur la notion de temps en danse contemporaine* (Pantin: Centre national de la danse, 2004), 132-133.

[7] Robert Morris, "Notes on dance," *Tulane Drama Review* 10:2 (Winter 1965): 179-90.

[8] Ann Halprin, "Yvonne Rainer Interviews Ann Halprin," *Tulane Drama Review* 10:2 (Winter 1965): 145.

[9] Ann Halprin, "Yvonne Rainer Interviews Ann Halprin," 143.

[10] For documentation of the "constructions," see *Handbook in Motion* (Halifax: Press of the Nova Scotia College of Art and Design, 1974).

[11] Sally Banes, *Terpsichore in Sneakers: Post-Modern Dance* (Middleton: Wesleyan University Press, [1980] 1987), 43.

[12] Sally Banes, *Writing Dancing in the Age of Postmodernism* (Middleton: Wesleyan University Press, 1994), 223.

[13] Lisa Nelson, "Sensation is the Image," In *Writings on Dance* 14 (1995-1996): 4-15.

[14] Patricia Kuypers, email to the author, June 6 2002. Gérard Genette would refer here to the "hyper-allographic," that is to say "works with a plural immanence." See Gérard Genette, *L'œuvre de l'art* (Paris: Seuil, 1995), 173; 228.

[15] Ann Halprin, quoted in Cynthia Novack, *Sharing the Dance: Contact Improvisation and American Culture* (Madison: University of Wisconsin Press, 1990), 28.

[16] Ann Halprin, "Yvonne Rainer Interviews Ann Halprin," 160.

[17] Sally Banes, *Terpsichore in Sneakers*, 47.

[18] This performance is documented in *Avalanche* (Winter 1973).

[19] Steve Paxton, "Drafting Interior Techniques," *Contact Quarterly*: 18:1 (Winter-Spring 1993): 66.

[20] However, one can only agree with Jérôme Bel as quoted by Geisha Fontaine and his skepticism regarding nudity as a demonstration of a "natural body" unmarked by cultural and social indicators. See Geisha Fontaine, *Les danses du temps*, 100.

[21] Steve Paxton, "Helix," *Contact Quarterly* 16: 3 (Summer 1991).

[22] Christine Buci-Glucksman, *L'Œil cartographique de l'art* (Paris: Galilée, 1996), 75.

[23] Christian Boltanski, "À propos de Dominique Bagouet," video-interview by Charles Picq, Maison de la danse de Lyon, 1995.

[24] Pascale Cassagnau, "Pierre Huyghe, le temps désaffecté," *Omnibus* 19 (January 1997): 10-11. Note that "appropriating" a score for a dancer, as for a musician, is almost impossible since choreographic scores are protected by copyrights. Thus the enormous variance between the fields of choreography and the visual arts, whose production modes and frameworks are very different. Here the author pleads guilty: it is not enough to trace "figures" or procedures used in the contemporary era. One should also trace what types of powers (or micro-powers) the different practices have to face in order to elaborate their field and to make these figures/procedures take place. But such a project would largely exceed the scope of this article.

[25] Jean-Christophe Royoux, "Remaking cinema," 220.

[26] Pascale Cassagnau, "Pierre Huyghe, le temps désaffecté," 10.

DANCING THE VIRTUAL[1]
Erin Manning

Think the body as an ecology of operations that straddles the flesh of its matter and the environmentality of its multiple takings-form. From such an environmentality retain the idea of technique. Think technique not as an add-on to a pre-existing body-form but as a process of bodying. Think technique as an in-forming of a mutating body. And then think that body as a field of relations rather than a stability, a force taking-form rather than simply a form. See technique as the mode through which a body can express, aligning into this expression qualities of its bodying (aspects of its motor tendencies, aspects of its existing experiential matrix). Make it, as Deleuze and Guattari would say, a body without organs. Make it more-than its biological organization.

Cleave the notion of the body beyond the human. Connect it to all that co-combines with it to create a movement of thought. Keep the movement of thought in the world (instead of putting it back in the body) and see what it can do. Consider this image: you are in the garden, your knees covered in mud, hands deep in the earth for an early spring planting. Instead of seeing the earth as a quality apart from the knee attached to a pre-existing human form, see the knee-hand-earth as a worlding, a force of form, an operative ecology. See this ecology as an active technique for creating, for the bodying, a taste of spring. Instead of thinking the body as separate from the earth, as separate from the arrival of spring, see the ecology knee-hand-earth in a spring planting as a technique for tuning the season. Notice that the more the knee-hand-earth constellation becomes its own intensive entity, the more the feeling of spring beckons even though it is barely two degrees Celsius. Were this November in Montréal, there would definitely be no such feeling of incipient warmth, the gardening assemblage in that season tuned more toward closing things in rather than opening them up. What is different between these two scenarios? In the spring, the knee-hand-earth assemblage is tuning beyond its novembering technique to encompass a quality of tuning-toward: this is a gardening with an anticipation of the feeling of spring. Incipient smells, the quality of a breeze, the texture of the earth, all of these tune the technique of gardening toward what it can call forth here and now, what its assemblage can become in this day in May. This is not just about sewing a seed, it is about reconstituting the relation climate-body-environment. It is about becoming co-constituted by an environmentality in the making. The technique of gardening for spring has transduced into an incipient call for the season to blossom.

Now that there is a sense of how the body evolves as an assemblage in this gardening scenario, consider the role of the object or "matter"—the garden spade, the earth, the tulip bulb—keeping in mind that, like the body, an object is a milieu of relations that are activated through vectors of association in the aliveness of a singular event. And yet, an object is also different from a body in the sense that it attunes toward roles activated by the implicit forces not only in its objectness but of the environment of which it becomes a relational part. An object is as much how it does as what it does. Think this object in relation to this multiplicity, in its competing orders of magnitude, as a speciation[2] that is never disconnected from the event of its coming-to-be (blade-density-resistance, rhythm-handle-forearm). Think the object not as this or that pre-constructed iteration but as that which calls forth implicit forces that affect not only the objects themselves but the environmentalities of which they are part. And think these implicit forces as the conduit, the vector or force of matter's inherent capacity to become more-than. Think the object not ontologically but processually. Objects in-forming are exactly co-imbricated with the implicit forces of their potential to become in an ecology of practices. This is their technicity. Technicity is the modality for creating out of a system of techniques the more-than of system. In the gardening example, technicity is the how of the ecology—the metal push of spade that calls forth the taste of a breeze that is felt as the leaving-behind of the impassibility of winter, an ecology which activates, in a kind of future presenting, the coming spring.

Technique and technicity coexist. Where technique engages the repetitive practices that form a composing body—be it organic or inorganic—technicity is a set of enabling conditions that extract from technique the potential of the new for co-composition. Think the new not as a denial of the past, but as the quality of the more-than of the past tuning toward the future. The new is a qualitative difference, already felt in the will have been. Time loops. The past now carries a potentiality that was always there but was backgrounded. Its implicit forces are coming to expression in a mutability that will in-form future relational constellations, eventually transducing into technique that which will be reiterable, repeatable. But beyond the technique something else can take place. A setting into eventness of implicit forces creates an opportunity for the coming event's technicity to express itself. Think technicity as the process that stretches out from technique, creating brief interludes the more-than of technique, gathering from the implicit the force of form. Think technicity as that which marks the difference in the event of gardening, an event, which, on the surface, uses the same techniques whether in November or in May. Think technicity as the field where movement begins to dance. Technicity as the art of the event.

Technique comes out of practice as much as it is what goes into practice. In this regard, techniques are hard to come by—they demand the patient exploration of how a practice best comes into itself. Technicity is the next phase of technique—it is the experience of technique reaching the more-than of its initial application.

Technicity is a craft—it is how the field of techniques touches its potential. From technique to technicity we have a transduction. Technicity is a shift of level that activates a shift in process. This is how techniques evolve. Without transduction we would have only mimicry, translation. The copying of forms. Technicity in-gathers the forms toward their implicit potentiality and squeezes from them the drops of the excess of their actualizations. Technicity captures the affective tonality of a process, a tendency, and catapults it toward new expression.

There are techniques for hoeing, for standing at a bus stop, for reading a philosophical text, for taking a seat in a restaurant, for being in line at a grocery store, each of these techniques both singular and general experienced as the "same" techniques but always with a difference. For example, there are cultural differences between modes of waiting in line, but all standing in line carries a certain number of general identifiers such as an implicit understanding that only one person can be served at one time. There are of course also techniques in a seed's germination, in the shift of the earth's axis toward the sun, and in the process of photosynthesis. And there are techniques that build on techniques—techniques for bowing the violin include implicit modes of standing as well as techniques for arm movement or wrist inflection; techniques for painting include implicit modes of seeing as well as techniques for manipulating light or texture; techniques for dance include implicit understandings of equilibrium as well as techniques for locating and moving rhythm and extension.

William Forsythe shows his dancers that, for instance, you can lift an arm across the body by using the extension of the limb creating a standard *épaulement*. Building technique on technique, however, he then shows that the amplitude of this movement's qualitative force is fundamentally altered through a movement of the rib-cage. Instead of pulling the arm, push the rib-cage and the body becomes a diagonal force, a torque, hip-shoulder syncing with an elasticity that dances almost without effort. The first option is a movement from the pretence of a stability. The second is a movement-moving. This is technique building on technique.

Something else is happening here as well. A technicity is developing that draws on the diagonal force of a moving body. Suddenly ribs become fingers, and shoulders become articulate. Forsythe explains: "When you move your shoulder, you can move it as expressively as the hand—the shoulder is the second most expressive part after the hand—the muscles over the rib are the serratus—they are like the finger ligaments going up the hand. Articulate your shoulder from the serratus."[3] When shoulder becomes quality of hand, organ becomes expression. The body acts in implicit relation with a movement that tunes to a different constellation of articulation. Body becomes bodying, and in this transduction, a series of new potentialities for movement are born. Think technique as that which perfects a system and technicity as that through which a process is born that composes the more-than which is the body's movement ecology.

Technicity is the associated milieu of technique. If technique is the learning of a certain kind of reach, a certain kind of pull or turn or spiral, if technique is the sounding of a voice or the rhythmic assertion of a step, technicity is the operational field of its expressivity. This field is co-imbricating. It is a lively interval, energized with all of the forces of movement-moving. The role of technique in the field of technicity is to create the potential for a singularity of forms to mutate toward a generative process. Technique is key because of its rigorous method of experimentation and repetition, a method that allays any passivity in the passage from the form of experimentation to its force. Technicity—the associated milieu where form once more becomes force, where individual gesture becomes individuation—is the process through which the implicit is acted upon to generate something as yet unthought.

The associated milieu of technicity is never given in advance, never conditioned before a process is under way. It is the event's process, never its mediation. Technicity is the field of incorporation in the making of technique's insistent difference and repetition. "The taking-form does not accomplish itself visibly in a single instant, but in a number of successive operations. We cannot strictly distinguish the taking-form from the qualitative transformation."[4] Technicity sets the conditions for successive operations, each of which incorporates the implicit, creating an opening toward an ecology of experimentation. It multiplies the form which "is but a fabricated intention, with a flighty disposition, [that] can neither grow old or become" toward an intensity that will always resist capture, but that will leave its trace. Technicity is an open field for structured improvisation. It in-forms a process of taking-form, gathering from that process the myriad levels of information. In doing so, it reminds us that form is in-formation, a complex tending-toward that momentarily resolves as this or that, but continuously preaccelerates toward the incipient nextness of its future-pastness.

Improvisation is not born of technicity, however. Technique is its grounding. It is born, paradoxically, through the repetition of a certain form-taking. Without the rigour and precision that comes of repeated, habitual activity, improvisation's potential vocabulary is too narrow, its implicit force too backgrounded to be functionally emergent. To create the new it is vital to have experimented with the outer limits of a vocabulary that is highly technical, and from there, but transversally, to invent. This invention takes place in the associated milieu—it is not I who invent, but the bodying process itself, across the activity of movement-moving. Remember that the associated milieu is the environmentality of the technique in its dephasing, the field where technique and technicity meet.

In the realm of the political, the question of technicity extends to the how of collective enunciation. How is a collaborative event orchestrated? What modes of process are created to assure that difference can be heard without succumbing to the end-game of debate? How to tweak collective individuation to give the group a voice that allows something to be said that is more-than individual but carries within it the germs of a multiplicitous individuality? How to operate at the level of collective invention in the tense of the not-yet, at the very edges where thought and practice meet? How to orchestrate a collective bodying—a society, in the Whiteheadian sense—that crafts its process from the very ecology that constitutes it, that merges technique with the more-than of its potential, finding within technique the implicit force that propels technique toward the excess of form or position?

Take the 2009 SenseLab[5] event *Society of Molecules*.[6] The goal of *Society of Molecules* was to find techniques that would allow a large group (between 60-100 people) from multiple countries to connect in the creation of an aesthetico-political event. This event was to occur in many countries at once, and so would have to work without a gathering in the form of a face-to-face encounter. The problem was how to distribute self-organizing creative energies while operatively interconnecting them at a distance. How to connect not simply at the level of content but also at the level of process?

This event had a lead-up of a year, during which "molecules" were created across the world. Molecules were defined as a group of 7-10 people who would take on a collective project. This collective project was defined as a local event that would creatively address a politico-aesthetic issue felt by local participants to affect the quality of their lives. The politico-aesthetic interventions would last between three hours and seven days, and take place during the first week of May 2009.

The early stages of the event were steeped in practices from earlier collective organizing: we read assigned texts, we created an internet hub for concept invention, we collectively thought about the relation between art and politics and we worked locally to develop ideas for our own molecular projects. Then we began to conceive of specific techniques for the larger distributed event, always with a focus on developing affective strategies that would allow us to connect at the level of our processes rather than focusing exclusively on content and thereby falling into the trap of "reporting." Three techniques were invented.

The first was the technique of the "emissary." Each molecule was invited to choose an emissary as well as to name a host. The emissary of each local grouping was paired with the host of another group. Sometime in the five months preceding the main event, the emissary would travel to the host group (virtual voyages were a possibility where resources did not allow physical travel). The role of the emissary was to make "first contact" with the other local (molecular) culture. To facilitate the unannounced meeting, "movement profiles" were compiled and distributed to the emissaries. The movement profiles described the designated host's habitual daily movements through the city, so that if the emissary so desired first contact could be made in a performative fashion taking advantage of the element of surprise.[7] Emissaries were encouraged to use standard forms of communication like cellphones and addresses sparsely, focusing instead being guided by the movement profile. Upon meeting, the host's job was to gather the molecule together and treat the emissary with a "relational soup."

The second technique involved collectively composing a recipe for the relational soup which would then be brought back to the "home" molecule. The relational soup could be anything at all. The enabling constraint was that whatever form it took, it should give the emissary a taste of that group's process.

The third technique took the form of a "process seed" brought by the emissary and left with the host group. The seed was sealed, and was to be opened only after the event. It could be an object around which a future group activity could be organized, or a set of procedures to be followed collectively.

The hope was that the techniques would activate a technicity that might orient the process in ways previously unimaginable. While there was a definite moment of aesthetico-political intervention (May 1-7, 2009), the emphasis of these techniques concerned both the specificity of the local events *and* what could be generated over time that might continue to feed a growing political process. Because the force of technicity is not measurable, there can be no "result" to such an event. How thoughts continue to resonate, how aesthetico-political practices created for local constituencies continue to evolve both actually and virtually—these are questions of technicity, and as such, they remain open. What can be said with certainty is that it is possible to create an environment that tends to the political in creative and unforeseen ways, and it is possible for techniques to breed into technicities that far outlive their local enunciations. Collective individuation in the realm of the aesthetico-political takes careful crafting, but it can have important effects on the field of the political.

Paired with the careful crafting of technique, improvisation can play an important role as an emergent procedure for the creation of new associated milieus of relation, milieus that subvert the linear time of if-then. What improvisation can do is texture technique to flesh out its potential. It does so by making "if" an open question, a time-loop, a folding proposition for the moving. From habit to invention, from technique to improvisation, the form becomes a folding-through of time in the making. The time of the if becomes an if...if...that lands only long enough to transduce, to in-gather the potential of the coming individuation toward the force of its already passing future becoming.

Technique remains here as the tool for the crafting of the movement's excessive share, of the more-than of form it continuously leaves behind. At this juncture of invention, technique, improvisation, and technicity are at close quarters—each builds on the other. Take an example from *Society of Molecules*. The technique may have been to collectively make a relational soup. And perhaps the decision was to follow conventions and buy vegetables at the market to actually make a soup. But at the market there is the sensation that the new-formed group (molecule+emissary) are somehow already in the process of crafting this relational intervention. Perhaps it's best not to cut this process by going home and beginning to cook? Perhaps a picnic on the side-walk is a better option? And then, in retrospect, perhaps the relational soup wasn't even the picnic but the movement improvisation that momentarily came to life in the market-gathering? Perhaps the recipe is not a meal at all, but an urban intervention? The point is that this intervention did not come out of nowhere. The technique was the spark that set it into motion. Improvisation then opened the movement to what it could become, unmoored. If the event was successful, it will have generated a more-than of its technique. This will have been its technicity.

It's not about designing the "never experienced before" but about creating an opening within the event for the outdoing of form. This involves a process of folding-through that activates a resonant fielding of different layers of dimensionalizing already in potentia. There is no reproducibility of technicity—it can never be generalized. Techniques, on the other hand, must to some degree be replicable—this very capacity for reproduction is what gives them their rigour.

Now think this in terms of a dancing body and consider José Gil's concept of overarticulation, which can be designed at the felt experience of the form outdoing itself. In rehearsal, William Forsythe asks his dancers to think about "what it was about the position that made it motion?"[8] Overarticulation is one way the technicity of movement-moving—movement beyond position—makes itself felt. The dancing body overarticulates not by bringing content to form or form to content, but by foregrounding the virtual share of technicity coursing through and across its movements in the making.

Overarticulation is steeped in technique, but to make itself felt it cannot remain on the strata of the technical. Forsythe calls it "looking for a chain of sensations rather than a chain of positions." Without ever referring to overarticulation as such, Forsythe speaks of refraining from "holding the sensation hostage to your expertise," thus making the experiential felt: "you're dancing in order to have sensations—you're looking for where that sensation is in your whole spectrum of dancing." Dance from the vectors of position where position is already becoming motion, ask, says Forsythe, "how you might get the most from that closed set of permissible positions: how can I take that movement as far as it can go?"[9]

Overarticulation is the surging forth of the potential of a movement's unfolding. It is the post of its preacceleration. It is the excess of the displacement, the making-felt of the expressive micromovements that populate all movements in the making. Think of the spiral as an example. A spiral as such cannot be danced. It is more duration than form. To spiral is to dance the future of a movement spiralling, to dance the overarticulation of the present passing. Each spiralling thus touches on the force of technicity, a technicity that can be amplified by emphasizing this tendency and composing with it. Take the spiral, diagonalize and torque it. "Follow the curves of the body—send the curve out from the hip to the arm raising and curving overhead, and note the hip is still moving when the arm is finished. Note the feeling of cross-attenuation (*tendu*)— find the cross patterns of the stretch—go for the feeling of the skin, the skin will tell you how to do it. Now add rotation: like an octopus who can do ballet" (Forsythe).[10] Seek not to locate the body in the afterposition of its having spirallingly diagonalized: feel its octopus. Dwell in the octopus and move it, leaving even this multiplying bodying-form behind. Move and exfoliate, as José Gil would say.[11]

The virtual share of movement—its technicity, its over-articulation—is not added-on to the spiralling body. Technicity is made tangible by the felt experience of duration within the movement itself. When a movement becomes habitual, its durational force is backgrounded to make space for its capitalizable economy in the time of the now. Get to the bus-stop, to the coffee-shop, to the store. End-point is everything. Everyday movements are reduced, compacted, overarticulations muted by overarching directionality and pre-dimensionalizing. A dancing body, on the other hand, learns to stretch out the force of duration, to express incipience, making palpable the force of form which is movement's procedural intensity. In the dancing, movement actualizes at the very limit of this intensity, making felt the activation of its in-formation as event.

To have moved is to have overarticulated in germ. Dancing is simply one example that brings to the fore the technicity of the body's overarticulating potential. To dance the virtual is to move while keeping alive the intervals that are the very compositions of an overarticulation that cannot be recognized or reproduced as such but that will feed every subsequent movement. Its mantra is: "Already go to what you think is your limit, and then go further" (Forsythe).[12]

Overarticulation, as the vibratory resonance of movement's excess—the felt surplus of its actualization—creates a field for durational movement that coexists with the timed event of movement moving. The more precise the technicity, the more complex the field movement leaves behind and casts forth. Technicity embeds margins of indetermination across systems of technique, activating the associated milieu of emergence itself. It is the practice that invents at the very edges of composition where the composition seems to have already come to its limit. To dance the virtual is to have been overarticulated as a mutating ecology that continuously moves beyond position. To dance the virtual is to have straddled the interval between technique and technicity, to have danced the immanent futurity of movement in the making.

[1] This text is excerpted from *Always More Than One: Individuation's Dance* (Durham: Duke University Press, 2013), 31-40.

[2] Throughout *Always More than One*, I am defining "speciation" in a way very different from the mainstream notion, coming out of evolutionary theory, that understands speciation as the evolutionary process by which new biological species arise. Here, speciation refers to the processual force of the not-yet that exceeds the concept of species. Speciations are what connect in the moving, I am suggesting, and not species in the sense of discrete categories of being. Speciations are neither organic nor inorganic—they are series, as Deleuze defines them, affective tonalities in act that merge tendencies for form and force.

[3] William Forsythe, from Forsythe Company rehearsal, Frankfurt, November 16 2010.

[4] Gilbert Simondon, *L'individuation à la lumière des notions de forme et d'information* (Grenoble: Éditions Jérôme Millon, 2005), 57.

[5] http://www.senselab.ca/

[6] For the documentation of the event Society of Molecules, as well as interviews on micropolitics with Isabelle Stengers, Bruno Latour, Maurizio Lazzarato, Barbara Glowzcewski, Julia Loktev, and Adam Bobette see http://inflexions.org/volume_4/n3_hamidamanninghtml.html.

[7] In cases where the host might leave during the five-month period, allowances within the movement profile had to be made. This became quite interesting as it required another member of the local molecule to move into another's movement profile for the duration of their absence.

[8] Forsythe, in rehearsals with the Forsythe Company, Frankfurt November 18 2010.

[9] Forsythe, in rehearsals with the Forsythe Company, Frankfurt November 18 2010.

[10] Forsythe, in rehearsals with the Forsythe Company, Frankfurt November 13 2010.

[11] Gil's concept of exfoliation is explored at length in *Metamorphoses of the Body*, trans. Stephen Muecke (Minneapolis: Minnesota University Press, 1985). Exfoliation suggests the creation of space through which a body-spacing, a space-bodying is co-composed.

[12] Forsythe, in rehearsals with the Forsythe Company, Frankfurt November 20 2010.

DANCE, THE METAMORPHOSIS OF THE BODY[1]
Boyan Manchev, Xavier Le Roy, and Franz Anton Cramer

Boyan Manchev: I shall begin by asking a question that is also a hypothesis, one that is probably a little daring: Is it possible to state that dance is becoming the art, if not the *techne*, emblematic of the contemporary world—and, if so, why? Yes, there's no doubt about it: today contemporary dance is bubbling with creative energy and attracts special attention from the public, but the phenomenon may have deeper roots than the internal logic of the development of an artistic field, in this case dance. One of the underlying questions that inevitably arises in relation to dance is that of the body, primarily the representations of the body as an object invested with cultural codes. Yet, at the same time, there is also the crucial question of the impossibility of inscribing the body itself within these codes as a place of resistance against them: the body as the place and power [*puissance*] of *ex-scription*. Let us suppose, then, that if dance is presented as the emblematic *techne* of the contemporary world, it is first and foremost as an expression of the innate transformability of the body and subject, and then as a form of resistance to the ambiguous radicalization and appropriation of this original transformability through the pernicious capitalism of the present day. This view proceeds from a more general hypothesis, according to which dance is defined as an experimental praxis of the transformability of the body—and thus as an autonomous sphere in which its techniques are invented. So let us consider the question of contemporary dance as consubstantial with the question of the body.

Xavier Le Roy: In Spinozan fashion, I prefer to substitute the question "What is the body capable of?" to "What is the body?" This question often underlies and motivates my work, just like questions related to the production of movement, such as, How do we extend our understanding of "movement"? How do we produce movements? What structure or organization produces what movement? These questions are pertinent to different fields, but they also cover dance. This is why I prefer to talk about choreography rather than dance. This thesis can be linked with the idea of the "current," of something that has taken place since the 1990s and that, I hope, is still active: what is vaguely and probably also imprecisely referred to as "conceptual dance." Use of the term "conceptual" is in fact a rather delicate matter and I'm a little reluctant to do so. I am part of this current, yet I do not consider myself a conceptual artist, though this may be a paradox as I think there can be no choreography without concept. I feel it is important to point this out in view of the terms we are using.

To return to Boyan's question about the body, I should first say that the notion of the body, or rather of representations of the body, has been expressed in different ways in a whole series of projects. For example, Jérôme Bel's proposition would be to offer a type of representation of the body as a signifier—the body as a bearer of signs, the body as a surface on which signs are placed, removed, replaced. It is more difficult to describe what Claudia Triozzi has proposed. Perhaps in her work the social aspect has prevailed over the representation of the body. That is a second possibility. My proposition is different again. For example, in my piece *Produit de circonstances* (1999), I have attempted to show that the representation of the body is something different from the envelope of the body: it might be a time and a space where there is *traffic*. It would thus be the traffic in time and space that we call the body, and this traffic results in the body passing through various representations.

Franz Anton Cramer: I think that the question you have just considered, "Which structures produce what movement?" also concerns the outward expression of bodies. For instance, what physical form is created through dance technique? This is not a particularly original reflection, but of course training in classical dance will form the body in such a way that it will afterward represent dance in a very particular manner. Structural developments of this kind result not only in a specific dance technique—there's the Cunningham technique, the Graham technique, the release technique, and so on. These are techniques that in some way structure and build the body. There are also certain historically determined expectations and images that relate to how dance should appear, to what it should do and, of course, to what our relationship with the body should be during the dance event. It is a matter of knowing if it is in fact the body or dance that is in question. What can the body have in common with dance if it does not dance? Or, conversely, what can dance achieve if it is not shown by and through the body in movement? It's a topic that comes up all the time and is a product of the complexity of the dance phenomenon, which itself constantly oscillates between visibility and disappearance, technicality and freedom. Hence this irritation that is almost inherent in what is called contemporary dance: but is what they do really dance? Does it really fall within the form and practice of movement that is supposedly identified as "dance"? My feeling is that this definitional field occupies a central place in our discussion. Moreover, there is always the artistic or discursive context, which is created in a fairly minimalist manner, with varying degrees of effort, and determines how bodies are presented in a particular manner, thus reproducing a certain kind of visibility. In my view, this is a subject that is of decisive importance to dance or perhaps to choreography. I prefer to use the concept of dance or contemporary dance since it doesn't exclude anything. In fact the concept of choreography doesn't exclude anything either, but it is more often thought of as a form of research, and thus does not focus on movement or technique. However, William Forsythe, for instance, also has a very distinct technique, one based on ballet technique, for expressing things very clearly and emphatically; for expressing things that are highly influential over the way we generally regard bodies in the cultural space of the theatre. You talked earlier about Jérôme Bel. I think that this was the exact point at which the world managed to enter theatre, by which I mean that Bel uses the structure and the methods, the signs and coding, that we associate with dance and the body, but he does so in relation to everyday gestures and situations, just so that we can ask new questions or at least prompt the audience to ask these same questions in the space of the theatre through the visibility of dance. The purpose is to attract attention to the fact that the dancing body can no longer exist alone. By that I don't want to say that dance is defined by movement. On the contrary, it is just the opposite; it's more that dance is defined by the absence of certain notions or observations. And even by the absence of the body. In fact, there are choreographers who don't work at all with the body, they work in the dark, with immobility, by which I mean that for them, movement no longer exists or is no longer to be seen. I think that dance—dance as I like to think of it—is currently much more about space or structure, a form of work in which several experiences can be fulfilled that react in a relatively clear way to the history of dance (and which often react to that history surprisingly little), but which also, despite that, fall within a historical continuity. Furthermore, movement is only one element. For example, thirty years ago the work of Pina Bausch caused a fuss though she worked entirely with dance and movement. She applied all of dance's conventional parameters (technique, theatrical setting, youthful presence) but simultaneously placed them in an entirely different context that was believed to have social importance, questioning the relations between the sexes and examining the problem of violence. She used the means available to her, including traditional ones, to make reference to a situation well outside the system she was using. She created another form of representation and another type of represented knowledge, but to do so she used above all the body as an individual agent. In bourgeois theatre, this was something pretty revolutionary that later became a staple: the presence of the body, removed from a certain system of stylization (like, for example, ballet technique), was transformed into an individual agent of a de-individualized discourse that nonetheless still belonged to the theatrical and spectacular dispositif. In a certain respect, the suppression of dance thus occurred both within dance and as dance. Today, it's no longer a question of movement or the absence of movement, of virtuosic or laconic technique. It is more a matter of choreographic experiences and artistic practices each finding their expression around a new form of questioning, a new apparatus.

BM: I would like to pursue the issue you began, first by coming back to the topic of the body's relation to technique, representation, and production. Xavier has just said something that I find very important, that he prefers to leave aside the question "What is the body?" in favor of "What can the body do?" Everything that has been said so far might be summed up as indicating that we cannot speak about the body as something identical to itself, as something substantial; in other words that the question "What is the body?" can no longer be answered: the question has no validity. In this sense, experiencing the conditions of the body's functioning turns out to be a central issue. Indeed, what you have just said could guide us in that direction, namely that contemporary dance intends to make the experience not so much about the body "in itself," as a presumed substance, but about the body in—or in relation to—the conditions of its functionality. In that sense it can be stated that the experience of Xavier Le Roy in particular, a radical experience, is as follows: to think of what the body can do, to rebel against all preconceived ideas about its functionality. By which I mean, showing a dysfunctional and disorganized body that, by means of the suspension of its organic functionality, also erases all the systems of identification and aesthetic, social, political, and biological codes attributed to the body. In this way, the body—detached from the order of representations and functionality—is revealed as a space where things become possible, such as metamorphosis, transformation, event. The resistance of this body against the fixed state of a finished product, that is to say against the principle of productivity linked to the principle of productive labor and the artwork, reveals an "original" power that sets itself at odds with its fixation in actuality, in action, and thus retains the capacity of the body to assume other forms of life, to attempt experiences that are not "its own." Perhaps the idea of the body's inability to be owned or to be assimilated by the subject offers us a possible perspective for considering the question "What is the body?" I am thinking in particular of Xavier Le Roy's work *Self Unfinished* (1998), in which the metamorphic body is possessed by the force of the radical outside, upon contact with which it loses its humanity and attains the sensation of the inhuman; that is to say, it discovers a staggering physical power resulting in the body transcending what is human, both in terms of certain archaic morphologies as well as in a transformation into a machine, an automaton. The rhythm of this piece is significant: the body of "Xavier Le Roy," the human body on the stage, is distracted, slow, I might say meandering. The undefinable bodies into which "Xavier Le Roy" is transformed—four-legged, headless—generally follow this slow rhythm, almost coming to a halt. My impression is that this slowness is actually the speed of power's resistance to the fiery logic of the piece; of the action and the fixed functional form that corresponds to these transformed bodies. Of course, this radical experience of the unknown also necessarily leads to a rejection of all known techniques of scenic representation, including the techniques of contemporary dance (which in a certain sense is also an ecstatic study of the techniques that probes the capacities of the human body, but which simultaneously transforms it into a super-instrument of still non-existent functions). Nonetheless it may also lead to a radical attempt to renounce *technique* in general (it should be remembered that the word technique comes from the Greek word *techne*, meaning skill, aptitude, or art).

XLR: Your comments on the question of technique bring to mind Jérôme Bel's piece *The Show Must Go On* (2001), structured around pop songs whose choruses provide the direction for the movements: for instance, in *Let's Dance*, they dance, with *Ballerina Girl*, they dance like ballerinas, and in *I Like to Move It*, they move something while smiling to show their enjoyment, and so on. The piece features about twenty participants who, for most of the time, are strung out in a line across the stage. At the end of the show, there are moments when they are more or less static: for the chorus of the song *I'm Watching You*, they just face the audience and look at them without moving. Sometimes some members of the audience think "I can do that too" and come up on the stage to join the line. I remember at one performance, someone went up on stage and joined the line as it watched the public, but you could see immediately that the interloper didn't have "the technique" that the others were using, that they had created for themselves. This example shows that it isn't at all just spontaneous and "simple," it isn't just ordinary movements that everyone does; they need to be executed in a particular way. I find this story interesting in relation to a discussion on technique: it demonstrates how important it is to reflect on how a technique is developed and what is done with it. That's inescapable. It's possible to begin a work from a technique or to do the opposite, that is to say, to not refer to one, but it will always emerge in a creative process. Then, the questions that arise are: What are we going to do with it? Are we going to transmit it, crystallize it, ingrain it? Do we want to transform it? Or get away from it?

BM: If we consider, as various philosophers and thinkers do, *techne* as being originally part of human nature, then the question of whether or not we can try to "get out" of technique, by which I mean the technique of performance, on stage is probably not very important. Because, when all is said and done, if you succeed in quitting one technique, you always find yourself in another. We are the product of different techniques. The question that then arises is: How would the opening of dance—which, since its origin, has consisted of technical experimentation with the power of the body, thus the demonstration of the body as *techne* par excellence, of the technological becoming of the body—how would this opening affect the supposed disclosure of the inorganic world, the coming out into the open of a radical modifiability, of a prosthetization that affects the very conditions of living? (I am of course thinking of the current condition of the inorganic world, of capitalism in the process of rendering life virtual so it can be marketed, a condition of radical biotechnological and biopolitical transformations.) The only challenge to this development would lie in a suspension of this opening, thus in the disclosure of the disclosure, in which the unlimited transformability of the human being would be seen as a condition that is both impassable and, at the same time, created there and then without an ontological foundation. Resistance to technique—or, more precisely, to technologies—would consist in the "revelation" of our "original" technical condition (or a transformation of it as origin), which consists precisely in transformability. However, transformability should not be understood simply as a fluidity, an affirmation that comes close to a vindication of the fluidity of capitalism today, or of its unlimited "permeability" and speed; on the contrary, the power of resistance assumes an immanent *resistibility*, an inertness if you like, the weight of experience. From this standpoint, Xavier Le Roy's piece *Produit de circonstances* is a perfect example, since it "illustrates" the passage from one technique to another, from one *techne* to another in a general sense: from "science" (medicine) to "art" (dance). At the same time, it is a transition that the character of Xavier Le Roy reflects on but, oddly, does not succeed in grasping reflexively; he is unable to explain it. Thus we find ourselves confronted by the idea of transformation and metamorphosis: the subject and the body are seen as an impossibility to be grasped, an impossibility of fixation. Let's also consider *Self Unfinished*, in which the incompletion of the self results not only in its entire elimination but also in the disappearance of all human, as well as animal, morphology. There is an immeasurable power that develops inside the body and transforms it into primitive forms of life, plant forms or simple organisms that only enjoy a radically reduced interaction with their environment due to the minimal actions of their "vital" functions. There is a headless figure, though not a superior being without a head, like the emblem of André Masson's group *Acéphale*; instead it is a morphologically primitive form, with undifferentiated organs, a torso or trunk and tentacles waving as if dying, belonging to a logic of interaction-reaction of a completely different order. However, this is not an archaizing nostalgia that harks back to primordial times, to the vegetable kingdom, even less than in the work of Bataille, Artaud, and Fabre. Le Roy does not revisit certain crypto-vitalist visions of the body as "pure" and substantial organicity, as the Thing that cannot be reduced to technique and representation. This is a risk run by many currents in contemporary art, in performance, and in dance in particular— research into excess, the radicality of the body, the return to animality and primitive passions, and risky and excessive states (see, for example, Jan Fabre and Wim Vandekeybus). It seems that these projects has two faces since they ultimately convey a substantialist, and thus conformist, idea of the body. Conversely, Le Roy's work researchs the conditions of life that exists *in* the metamorphosis, the passage of the forces, the *traffic* of intensities, forces and rhythms:

it's the body as the open and not as figure, even if the figure is that of a monster. Le Roy shows the body in permanent transformation, always a transformation of certain *technai*, of certain techniques. In other words, to get away from technique, he shows us the impossibility of ridding ourselves of techniques. At the end of the day, the most difficult question posed by *Self Unfinished* is not that of other forms of life and representation, but the question of force or power of transformation that permeates these forms. What is the force that makes a body transform itself? Is it the infinite metamorphosis of the living being that goes as far as suspending the concept of life itself?

XLR: On the one hand, there is the impossibility of fixation, and, on the other, the fact that without fixation we can neither understand nor move forward. This is a paradox posed—in relation to these issues—by the research undertaken on representation and movement. Dance is an active and fascinating practice of this paradox.

FAC: I think that when we talk about the technique of dance, it does not have so much to do with different styles, but instead with a question of knowing if and to what extent it is possible to systematize the practices of the body or the practical work with the body. We should reconsider the 1930s. On one hand, Marcel Mauss's famous treatise *Les Techniques du corps* was published in 1934, in which he defined these techniques as a means for the ethnographic analysis of the manner in which cultures communicate either by means of or with the body, and how in general this gives rise to a culture. Here, technique is understood as a technique for using the body in life. Secondly, in Paris in 1935, a series of lectures was given on the subject of the technique of dance. These were then an attempt to represent all of the contemporary diversity and scope of dance—

"contemporary" is after all a notion that travels across time. Thirty-five lectures were given in which every Parisian school that taught dance had the opportunity to present their system. By this time a great degree of specialization had already become established within the different techniques, while, in parallel, it has always been understood that there is only one technique, the "technique of dance." In that sense, dance as a whole is one form of the manifestation of the diversity inherent in culture. Movement is thus always also a form of production. As Xavier has said, "What movements can we produce with our bodies?" These movements are also always cultural manifestations, the result of certain states of culture, so to speak. Perhaps today the interest in contemporary dance is so great precisely because it is about producing things that, in today's global capitalist context, cannot be owned. Dance produces effects that, as facts and relations, always disappear. So, it can develop a certain strength of resistance to production (the production of sense, materiality, stability) as it is not something that can be stored. Of course, there is also commercial dance, like the *Lord of the Dance* and all possible kinds of dance calculated to make money: show business, variety performances, entertainment. But contemporary dance defined as a form of art in its own right cannot be owned. This production of nothing, of something that transforms itself into nothing, is a central element in the form of cultural expression that is dance.

BM: To re-emphasize what Franz Anton said about actuality, which is even more true when placed in a historic context, something I consider crucial, I'd like to bring things to a close by returning to the hypothesis formulated at the beginning on the supposed emblematic value of contemporary dance today. Following the critical discussion we have had together, I maintain that contemporary performance and dance emerged at the time of the society of spectacle as a reaction to the presentation of capital as spectacle, to the merchandizing of the image of the body, and to the prostitution of representation. These opened up a field of resistance in which a body materialized that rebelled against the constraints of representation and the principles of productivity and functionalization, a space characterized by freedom and non-submission. However, this situation has been radically transformed by the pernicious capitalism of the present day. This capitalism has taken over the space of resistance and the autonomy of life, the space of freedom and the autonomous hedonism of the body, reducing the latter to a form of commercial sex appeal, an added value. Late capitalism has also taken over the "plastic" form of life—in performing it, it produces the plasticity, modifiability, and inorganicity of the body, the subject, and life—it reduces to profit-making productivity what used to be the domain of invention and resistance, the criticism of dance and performance from the start. Now, competitive capitalism can be thought of as the appropriation and universalization of alternative models of experience developed during the last few decades within the artistic practices of dance and performance. The current obsession with the term *performance*, which thirty or so years ago denoted a pioneering artistic practice, is more than eloquent. The paradox consists in the fact that in our recklessly capitalistic society—whose primary traits are the unlimited transformation of the subject, and the virtualization and standardization of forms of life into the latest form of merchandise, or rather into an added value of all forms of merchandise—performance and dance risk not only seeing their critical potential reduced, but also finding themselves become perfect examples of perverse capitalism. If perverse performance establishes itself as the new model of the social contract, then performance and dance would find themselves, against their will, in the position of being the favored figures of competitive capitalism. Apparently, performance in the traditional sense is no longer able to carry out its critical function, which placed it in the spotlight several decades back as a pioneering artistic practice. It is now more urgent than ever to open a critical debate on dance and performance. To repeat our question one more time: How is it possible for a critical artistic practice to exist in this situation? Is it possible in general? How can artistic practices react to radical transformation if they are in a position to? Contemporary dance practice—or rather some practices, certain praxis and certain *technai*—make these questions the basis of their critical, courageous, uncompromising, intransigent, and radical experience. And it is with these questions that we should "close" our discussion, that is to say, keep its critical nature open.

[1] This conversation took place during a round table held in November 2004 at the Sfumato Theatre in Sofia, Bulgaria within the context of the program *Le Passage des frontières* organized by the Goethe Institute in Sofia (directed at the time by Peter Anders). The participants in the round table were Agnès Izrine, Franz Anton Cramer, and Xavier Le Roy, followed by Margarita Mladenova and Peter Anders, with Boyan Manchev as moderator. Franz Anton Cramer, Xavier Le Roy, and Boyan Manchev then rewrote a part of the conversation for the purposes of publication. First appeared in *Rue Descartes* 64 (2009), in an issue on *La métamorphose* edited by Boyan Manchev.

WRITING IMAGES AFFECTS

TOWARD A CRITICAL READING OF CONTEMPORARY DANCE[1]
Yvane Chapuis

With regard to artists hailing from the plastic and visual arts, it is relatively easy to find documentation about their work and the issues raised by it, but when it comes to choreographic artists this presents a challenge. Why, in the case of Bruce Nauman's oeuvre, are there several hundred articles and a dozen or so monographs in six or seven different languages—like so many possible readings capable of echoing various intelligible forms of our presence in the world—when Yvonne Rainer's, for example, merits not even a tenth of this attention? And the same applies if you make a (sort of) chance comparison between Marcel Duchamp and Vaslav Nijinski, Jackson Pollock and Martha Graham, Joseph Beuys and Pina Bausch, Dan Graham and Ann Halprin, Maurizio Cattelan and Marco Berettini, Carsten Holler and Xavier Le Roy, and so on.

Why does dance thus resist critical analysis and have journalistic discourse as almost its sole feedback?[2] Here one of its qualities comes to the fore: its immateriality. Dance has this particular feature of vanishing as quickly as it appears. In this way, it creates an event. To see it, you have to make an appointment, usually of an evening in a theatre or some such venue. Dance may also happen in other places: museums, art centers, and galleries try to showcase dance. All the same, not without certain ups and downs, because these places, which have the habit of handling objects, are discovering another economy made up of men and women who will leave nothing behind them to hang or conserve, and whose production is determinedly inseparable from their presence.

As Peggy Phelan notes about performance—"representation without reproduction"[3]—dance cannot take part in the circulation of representations, for then it would become something else. It can be remarked, but this repetition marks it as different. There is nothing to be gained through it, just expenditure. In the late 1960s, this is precisely what would prompt such artists as Bruce Nauman, Robert Morris, Vito Acconci, and Dan Graham to incorporate within their praxis certain forms and procedures peculiar to it, while questioning the end result of artistic activity, and taking part in the questioning of the validity of the work of art as an object. The performative dimension of dance offered them at one and the same time a chance to extend the research initiated by Minimalism by coming up with an art where meaning is created during a precise, concrete time-frame—put differently, an art relieved of any idea of transcendence, where the work is not an autonomous entity, but the component part of a situation.

It goes without saying that dance does not in any way dodge economics. Each choreographic piece, perforce, involves production wherewithal, something that Marco Berrettini unfailingly reminds the *Multi(s)me* audience when, with the irony that hallmarks his work, he plays a samurai whose sword, in sci-fi fashion, has been turned into a lit neon, and several times repeats the hara-kiri gesture, declaring before the fatal act: "*Multi(s)me*, 5800 euros." Quite simply, the circulation of dance works cannot be imagined in terms of profit, or increased value. Unlike Gabriel Orozco's *Yielding Stone* (1992)— that ball of plasticine that picks up dust and debris as it is moved, keeping the marks of the fingers and hands that have pushed it and the obstacles it has encountered, getting richer all the while in its movements toward the exhibition—each presentation of a dance work, each reiteration, is a new production of gestures involving bodies (thus people) at work.[4] Within art institutions this is not always self-explanatory. It is always surprising to note that those who become champions, even only within the walls that enclose them, of "on-the-move" forms (in both senses of the term: process-based and in the mood of the times) adopt an extremely romantic attitude as soon as what is involved is the economic reality of artistic activity.

Today, within institutions whose mission is to make art public, there is actually a line of thinking about the strategies of its presentation inspired by art praxes that are more concerned with production and manufacturing activities than with the making of an object, where the research and development processes become more interesting than the end product. Many art projects which thus take the form of events, workshops, and contextualized interventions, operating through methods of communication and interaction with audiences, have led to exhibition praxes and evolving configurations for museum institutions, running counter to an untouchable and closed unity. There have thus emerged conceptions of the exhibition as an experimental production space, capable of overtly thematizing the parts, stages, stops, and overlaps of the processes of work; where, in comparison with an experiment, the beginnings and ends of exhibitions are blurred, with the first results capable of mixing with the considerations that preside over the formulation of the following ones. Otherwise put, everything contributes to make the "theatricality" of the exhibition transparent. It is now enacted like an event (a performance?) in real time and space – precisely the two coordinates that the white cube did away with, by definition placing the work of art in an allegedly neutral and timeless context.

Now, this reconfiguration of exchanges with the public rarely goes hand-in-hand with its counterpart exchanges with artists. What is promoted on one hand (the opus at work) is only reluctantly considered on the other. People go on soliciting artists for nothing (at best, at worst at their own expense; and, if there be an exception, the more important the institution the more the issue of an honorarium does not come into it) by reverting implicitly to the good old commercial system to take over. However in the absence of any product, it just so happens that the labeling for a fruitful future on which the institution was counting no longer stands up. The contradiction, not to say the double game, in which the institution thus finds itself involves, on the one hand, the risk of installing the artistic production in a schizophrenic state, and leads, on the other, to raising questions about the reality of what it is promoting as art. It is not a matter of doubting the interest in performative art forms, but of pointing to the urgency there is in considering the economy on which they rely, in order for them to remain operative. If art's audience is becoming here an integral part of the work's elaboration, why can't the role of the purchaser be subject to the same transformations and take part in the production of the work? The game is probably here tighter than the institution should assume— the interlocutors are less docile. However, not re-playing this game is tantamount to defending an illusory model, one that is disconnected from the economic reality and thus devoid of political reverberations.

In this context, theater (as an institution) may indeed seem archaic, insomuch as its dispositif for presenting works has not altered since Antiquity, and yet it is instructive. Here, probably because performativity is not experienced as concept but as reality, each one of the actors in the process at work is awarded his or her share. Artists (authors and actors) benefit here from a status that, in France in particular, incorporates them into the job market. Something which gives shivers to the advocates of the figure of the artist as dandy, who, as such, models himself on his time and turns himself, depending on the circumstances, into a "producer," "go-between," "dj," and the like.

Seen from this angle, the visual arts territory does not constitute an asylum for artists known as choreographers. This is a fact that should cut short any tendency to believe that an undisciplined movement is currently being (re)enacted in the dance scene, a movement that consists in leaving the stage. But for where? Those who left the theater in the 1970s, like those who are leaving today, are coming back to the stage—it is a question of survival.[5] When a choreographic artist creates an off-stage initiative, the issue should have to do more with what she or he has not resolved in relation to this dispositif, than some subversive kind of attitude that no longer has any currency these days. This does not involve any value judgment, but, on the contrary, makes it possible to concretely envisage dance in terms of hesitation, questioning, and experimentation in relation to its own system of representation.

What is more, the forms that are currently being developed as a (temporary) alternative to the theatrical apparatus are still choreographic—in the sense of staged artificial actions in which the central concern is not so much the body as what animates it. In this way, they stand apart from the performances that emerged three or four decades ago within the visual arts field that people are quick to associate them with. This differentiation is important. On the one hand, it stops dance from seeming like a latecomer, and, on the other, it stops us from resorting to the old refrain of interdisciplinarity, capable, it has to be said, of giving rise to works whose artificiality stems from a kind of *in vitro* culture. In a tone of connivance, people ask (people produce) the choreographer, the musician, and the writer to produce visual works, with no awareness of the violence, or stupidity, represented by such a denial of each person's culture. There is another variation on the same theme: you put two artists from different cultures in the same tub, preferably people topping the bill (if the stock is promising, the results are optimized), and you wait to see what happens. Usually, the absence of any encounter.

Unless, of course, this interdisciplinarity sheds formal (formalist) concerns and sticks to questions of the strategies, rules, and artistic forms of the *modus operandi*. A few years ago, in an interview,[6] Marco Berettini remarked upon the lack of theorization in dance, and took as an example a meeting between Jean-Luc Godard and Fritz Lang, where the two directors agreed to an exercise: on a sheet of paper they drew a room with a chair, a table, and two doors. Having decided that a man should enter, sit down at the table, and then exit through the other door, their discussion started by dealing with how each of them would have filmed the scene. When we question dance in these terms, we realize that its movements have already for a long time been permeated by other approaches: from film to the other arts, from the sciences to sports, as well as everyday activities, clubbing, comic strips, and so on. But it is even more interesting to note that the variations that are of interest to the two directors here are also at work in dance as it is practiced by a broad range of contemporary artists. When one tries to grasp, along with them, how the possible forms of dance appear, one actually realizes that these forms are being played out in the repetition—obsessive, experimental, or playful—of a gesture or a word, always borrowed, and the differences it produces. This perspective calls attention to fundamental research that cannot be undertaken here, but which should privilege the singularities of these possible forms of dance through multiple opinions on one and the same object, be it the work of an artist or a specific question.

This said, the issue of the shortfall of criticism on choreographic works remains an open one. If dance's immateriality complicates the feedback needed for analysis, these difficulties do not suffice to explain criticism's absence. Performance, for example, which might be said to have similar qualities, does not suffer from any such shortfall. This form, recognized as a fully-fledged medium during the 1970s in both the United States and Europe, whose history finds its foundations in certain experiments carried out by Futurism, Dada, the Bauhaus, and Surrealism, has since its outset been documented and discussed—first and foremost by the artists themselves. The nature of the shortfall is thus cultural: the fine arts have, for almost two hundred years, produced a reflexive discourse that dance knows little about. This interpretation is confirmed when you take a look at the university, especially in France, where the history of the discipline is only in very rare exceptions incorporated. As far as specialized schools are concerned, and as Boris Charmatz, Isabelle

Ginot and Isabelle Launay remind us, it would appear that the tradition consists of obscuring the field of thought, because "too much thought might hamper dancing."[7]

Nevertheless, even out of its context, dance remains undiscussed. If, these days, certain museum institutions, and not the least among them either, in both France and abroad feature dance on the list of their public activities, nothing (or next to nothing, depending on the example)[8] is done in terms of writing and critical accompaniment. Whereas any old exhibition comes with a catalogue. Idleness? Incompetence? Inconsiderateness? An oversight in their heritage-oriented mission in every instance. This responsibility with regard to the formation of a history of dance and the thinking it introduces is nonetheless the object of specific art projects such as those developed by the Quatuor Knust and Les carnets Bagouet. There seems to be a very widespread idea at work whereby dance is considered inexpressible—some would say it cannot be recounted—and yet, paradoxically, gives rise to words. The shortfall I have pointed out does not have to do so much with the discourse about dance (this exists fairly and squarely) as with the discourse being constructed on the basis of an analysis of works. But would the first person who often strives to locate in dance that which dodges language, sometimes making of it a primitive form, at others an expressive form, stifle the second? For, as is observed by Christophe Kihm in his text devoted to this issue, "we will always gain by precisely specifying the object being described when we mention 'dance.' We should thus avoid drawing in speculations that, no matter how dazzling they might appear, are all the more easily detached from the object that they are meant to describe when their goal is not so much to consider the active part of it and its praxes, but its nature and ontology."[9] The fact is that this ontological perspective has the shortcoming of making no differentiation between what was danced yesterday and what is being danced today, what is being danced here and what is being danced there, because dance apparently exists *per se*. But dance *per se* does not exist. Like all reality, it is dated and historically and socially situated.

When Nauman, Acconci, Morris, and Graham, to take the example we have already mentioned, are interested in dance, this is precisely because at the same moment and in the same place (the American art scene of the 1960s), there appeared in the field of dance a similar refusal to separate art praxis and everyday activity, as well as a disinterest with regard to technique that encouraged amateur praxis. When, in a surprising way, Mike Kelley juxtaposed Martha Graham's ballets and Nogushi's sets with certain scientific experiments on the emotional responses of primates conducted during the 1950s in the United States, this was precisely because that repertory of historically dated forms (abstract Expressionists, inspired by Jung's psychology) enabled him to weave relations where it appeared that meaning and understanding were only revealed within a given ambiguous space, whose outlines were perforce cultural, social, and political. With the artist specifying, *inter alia*, in the work titled *Test Room...*(1999), the unconscious mise-en-scène in the field of experimental sciences, where, on the face of it, there was a quest for a real explanation, an Oedipal model, or, otherwise put, certain ideas of the moment.[10]

This questioning of the referents at work in the manner of formulating a thought, be it scientific or artistic, echoes the analysis of the use of the score—understood as a program of activities—proposed by Laurence Louppe in "Du partionnel."[11] For the author, the score-related option appears in the dance arena as a means, possibly a chance, for elaborating a non-Oedipal framework, where adherence to a model is no longer necessary, nor the transmission of values and above all of pre-established beliefs. Her proposition is all the more interesting because she extends it to contemporary art, where the score acts as a scenario or script. With regard to the alignment of systems for representing art and science, in view of questioning the possibility of an objective definition of reality, we refer readers to the score of the Xavier Le Roy's performance-lecture titled *Produit de circonstances* (1999).[12]

When Alexandre Périgot organized *Free Style* (1998/1999) in Paris, and then in Tokyo, inviting local dancers to come and "give their best" on the model of that figure borrowed from hip-hop, there did not appeared a common dance on each occasion but instead singular dances in which you could read differences of paths and of cultures. It would thus be possible to multiply at leisure the examples where dance turns out to be neither neutral nor timeless.

Because dance has that specific feature of being borne by bodies (people), we see here, more than elsewhere, the danger represented by generalization. And if it is legitimate, not to say indispensable, that philosophy, like any other field of thought, provides tools to be at dance's disposal, it cannot, on the other hand, turn around and define what dance is. Because this introduces a relation of hierarchy (I know about you what you don't know) that, according to Deleuze and Guattari, one had thought abolished, once and for all: "It is thought that philosophy is being given a great deal by being turned into the art of reflection, but actually it loses everything. Mathematicians, as mathematicians, have never waited for philosophers before reflecting on mathematics, nor artists before reflecting on painting or music. So long as their reflection belongs to their respective creation, it is a bad joke to say that this makes them philosophers."[13] There is similarly formulated in dance, in which there is a self-reflection that proceeds through a critical appropriation of its history, its praxis, and its gestures, as well as its apparatus of production and cultural mediatization, without which it could not exist, or even be visible. And yet does this propose a conceptual dance, as it has been said? I do not think so. Because, as Deleuze and Guattari define it, producing concepts and reflecting are not the same thing. Even though it intends to expose the dialectical processes whereby its forms may appear, dance, as it appeared on the French and European scene throughout the 1990s, does not have the aridity, either, of what we commonly understand by "Conceptual Art." Though, wit and irony are its hallmarks on more than one occasion. It is certainly post-conceptual, but it is then likewise post-minimal and post-pop. Artists tell us this in a more or less explicit way, because their history is not reduced to that of the medium they use. Just as it is not reduced, either, to the history of the arts, or to that of thought. Their history is also individual. Each work, each project gives visibility to vestiges, even fictitious one, of the people who make them appear. Here death in fact finds its place, probably because dance is a living art. This capacity to "live death" and "die life," as described by Jacinto Lageira in a text on Marco Berrettini's *Multi(s)mes*,[14] specifies dance in such a way that, from this side of the globe, death always seems to have to leave our reality.

[1] This is an edited version of "Pour une critique des oeuvres chorégraphiques," first published as the introduction to Médium: Danse, edited by Yvane Chapuis, in *Art Press* 23 (2002): 10-14.
[2] According to Claudine Guerrier, author of *Presse écrite et danse contemporaine* (Paris: Chiron, 1997), the press in France has helped the emergence of contemporary dance, and its subsequent legitimization, meaning the importance attached to it. For our purposes, the tenor of the journalistic discourse on dance often raises doubts about the value of the any information that is printed in the daily papers that were hitherto taken seriously.
[3] Peggy Phelan, "The Ontology of Performance," in *Unmarked: The Politics of Performance* (New York: Routledge, 2001), 146-66.
[4] Dance is thus based on a food-like economy. The price of works is indexed to the cost of living. What increases with the fame (visibility) of an artist are the means of production made available to her/him. The time allotted to rehearsals, the number of performers, and/or the sophistication of sets and lighting thus depends on these means.
[5] On this, see Lucinda Childs in an interview with Patricia Kuypers in *Nouvelles de danse* 42-43 (Summer 2002): 117-133.
[6] Marco Berrettini, non-published interview with the author, 1998.
[7] See Isabelle Ginot and Isabelle Launay, "L'école, une fabrique d'anticorps?" and Boris Charmatz, "Il va falloir faire vite," in Médium: Danse, *Art Press* 23, (2002): 106-113.
[8] Here we must quote the catalogues for the exhibitions *Danses tracées, dessins et notations de choréographes*, Centre de la Vieille Charité (Paris: Dis Voir, 1991), *Trisha Brown, Danse, précis de liberté*, Centre de la Vieille Charité (Marseille: RMN, 1988) and *Art Performs Life: Merce Cunningham, Bill T. Jones, Meredith Monk* (Minneapolis: Walker Art Center, 1998).

[9] Christophe Kihm, "Geste, découpe, mouvement, image," in Médium: Danse, *Art Press* 23, (2002): 72.

[10] See the exhibition catalogue for *Mike Kelley* (Grenoble: Le Magasin, 1999).

[11] Laurence Louppe, "Du partionnel," in Médium: Danse, *Art Press* 23, (2002): 32-40, and published in the current anthology as "On Notation."

[12] See Médium: Danse, *Art Press* 23, (2002): 114-126.

[13] Gilles Deleuze and Félix Guattari, *What is Philosophy?*, trans. Graham Burchell and Hugh Tomlinson (London: Verso, [1991] 1994), 6.

[14] Jacinto Lageira, "Cristalliser et/ou désorganiser," in Medium Danse, *Art Press* 23 (2002): 64-77.

TO END WITH JUDGMENT BY WAY OF CLARIFICATION...[1]
Bojana Cvejić

Xavier Le Roy: Because we cannot escape this terminology any longer what is your understanding of conceptual dance? What is it in relationship to dance? In relationship to conceptual art? When have you read, heard the terms "conceptual dance," "non dance," or "anti dance" for the first time? How do you think these terms are understood in the field of choreographic art? In other fields? What is your understanding of these terms? Or why do you think they where chosen?

Bojana Cvejić: The term "conceptual dance" has never been theorized, introduced in a programmatic way by the makers, i.e. the choreographers who are attributed the label, nor has it been elaborated theoretically in the European or American discourses of performing arts who would be following the so-called conceptual dance practices today.

So far I have been convinced that the term is so inappropriate that it should be dismissed, its usage being more harmful than supportive of the development of these practices. But as the term stubbornly recurs, and more and more with the negative intention of closing a paradigm down, perhaps it is important to use this panel as the last opportunity for contesting the grounds on which the denomination "conceptual dance" in regards to Conceptual art has been made. I would very systematically and concisely divide arguments in two: what makes the content of the concept "conceptual art" the grounds for "yes" (which are definitely not the reasons why the term conceptual dance was coined, because the usage of the term shows that it isn't informed by knowledge about Conceptual art), and the grounds for "no"

YES

1.

Conceptual art developed the new aesthetic of *the speech act* in the late 1960s. The artist representative of minimal sculpture, Donald Judd best exemplified it with the statement: "This is a work of art if I say so." Indeed if some recent dance practices use the performative of "this is choreography, this is, this could be dance" to constitute their novel propositions on dance, they nevertheless move away from the aesthetic of declaration and intention.[2] The proposition "this is choreography" is never neutral and arbitrary, for it is devised to meet the resistance of Dance in singular, the dominant essential views on dance, the institutional resistance to not only proposing other propositions, but to the form of proposition as such.

2.

When a work of dance or choreography is considered a kind of proposition presented in the context of dance it issues a comment on dance. Here we have to reconsider how *the proposition "this is choreography"* relates to Joseph Kosuth's definition of artwork as an analytic proposition. In dance there has never been a determination of analytic critical conceptualism of the kind of Kosuth, which would analyze the types of propositions using positivist logic, or linguistic or semiotic models and replace the matter of performance with a metalinguistic discourse on the nature and concept of dance. However, the propositional form of the so-called conceptual dance practices shares with Conceptual art self-reflexiveness, much less discursive or epistemological and much more perceptual/antiessentialist, thereby working mainly with the materiality of dance and the perceptual experience and interpretation of the spectator. Self-reflexivity in conceptual dance is directed towards the dispositif of theatre, the conditions, roles and procedures whereby a spectator is presented something as dance, which becomes the object of its own performance. Such a reorientation promotes a radical stance: if dance tries to tell us something about the world it is bound to fail... it can only represent representation, in other words, its means, mechanisms and ideologies of producing meaning and status in contemporary culture.

3.

The self-reflexiveness should better be replaced by *spectatorship,* when it addresses the frame of perception, and in some rare cases, receivership, when it requires that the spectator discursively engages in the understanding of what the work proposes as choreography. Meaning is created in structural relationships between the work and the field of dance and choreography, the conditions and roles of the author and the spectator.

4.

Does conceptual dance share with Conceptual art the *institutional critique*? only in respect of critiquing the ideological fetishism of the status of object and commodity status. Nevertheless the so-called conceptual dance participates in the institutional distribution; there is a necessary collaboration between the programmer and the choreographer to a certain degree; some programmers strive to co-create concepts or rather contexts of festivals which will support the propositions of the conceptual dance.

NO

1.

The work of the so-called conceptual dance isn't based in *the withdrawal of the perceptual*. It doesn't map the linguistic onto the perceptual, even if it is influenced by the so-called Duchamp effect, the word does not prevail over the movement. There is no dogmatic prohibition of physicality (like it was the case in Conceptual art that the art object was replaced by the theoretical object). On the contrary, the practices are based in configuring other materialities of movement and body expressivity, which would no longer rest on the Romantic notions of the ineffable and unfathomable, the speechless anonymity of the body etc (I'll return to these notions in regards to Dance in singular). The fear of the ugly words "tautology" and "self-referentiality" associated with Conceptual art and used against the so-called conceptual dance comes from relying on the entrenched hope in Western culture that dance would be the event of thought before it acquires name. This is where Western philosophers like Alain Badiou, theorists and intellectuals take pleasure in dance, and become complicit with dance practitioners who aim to preserve dance as a medium-specific practice of the sublime and ephemeral self-expression of a free individual. Badiou confirms Mallarmé's definition that dance is poetry emancipated from the writing tools. The practices called "conceptual dance" approach dance as writing in Derridean sense, which doesn't and cannot reiterate the writing of a text in the domain of theory.

2.

No utopia: conceptual dance cannot be seen as part of the historical project of Modernism, as it was the case with Conceptual art. It doesn't belong to the same lineage of abstraction which would make it the last instance of abstraction (Merce Cunningham – Yvonne Rainer – Xavier Le Roy, Jérôme Bel or Tino Sehgal; Marcel Duchamp – Donald Judd – Joseph Kosuth) or reductionism and self-reflection, where the use of language substituting for movement would be a form of dematerializing the object and the commodity dance. There is no goal in transforming the format of presentation (theatre performance of dance), audiences or institutional market. These practices operate from within the institutions, emphasizing a critical use of the theatre dispositif.

3.
However, the practices bundled under "conceptual dance" propose a *plurality of configurations* of movement, body, subjectivity, cultures, beyond self-referentiality and homogeneity that could be associated with rational self-reflection from only within the medium. We couldn't speak of an artistic movement or formation, we would even have difficulty to make one paradigm, which would include Bel, Le Roy, Boris Charmatz, Vera Mantero. This proves two things: the heterogeneity points to a hybridity of different influences, strands, disciplines, media and genres (hybridity against the purity of the pure modernist dance) and an openness of differences, many not only concepts, but conceptualizations of dance beyond Modernism.

The next step in this discussion would be to consider how a concept is formed: how it emerges, starts to regulate a practice, projects itself onto a practice. My thesis is that conceptual dance was so ill-named for it proposed an open, unbounded concept of Dance as Choreography, which contradicted or showed that choreography was used as a closed concept of Dance. I will explain the difference in the following paragraph.

XLR: Do you think, and if yes, then why dance always needs to be defined in a binary mode. There used to be Ballet/Modern, Modernist/Post-modern or Postmodernist, or Modern/Dance theatre. Or was it Ballet/dance theatre [Tanztheater], and how is it now: conceptual/pure dance?

Is binary logic specific for dance? Do you think that it can have something to do with the fact that choreographic art is not a well-established or recognized art practice in comparison with visual art or music for example?

BC: Until the '90s, one could go away with talking dance performances by way of asking what kind of object "dance" a performance is: what is its dancing "matter," body-instrument-technique-style, and then, perhaps, some subject matter, what the performance speaks by way of a metaphor. In the '90s, this question was no longer sufficient, and another approach settled in. Not what kind of object a dance performance is, but what kind of concept of dance is performed, or put forth in the performance. This entailed that the new practices could not be defined essentially, by grasping and reasserting the same properties or distinctive traits, which constitute the work. The work of, say, Vera Mantero and Jérôme Bel, or Jérôme Bel and Xavier Le Roy, can never make a perfect community of aesthetic properties, but can belong to a family of resemblances, properties which appear similar but in fact configure the work of each one differently. An example. We can speak of transparency or clarity of procedures in the case of Bel and Le Roy. In the case of the former the clarity of procedures comes from linguistic operations and speech acts (cf. *Le dernier spectacle*, *Shirtology*, *The Show Must Go On I & II*), and with the latter, it is the means to provide a direct access to the body materiality, a posthumanist vision of what a body can do (cf. *Self-Unfinished*, *Giszelle*). The wrong conclusion to draw is to make this feature (transparency) essential, to treat as an aesthetic ideal.

What was so different in the works of the aforementioned choreographers is how they conceived concept for each performance. Now, concept has become either an overrated or an inflated term: hated by those practitioners, critics or programmers whose ethic of work implies a non-reflexive studio craftsmanship or degraded by those proposals and applications for subsidy where a certain theoretical or political agenda is expected in the written proposal (not always making it to the work). This only shows that concept is a poorly understood term in dance.

Every work of dance has a concept, of course, because it is founded on a conceptual order of ideas, beliefs, values, procedures and meanings even when they are generated by intuition. However, from the '90s on, concepts are being thematized, and discussed for every choreographic work of the new practices. So it was no longer understood that the choreographer—her style, language, technique, represented themes—is sufficient to stand for her object dance with her concept of it. Choreographers began to conceptualize choreography as the object of work. In other words, they don't treat it any longer as a self-evident notion, a concept that is closed. A close concept defines choreography as composition, and identifies composition with inscribing a form or structure, but in any case a notion of a whole, by bodily movement in time and space. Inscription of movement in time/space is rather a vague, empty signifier, but vagueness is exactly how regulative concepts function. They fulfill a normative function, especially because their content is elusive. So such a closed concept of choreography rests on an agreement ("whatever your composition is, it necessarily has to pertain to bodily movement and parameters of space and time"), and a hierarchical apparatus of production (choreographer transferring knowledge to dancers by show-copy model or material molding).

The choreographers in the '90s contested the idea that choreography is the writing that follows, resembles, represents the speech of dance, like the written following the spoken word. They insisted on the separation between dancing and choreographing, so that writing may precede dancing. Writing isn't only language for action, movement, thought, reflection, consciousness, unconsciousness, experience and affectivity; it is all that, but also the totality of what makes it possible, in other words, it can include a deconstruction of the assumptions, rules and values which guide writing.

To claim that choreography is an open concept implies that the notion of choreography (composition) be expanded and modified. Choreographic practices start using other tools than the so-called immanent, but actually inherited beautiful forms of eternal value, to derive itself. The new tools have been so far: language and theory, history and historicity, sign communication, visual arts, secondary effects of other media like film (cinematic technologies), music, digital medium, then the theatre dispositif in relation to popular culture, the spectacle in both senses of the society of spectacular commodities and the spectacle of performance.

So when we speak of the concept as unbounded as a language game (Wittgenstein), it implies that a performance sets serviceable rules given for the present case. An open concept of choreography accounts for an unforeseen situation to arise and lead us to modify the understanding of it. This is not an academic sterilization of the process of concept formation. If we behaved according to the politics of this argument, then the simplifications of what conceptual dance is and why we should disregard it would not stand a chance.

One more charge to consider. We too often hear that the practices under the name conceptual dance are the result of a belated influence of the Judson group of choreographers in Europe, mediated not so much via Steve Paxton or Trisha Brown, but more indirectly via Yvonne Rainer who has stopped choreographic work already in the early '70s. Sitting in this panel here with Christophe Wavelet and Xavier Le Roy who worked on reinterpreting works of the Judson choreographers within the project Quatuor Albrecht Knust, of course, we cannot deny this influence. However, we have to be careful when pronouncing the judgment that European dance only now experiences the influence of the American so-called post-modern dance and therefore, is somehow a bastard child of the '60s.

There is something more to understand here about the open, unbounded concept and its temporality. Prior to the point at which we would say a concept has emerged, it might be that many if not all the threads of what becomes the content of the concept already exist. This is why new appears as much continuous as it is discontinuous with the old. So it is a case of transformation, and not repetition. Continuity is crucial to the functioning of open concepts, weaving through a living and changing practice. Modification, continuity and expansion suppose that we cannot make paradigm examples, which we would treat as ideal types for an aesthetic, and we have to give up the so-called "monster-barring" (excluding difficult borderline examples), because all cases become more or less monsterous, connecting unreproducible connections. What does Thomas Plischke have to do with Juan Dominguez, Christine De Smedt with Alice Chauchat, Mette Ingvartsen with Antonia Baehr? Not much, except that their work stands outside of a closed concept Dance. In other words, it betrays an essentialist view that has been dominating dance since Classical Ballet to the still Modernist established practices of the choreographers who emerged in the 80s and who are desperately clutching to the idea of Dance as the invention of body. And to illustrate this view I will quote an excerpt from the infamous essay "Dance as a Metaphor of Thought" by Alain Badiou.[3] It offers a philosophical sublimation of what is the doxa haunting contemporary dance: "Dance is innocence, because it is a body before the body. It is forgetting, because it is a body that forgets its fetters, its weight. It is a new beginning, because the dancing gesture must always be something like the invention of its own beginning. And it is also play, of course, because dance frees the body from all social mimicry, from all gravity and conformity. (...) [Dance] makes the negative body—the shameful body—radiantly absent."

This view favors two notions:

1) *presence*: The meaning of being, captured by the interiority of the subject; by virtue of hearing oneself speak, by virtue of feeling oneself dance, the subject affects itself and is related to itself in the element of ideality. The frequently asked question about how one experiences one's own dance solo

2) *the ineffable sublime*: Dance shares the same cultural destiny as music. The ideal music was for art and its culture in the XIXth century is dance in the end of the XXth century and today. The ineffable, inexpressible, universal, infinite in the finite form, transfigure in the values (Romantic illusion) that dance promises in the age of liberal capitalism. Defying these assumptions is what connects the non-similar practices of these choreographers. Calling them conceptualist choreographers means subtracting dance out of their practices for the simple mistake of overlooking that their procedures only target the body, the materiality of performance calling for sensation inasmuch, or inextricable from communication. In other words, their work isn't conceptual because it doesn't dematerialize the concept from its object.

XLR: How and why at the same time that the terminology concept dance, non-dance, anti-dance etc. appeared we could observe focuses on other terms such as: "process", "laboratory" and "research"? If you agree with this when did you notice that in your environment? Would you relate this to the word or questions about collaboration? What is Research?

BC: Investigation is a set of procedures of discovering, developing, describing, explaining and interpreting the functions, methods, values and sense of art. This term was introduced by Giulio Carlo Argan for Neoconstructivism in the '50s, but it also applied to a branch of Conceptual art that focused on addressing the question: what is an artwork, how is it being made and how does it function in the art world. Art as research presupposes the following:

1.

that art has a cognitive power—to produce knowledge, specific to that art; and a power to theorize, to produce a problematic and resolve it

2.

that art based in research doesn't find its purpose in the artwork as the final result of the process of making or producing, but in the process of investigation. The result of research need not be achieved, or isn't worthwhile mentioning or is overcome the moment it has been achieved. The process of research shows itself as a thinking model, a model of working and behavior of the artist.

3.

that there need not be any homology between the scientific methods and the methods of producing an aesthetic object.

But what is the specificity of research in dance, especially in regards to the currency of research, process, laboratory or collaboration nowadays?

4.

Here I would give an opinion, or an estimation. It seems that work came to be represented (not necessarily conceived so) as research in the '90s with the growing number of the so-called independent artists. Entertaining that development, a new model of venue emerged, where the programmer undertook the role of a patron of research, not always of a curator. With patronage I mean parenthood, the programmer authorizes a work as a process of research: (s)he first invites artists who (s)he thinks need the support of a so-called independent venue, then (s)he talks to them in order to find out whether their topic, concept of work or model of thinking smells like searching for something (not that it has to pertain to a particular area of research that the programmer is curating), and finally (s)he decides on the format of presentation, which often needs a festival or another kind of special manifestation: "opening-doors." When a parent-patron, the programmer takes the responsibility of the shown process or product (usually, it is presented as a work-in-process, promising and postponing the final result). As the presentation likens the performance, it doesn't offer an insight into its research methodology nor its objectives of research, or to anything that would make it different from product. It differs from a performance-product only in the degree of completeness. The work seems to finish the process of making when it acquires the satisfying looks of searching for something. Ethics of research, experiment and critique transfigures into an aesthetic of indie-work, foreclosing further development when the outlook of research is achieved.

However, there is an entirely different usage of the term research and laboratory, much less specific and contemporary than what I outlined here, but maybe more general and common for contemporary dance practices in Western Europe. Research is understood as the process of inner necessity of the dancer searching for her proper authentic body movement and language in self-expression. Studio seems an indispensable site of the reinvention of the human body through dance. This shows that the ideology of Expressionism has been negotiated into a kind of hidden matrix, or mode of production in dance, similarly to what happened to the conversion of Romanticist XIXth century music into pop music or XIXth century opera to Hollywood film production. But to say that dance specifically requires a search for the original, authentic movement of an individual body is to romanticize the basic definition of poetics as the principles of making which always entails a process of searching for something. The condition of art since and after Modernism presupposes that artist searches whenever she makes work.

If we consider the concept of art as research as introduced in the visual art theory by Argan and explained above, the common use of research in dance as we know it is inappropriate. We still may need to discover which practices in contemporary dance have developed problematics, methods and techniques in the mode of investigation and not poetic search for the means of expression.

[1] This writing took shape as part of the conference *"INVENTORY: Dance and Performance Congress / Live Act / Intervention / Publication,"* 3-5 March 2005, Tanzquartier Wien. Invited to curate a panel around questions of research and laboratory, Xavier Le Roy set up a public discussion with Gerald Siegmund, Christophe Wavelet, Mårten Spångberg, Bojana Cvejić, and himself, in a dialogue with the audience, around the terminology of "conceptual dance," "research," and "laboratory." What follows is an excerpt of the conference proceedings by Bojana Cvejić and Xavier Le Roy. This conversation took place at a time of fierce debates over the legitimacy of conceptualization in dance: if the views of the author have somewhat altered since, these crucial questions around wordings and choreographic practices still are resonant today.
[2] See Benjamin H. D. Buchloch, "Conceptual Art 1962-1969: From the Aesthetic of Administration to the Critique of Institutions," *October* 55 (Winter, 1990): 105-143.
[3] Alain Badiou, "Dance as a Metaphor for Thought," in *Handbook of Inaesthetics*, trans. Alberto Toscano (Stanford: Stanford University Press [1998] 2005), 57-58.

A COMMON PLACE[1]
Isabelle Ginot

"What is your opinion of contemporary creation today?" I was asked this question, which was in fact an invitation to write something, a few months ago by Michel Caserta—dance curator and institution director, among other things—following an earlier collaboration that had already given rise to an article.[2] Open, to say the least, this question did not appear straightforward during a period in which "contemporary creation" and its criticism (and thus "my opinion") were undergoing far-reaching change. The "contemporary creation" I shall discuss in this article represents only a part, and perhaps a marginal one at that, of the current choreographic scene. However, and this is why it interested me here, it constitutes a very visible part, one that might even be considered to overshadow the rest of the creative sphere: that is the very poorly defined and badly named domain of "the new forms," those that can be seen in a range of fashionable places—alternative or intermediary spaces, etc.

To my mind, this movement is above all characterized by a twofold critical production: first, it questions the choreographic legacy of, as well as the discourses "on," dance, since it is clear that aesthetic and critical thoughts are closely linked, and that it is not possible to engage with one without becoming bound up with the other. It is well known that the end of the 1990s was affected by a crisis of every value that underlay the choreography of the previous decade. Today a new generation of dancers, choreographers, and performers offers an analysis of, and reaction to, the system as a whole, whose principal failing was its stifling uniformity. One of the qualities of this critical movement is that it tackles the system as a whole, showing how it operates in terms of aesthetics (which aesthetic norms are now dominant?), politics (what connections govern the relationships that exist between artists, artists and regulating bodies or curators, spectators and dancers, etc?), and economics (how the development of a market for the performing arts is indissociable from the development of an aesthetic). With the market saturated and the system hardly allowing any new names to enter, this period of theorization is being accompanied by political actions involving artists themselves taking up new spaces and modes of production.

A new community of dance has therefore emerged, coexisting with the previous generation and somewhat masking it. Whereas the '80s had brought "the new dance" to attention via institutional spaces (such as national theaters, festivals, etc.), the turn-of-the-century avantgarde began in alternative (soon to be termed "intermediary"?) spaces before more official programs and curators realized they had to change direction and slowly include these rebels.

An inherited "degree zero of dance"?

Since Yvonne Rainer has become the authority for many of these young artists, her own terms can be used to sum up the issues that predominantly concern this movement: no to spectacle, no to choreography, no to interpretation, no to drama...[3] Thus, anti-shows are proliferating at the Ménagerie de Verre, in various industrial wastelands, in studios, etc. Myriam Gourfink, whether solo or in a group,[4] moves so slowly that her motion is hardly visible as she follows a mysterious score created by a digital device and derived from yoga postures. Jérôme Bel, in *Jérôme Bel* (1995), shows naked bodies, debased by elements of everyday life: creases and red blotches on the skin, urine, and so on. In *Distribution en cours* (2000), Emmanuelle Huynh fills the stage with an implausible set of objects collected by her dance colleague Christian Rizzo. Rizzo himself turns the stage and the dancers' bodies into showcases in *Et pourquoi pas: "bodymakers," "falbalas," "bazaar," etc., etc...?* (2001). A number of non-dancers appear on stage, revealing their non-virtuosic presence, but also displaying their intellectual, technical, or other capacities (for example, in 2001, Laurence Louppe, a critic and historian, appeared in Alain Buffard's *Dispositifs*; the psychoanalyst Sabine Prokhoris appeared as a fortune-teller in *Boissy 2* by Cécile Proust, and Isabelle Launay and Hubert Godard "performed" a reflection on the history of dance in *Faculté* by Boris Charmatz). In consequence, the traditional boundaries between spectators and performers are dissolved by the sensational use of manifestos, gatherings, texts, and performances. Dancers and non-dancers (especially critics) share the stage, but also the right to speak, creating new modes of production and presentation for the works. Of course, the traditional separations between disciplines (dance, theater, the visual arts) are once again abolished: Mark Tompkins (to take only one example) works alongside dancers, artists, actors, circus artists, and others.

These works owe a lot to what was perhaps wrongly considered as "the given knowledges" [*acquis*] (and which for this reason lost interest) of the 1970s. The heroes of the young French generation are the main avant-gardes figures in New York from the '60s and '70s. Laurence Louppe, exegete of the postmodern Americans, has become a leading reference for the French movement; in 1996, Yvonne Rainer was called back to dance by the Quatuor Knust when it recreated her *Continuous Project – Altered Daily*, as well as Steve Paxton's *Satisfyin' Lover*, thereby stimulating immense enthusiasm for the period and its masters. A stay with Ann Halprin, a legendary figure at the origin of the American movement, was of fundamental importance to Alain Buffard, formerly a performer in some of the "leading French companies."

A study of the history and aesthetics of the two periods and movements in order to understand the effects of this proximity still remains to be undertaken. However, some aspects are of particular interest to us here. First, the young artists' thirst for theory in both generations: dance broke the silence that has been claimed essential ("the dancers chose silence, they voiced their message with their bodies, not words...") and dancers took up the theorization of their work themselves, starting with a systematic critique of the aesthetics and economics of earlier choreographic productions. It is therefore clear that "creation" (i.e., artistic labor) means at once an intellectual and tangible [*sensible*] labor, and that it is not just gestural but also conceptual and discursive. Another element that these two generations have in common, and which is of special interest to this essay, is the trend toward the collective: we often hear of Judson Dance Theater, whose mythology has been a major influence on the works created by the new generation, as a collective. The '90s saw a resurgence of collectives, in particular groups with political agendas: the "reunions de Pelleport," the Signataires du 20 août, Espace commun, Prodanse, among others, brought together artists, curators, administrators, and others. In addition, a phenomenon arose of what Christophe Wavelet coined "temporary coalitions."[5] The distinction between the choreographer and performer has been dissolved in the simple fact that works are produced in a fashion in which the division between the two roles no longer makes any sense—authors, actors, and performers all work with and for each others. Thus Christian Rizzo can be both a "performer" and "costumer" for Emmanuelle Huynh, be part of a project by Rachid Ouramdane, and also choreograph a solo "for" the latter (*Skull*cult*, 2002), while continuing to create projects of his own that reunite the same colleagues, friends, and collaborators. *Morceau* (2000) "by Loïc Touzé" is described as being "conceived and realized by Jennifer Lacey, Latifa Laâbissi, Yves-Noël Genod, and Loïc Touzé." This piece brought together four performers (who are also authors of their own projects elsewhere) who bring to this work "by" Loïc Touzé not just their own contributions, but probably also common aesthetic questions. The examples of such collectives are endless: the formation of a tight network gives a number of dance groups the appearance of being a family. The phenomenon is closely associated with the dissolution of the hierarchical relationship between the choreographer and the performer (though it has probably been replaced by other hierarchies that might soon become apparent). And to this can be added the fact that the audience is filled with the same faces and names when they are not performing on the stage. Trisha Brown's remark concerning her early works is still very relevant to the new generation: "The people who watched my work were my peers, they made a very intelligent public."[6]

This "new dance community" is thus bound up in a common project in which one of the major issues is the notion of the work. In fact all of those characteristics of what constituted "good choreography" in the 1980s seem inapplicable to these recent productions: choreographic composition gives way to the "dispositif" (*Bord* by Emmanuelle Huynh, 2001), and gesture to improvisation constraints (*Algo Sera* by Nathalie Collantes, 2001). The nature of what delimits a "work" has changed, just like it changed with the aleatoric compositions of Merce Cunningham, the gravity-inspired adventures of Trisha Brown, and so on. And since then, of course, the nature of perception has changed too, as did the status of the spectator, the critic, the curator, and the producer. These last two are in a particularly difficult position: required to pay but also blamed for doing so (never enough and always in a suspicious fashion), they are considered to be domineeringly exclusionary if they do not provide funds for the show to enter the dance market, and manifestly mainstream or if they do. As for the critic, he sort of disappeared along with the dissolution of the boundary between him and the artist, who offers a discourse on the work while the work is being produced, unless his discourse is of course the work itself.

Under such conditions, the original question of "my opinion about contemporary creation" disintegrates due to lack of a vision, lack of criticism, and lack of creation, at least in the traditional meaning of this term. However loads of other questions remain open. First of all, that of the works themselves (which we should probably call "*dispositifs*" or "processes" to be sure not to confuse them with the earlier "works" that they wish to criticize). This new era is also striking for the redundancy that exists between the discourse and the works, and sometimes between the works themselves. It is tempting to lump all these works together, as I have just done, and describe the whole without attending to each piece's details. Furthermore, though these pieces are based on the criticism or deconstruction of earlier models, they are also unquestionably dependent on them. Thus, the numerous performances that attempt to re-invent the "visible" (what is shown) fail to reconsider the conditions under which the piece is viewed, and present in the frontal perspective of traditional stages materials that are obviously conceived for a different use of space. Likewise, harsh criticism of the effects on aesthetics of the performance market (the system that underlies subsidies, production, distribution) does not thwart the presentation of pieces in places as symbolically and economically powerful as the Théâtre de la Ville. Is it that the negative effects of these presentation models are only prejudicial to the "old" dances from the 1980s, whereas those from the 2000s are immune, impervious to the effects of commodization? The impression is given that this is all cyclical, and that we are witnessing the endless return of the same old causes and effects. But can the trends of the dance scene be considered differently, and can they be analyzed in a productive, rather than in a disillusioned, way?

The non-originality of the non-avant-gardes?[7]
In a "very postmodern" spirit, this milieu (in the sense of both "professional milieu" and ecosystem, with its own laws, and forms of exchange and circulation, expenditure and compensation) is exceedingly devoted to the deconstruction of originality, the demiurgic creator, and authenticity, in order to replace it with copy, ersatz, and sham, thus reinstating issues at stake thirty years ago. One of the paradoxes of the present phenomenon, I think, is to be found in the crystallization of positions in contradiction with these values. What

164

are we to think of the questioning of the status of the choreographer and the performer (*Xavier Le Roy* "conceived by Jérôme Bel and directed by Xavier Le Roy") in a piece made available through the traditional distribution channels and presented in conventional conditions to an audience invited to attend in the usual manner, when it is difficult to understand how the category of the "audience" can resist while that of the choreographer and the performer is dissolved? How can these works be coproduced without their subversive impact being defused? How can they be presented in our theaters without their significance being reframed? Similarly, critics offer their discourse in an attempt to stay in step with this movement but in so doing double the overall quantity of discourse since these days artists produce their own. Yet how can the critics associate with the movement without producing "an author's discourse" that maintains the usual categories of critic, creator, and work of art? Conceived in this way, preservation of the traditional statuses of the artist, critic, and curator leads to fossilized or meaningless relations between the different functions: by producing pieces that are both "creative works" and "discourse on the works," and by producing "criticism within the community" (Jérôme Bel asks Alain Buffard and Xavier Le Roy to comment on his work;[8] Christophe Wavelet analyzes Alain Buffard's work, and so on[9]), artists neutralize the traditional function of critics and appropriate for themselves the power that the latter normally hold. Perhaps it is precisely because artists want to secure this power that they sometimes offer views characteristic of traditional criticism (judgments, canonizations, excommunications, etc., using a vocabulary so specialized it smacks of the language of a cult). In so doing, they consolidate a form of perfectly harmonized discourse that *a priori* discredits any alternative thinking that might arise in relation to the works produced. Does this new radicalism lead to anything else than the advent of "a new generation" of artists (whom we must be careful not to call choreographers), the authors (despite their denials) of creative works produced on the back of endless subventions, co-productions, and communications? For their part, critics hardly have any other choice than to imitate the artists' discourse on their own work (a hagiographic stance) or to disparage their work (a negative standpoint that only confirms to the artists the need to do their own criticism). In spite of the apparent dissolution of any sort of boundary (between disciplines, functions, or discourse and creation, etc.), other less conspicuous confines subsist between the different but overlapping conceptualizations from the two time periods. In other words, the indictment of models at once aesthetic, political, and economic by a new generation of artists undoubtedly answers a vital need in the choreographic community. However, this "new era" overlaps with a rationale that is still derived from the time of the earlier models, even if the people involved seem to have moved on. Does the fact that it is "artists" who deliver most of the legitimating discourse on other artists and on themselves change anything in the content of the critical discourse as a ruling rather than legitimating one? Is the advent of these new models (a "re-advent" of old ones) opening other horizons beyond the recognition of a certain number of artists, to the detriment of those who will not be champions of radical attitudes? Is there anything else happening other than the creation of a new "milieu," of a new dandyism based, exactly like the previous one, on an aesthetic consensus and signs that make it possible to distinguish between those who "belong" and those that don't, as much among the artists as among the professionals, not to mention the audience?

These ambiguous conceptual stances as a whole, as well as the growing feeling of being personally invaded by the vague, abstract, "elusive" language used to describe these new forms—language the works themselves and their surrounding communication are composed of—lead me to attempt in this essay in order to catch hold not of "what does not work in the system," but rather "what does not work in the way we think and devise the system." Besides, how does one understand the phenomenon of "elusive language"? In the middle of the era of copying, duplication, and the destruction of anything to do with the notion of origin, the critic that I am would very much like to not be cornered (either by herself or by archetypes of thought) into making judgments, however justified they might be, on the validity or "originality" of works, nor into taking responsibility for her own discourse, invaded as I feel it is by the discourse of "all the others." And the educator that I am would like to be able to lay down her weapons in her fight against all clichés, stereotypes, and received ideas, a fight that is the base of my experience teaching on dance.

Dance as doxa and doxa as envelope

That is why today I am trying to shift my attention on "contemporary creation," moving away from a focus on its subjects (choreographers, performers, curators, etc.) or its figures (the works) to analyze it as "*doxa*." To Anne Cauquelin,[10] doxa is an autonomous form of learning, not a false or inferior one, but a specific register of knowledge: a "common place"—a place that is shared—and a common thought. Or perhaps, says Cauquelin, an envelope: what surrounds us, a fluid and fleeting discourse of knowledge that permeates, and above all engenders, our overall acts, perceptions, and discourses. In addition, doxa is what is passed by word of mouth, what is not only constant and continuous, but also partial, heterogeneous, contradictory, and, most importantly, always in movement. Thus the doxa is an envelope. Cauquelin also notes that what recent debate has called "the end of art" is actually more akin to the crumbling of the difference between container and content—or between a work of art and its exhibition, between creation and communication, and so on. What is contemporary art? A doxa, she suggests, and gives numerous examples: a shopping list, catalogues, commentaries on a work of art in place of the artwork itself, an exhibition as a work of art, etc. Therefore, the true avantgarde standpoint is to acknowledge that the discourse on an artwork is part and parcel with the work itself, that the envelope and its content have long mutually penetrated one another, and that in reality only the envelope exists, not as an empty container but rather as connective tissue. Contemporary art has done away with the separate elements of artist and artwork by turning the art world into a "*réseuil*"[11]: "[confining] works, artists, and professionals as well as any viewers/buyers in this increasingly tight net, so much so that this *réseuil* ends up being identified as art itself. Thus art is nothing other than this network, which would be unable to exist if it did not perform the functions of a network, that is to say, if it did not form, deform, and transform itself at every moment."[12]

From the viewpoint of contemporary dance, it would be possible to draw a history of the movements taking place within doxa (Anne Cauquelin devotes her book to describing the "physical nature," "logic" and "aesthetic quality" of doxa) and to observe them as such, rather than lamenting (as it has long been a "common place" to do) the damaging effects perpetrated by "fashion" on dance. It would be possible to describe how "the contemporary dance of the 1980s" developed on the basis of a common discourse, a common language (an envelope) in which artists, critics, curators, and spectators either shared, or were excluded from, a particular form of thought. And rather like a meteorologist, Anne Cauquelin goes on, it would be possible to monitor the direction of the currents and alterations of form that led to new semantic or aesthetic constellations (or nebulas) during the 1990s. It would also be possible to draw up a list, though inevitably incomplete, of the "key notions" and, above all, the vocabulary used in the transmission of this doxa ("radicalism" [*radicalité*], for instance, seems to have played a major role in the transition of the choreographic doxa's figures from the '80s to the '90s). But that is not the aim of this essay. Our interest is more in the effects perpetrated by this "new figuration": contemporary dance as a common place.

We cannot be certain that the observations inspired by the contemporary art scene can simply be transferred to the contemporary dance scene. In particular, as we have seen above, the crumbling of the figure of the artist and of the status of the work in such a dance scene is far from actual. Moreover, the choreographic milieu that this essay attempts to draw "a different fiction" of may not be the totally uniform and perfectly fluid network that the term "*réseuil*" seems to describe, as it also includes stones, countercurrents, and pockets that create resistance. Beyond these questions of texture, which might appear abstract to the reader, in what way does this vision of the choreographic scene change the present order? Is seeing the ensemble of our activities as spectators, artists, critics, political decision-makers, and curators as just so many aspects of the same thing, or as the multiple faces of a Möbius strip (the envelope) not the same as repeating (another trick of doxa) what contemporary artists and critics keep asserting: that there is no divide or essential difference between the artists and non-artists, between the works and the world itself?

What I am interested in doing here is observing in what way identifying the features of this strange body that we all belong to—the doxa—would allow different ways of seeing or communicating to be initiated; to observe not the individuals involved in the action (artists and critics observing and commenting on one another; the subjective choices of curators affecting the career path or the potential of a particular artist, etc.), but rather the actions themselves and their effects. If we now consider artistic gestures, discourses, actions, and texts as different aspects of the same fabric of knowledge—the common places—then contrasting a certain register of critical thought against a certain aesthetic choice by a certain artist no longer makes much sense. This standpoint radically blurs the status of the subject, whether artist, curator, or spectator. Therefore, the issue for critics would no longer be to "produce discourse" on a particular work or artist, but to consider, for instance, what kind of force underlies and organizes the work in question; or to understand what intention or inclination gives rise to both the creation of a piece and the programming or coproduction of a theater. And finally to recognize what movements are at work within this milieu, such as are revealed by certain moments of creation and reception...

Making things possible

Thinking of choreography as a whole in terms of the "movement of things" would make it possible to untangle the causal relations that organize and order our vision of art, and to pose the question of ethics again (why and for whom does art exist?), which is crucial in a field where aesthetics and politics are tightly bound up by public services. Belief that the curation, the production, the financing schemes, the architecture of the performance spaces, etc., exist to promote or impede the birth of creative works leads "contemporary creation" to become the Holy Grail that all actions of the professional network are trained for. But the proposal could be reversed: What does a particular work make possible? From what potential has it emerged? And what potential does it offer in return?[13] This question would not only allow the principles of causality to be reattributed, and their links with whichever revered creator is under consideration (artist, author, etc.), but also the questions of responsibility, and therefore of ethics.

In the present period, numerous discourses (particularly those of artists) aim to get choreographic work considered on a critical register: considered with respect to earlier works or periods, or a number of aesthetic conventions, or to political and economic standpoints. These discourses are used to reflect on other works, other discourses, other actions, but in so doing, they either turn attention away from the works themselves or focus strongly on a particular aspect. The change of viewpoint offered here has the aim of activating other registers, other choreographic "potentials"—not to replace the critical register, but to present an alternative. If the thought and practice of dance are a form of doxa, it is therefore the study of its movements, rather than the study of its objects, that might be of interest. Especially what I shall call flows: gestural, economic, and semiotic flows (regarding the latter, the phenomenon of abstract, elusive language would be effectively described, I think, starting from "the epidemiology of doxa," as is also described by Cauquelin: how words and concepts flow from person to person, and from article to conversation, and become simultaneously commonplaces and de rigueur in dance theory). For example, the question of speed seems to be particularly topical (Jérôme Bel talks about his "immobile years"[14]) and a large number of pieces can be considered from the perspective of the slowing down that they entail. A slowing of gesture, but maybe also the slowing, or even interruption, of the semiotic, economic, and other activities of which these "works of art" are traditionally the driving force (what is implied here are the activities initiated by any production project, and by the piece itself, such as its presentation, audience gathering, spectacle economy, distribution, comments on the piece, among others).

An example is given by the solo developed by Portuguese choreographer Vera Mantero: *Une mystérieuse Chose, a dit e.e. cummings* (1996). In many respects, it belongs to the traditional economy of spectacle. This piece tours and is presented regularly, and therefore follows standard economic activity. In retrospect, one can also envisage this solo as a moment of the shift and re-composition of the aesthetic and political issues that were to become central to the majority of pieces in the years that followed (the rejection of dance, the questioning of the norms relating to the dancer's body...). It has therefore become a "reference" piece. However, even though it was explicitly loaded down with layers of meaning (in terms of the costume, make-up, text, references indicated in the theater program, etc.), this piece seems to produce a slowing-down effect, even one of stasis, in what I will call the semiotic flows—the generation of discourse and thought about itself—since it simply resists interpretation. As one watches the solo, all thought comes to a halt, only to start again and be enveloped in a discursive flow. As Vera Mantero, paralyzed by the goat hooves she wears that threaten her balance, reels off a long list of impossibilities ("a sorrow, a dreadful impossibility, a sadness, a lack of conviction, a fall, an absence"...), any potential interpretation is blocked as soon as it starts. Thus this form of immobility is not just an absence of movement, but an interruption of movement: a gesture begun but quickly blocked, a hint of meaning given but then dismissed. In consequence, I see this solo as stasis, an interruption in the economy of meaning: *Une mystérieuse Chose...* does not get involved in the networks of commentary, interpretation, or the commodization of meaning. Of course, it is possible to see in it (some did) a criticism of the economy of spectacle and choreography, or perhaps the symptom of a crisis in the artist herself, who seems to be affected by the "impossibility" of dancing. But can we consider this non-dance from the viewpoint of what it makes possible, for example, a diversion (like a stone diverting a stream of water) in the economy of meaning? A moment of standstill and resistance (in the physical sense) to movement, which is no longer seen as an "ideal" of liberty, but rather as a "compulsory direction of circulation." Stasis here is a moment of immobility in reaction to the economy of flows.[15] Any attempt to reconstruct a coherent interpretation of this solo seems like an effort to reduce its power,[16] to counteract its potential or, to use François Jullien's term, its "inclination," meaning the effect of tension generated by the work.[17]

It might therefore seem paradoxical to choose an example that deals with immobility and stasis to illustrate this notion of the "movement of things." Dancers know well the first reason for this choice: immobility is a state of movement (a "small dance" according to Steve Paxton, or a tension more or less strong yet balanced between two directions of movement). The second and more directly illustrative reason is the increase in instances of immobility or extreme slowness in recent pieces (Jérôme Bel, Myriam Gourfink, among others). Finally, it also seems to me that this slowing down of physical gesture, or "still acts," relates to a "movement of things" that the established order would want to have remain "free": free trade, flow management, globalization, etc., incessantly stimulate the fantasy of rapid, free, and unimpeded movement—see, for instance, ATAC's economic analyses. Stasis may therefore be seen as an imperceptible action, but one that disturbs the flow and circulation.

And since this long reverie is a response to an invitation from the Val-de-Marne Biennial, might it be possible to imagine "the place"[18] (and all the structures by which it is affected, such as financial schemes, political proposals, architectural spaces, functions, and public attendance) as a response to this question? To which "inclination" is this place a propensity, and of which dynamics is it a result? What would the effect be, in terms of cultural policy, if it were conceived of as a place "dedicated to dance" that was not based on its potential output (the hosting, production, and presentation of pieces to the public; giving classes, etc.), but envisioned in terms of work and process? Would it be possible to conceive of such a place taking speed as its starting point? Since the idea of a place as a "container" to accommodate "any kind of creation" (the revival of the famous multipurpose spaces of the 1970s) is an illusion, might it be possible to, rather than continuing to ignore the prospect, conceive a "place for dance" as a process that, like the works themselves, defines or indicates certain inclinations or dynamics? And, if we can take that as a given, perhaps we could cease to think of the place as a location (the theater being a sort of sealed container at the door of which "dance" either becomes available or ceases to become available) and consider it rather as moments, a space that could be "activated" when required and is no longer permanent... A space that could be thought of as work and movement rather than as a building.

[1] This article was first published in *Repères* 11, National Dance Biennial of the Val-de-Marne (March 2003).

[2] "Vingt ans... à venir?," *20 ans*, National Dance Biennial of the Val-de-Marne (on its 20th anniversary, 1999).

[3] "No to spectacle. No to virtuosity. No to transformations and magic and make-believe. No to the glamor and transcendency of the star image. No to the heroic. No to the anti-heroic. No to trash imagery. No to involvement of performer or spectator. No to style. No to camp. No to seduction of the spectator by the wiles of the performer. No to eccentricity. No to moving or being moved." Yvonne Rainer, *NO Manifesto, Tulane Drama Review* 10:2 (Winter 1965): 178.

[4] Solos: *Waw* (1997), *Glossolalie* (1999), *Taire* (1999), *Too Generate* (2000); group pieces: *Überengelheit* (1999), *Écarlate* (2001).

[5] Christophe Wavelet, "Ici et maintenant. Coalitions temporaries," *Mouvement* 2 (1998): 18-21.

[6] Interview with Trisha Brown: "Entretien avec Trisha Brown: en ce temps-là l'utopie...," in *Danse et utopie*, Mobiles 1, Arts 8 (Paris: L'harmattan, 1999), 109. Ramsay Burt commented on the effect of this phenomenon in "Politique, communauté et la relation entre le public et les interprètes dans *Trio* A d'Yvonne Rainer et *Roof* Piece de Trisha Brown," Symposium "Pratiques, figures et mythes de la communauté en danse depuis le XXᵉ siècle." Centre national de la danse, Théâtre de la Cité internationale de Paris, 4–6 October 2002.

[7] In tribute to the book by Rosalind Krauss, *The Originality of the Avant-Garde and Other Modernist Myths* (Cambridge [MA]: The MIT Press, 1986).

[8] "Dialogue sur et pour Jérôme Bel," *Mouvement* 5 (June/September 1999): 29-31.

[9] "Appropriations singulières," *Mouvement* 6 (October/December 1999): 61-63.

[10] Anne Cauquelin, *L'art du lieu commun. Du bon usage de la doxa* (Paris: Seuil, 1999).

[11] An ancient word for net or netting, including handcrafted nets to decorate tables, bed linens, etc. Source: *Dictionnaire Universel*, compiled by Antoine Furetière, 1690.

[12] Anne Cauquelin, *L'art du lieu commun*.

[13] This issue is borrowed directly from Chinese thought as François Jullien theorizes it in *La Propension des choses* (Paris: Seuil, 1992).

[14] "Les délices de Jérôme Bel," *Mouvement* 5 (June/September 1999): 27.

[15] André Lepecki inspired this perception of Vera Mantero's piece as stasis from his commentaries on another of her solo works, *Dança do existir*. He borrowed the notion of "still act" from anthropologist Nadia Seremetakis: "for Seremetakis, 'still acts' represent moments of pause and standstill in which the subject—by physically creating a break with temporality—questions what she calls 'historical dust'." In "Le Miroir éclaté," *Protée, Danse et Altérité* 29:2 (Fall 2001): 68.

[16] This viewpoint is developed in "Dis-identifying: Dancing bodies and analysing eyes at work," Discourses in Dance 2:1 (Spring 2003): 23-34.

[17] François Jullien, *La Propension des choses*.

[18] Over the next few years, the Biennial will be constructing a new place for dance out of a disused factory. See the article "2003" by Philippe Verrièle in *Repères* 11 (March 2003).

THE PERFECT DANCE CRITIC[1]
Miguel Gutierrez

The perfect dance critic does not exist.

The perfect dance critic works for the perfect arts editor, who does not exist. The perfect dance critic writes in the perfect arts publication, which also does not exist. The perfect dance critic doesn't secretly wish that everything was the way it used to be. The perfect dance critic doesn't secretly love ballet more than anything else and feel like she's just slumming when she sees "downtown" work.

The perfect dance critic can talk about individual pieces in relationship to the pieces that the choreographer has made before, and can write about how the piece fits in terms of the evolution of the work. The perfect dance critic understands that "technique" is a vast term that applies to the ways in which dancers can access effectively and intelligently the numerous expressive possibilities that are available to them in their bodies. The perfect dance critic understands that "virtuosity" can apply to the most idiosyncratic of weight shifts.

The perfect dance critic has an awareness of what the postmodern movement in dance expressed, achieved, and how it lives in our consciousness today.

The perfect dance critic does not live in a time warp that shuttles him between now at City Center and 1950 when he irreversibly decided what dance was, is, and can only be.

The perfect dance critic can describe movement vocabulary, and speculate as to what the choices of movement vocabulary mean in relationship to or how they help to shape the larger vision that the dance artist offers.

The perfect dance critic knows that the choreographer's choices are integrally related to the selection of dancers that she has working with her. The perfect dance critic understands that the dancer is an artist and not merely a tool of the choreographer's or director's work. The perfect dance critic can articulate the qualities of individual dancer's energetic presence in the work.

The perfect dance critic understands that beyond movement vocabulary, dance work is a total aesthetic experience and can therefore elaborate on the contributions or selections of music, set design, costumes and lighting in more than one-sentence toss-offs. The perfect dance critic can write about these aspects of performance with ease and intelligence because the perfect dance critic is well-informed has a comprehensive interest in all aspects of performance.

The perfect dance critic can make references to artists and ideas from other forms of performing and visual arts when trying to contextualize work.

The perfect dance critic discusses the implications of the different cultural representations of gender, race, sexual orientation or class in the work. The perfect dance critic acknowledges his own cultural position when addressing these issues, and how that cultural position may shape his feelings or responses.

The perfect dance critic gets excited when she sees something that's different, unusual, challenging, or thought provoking, rocks her world, and writes about it with accompanying vigor.

The perfect dance critic writes in a way that is contemporaneous with the time we are living in.

The perfect dance critic knows when it's time to quit, change careers or retire.

[1] First published in *Movement Research Journal* 25 (Fall 2002).

JENNIFER LACEY & NADIA LAURO:
CHOREOGRAPHIC DISPOSITIFS[1]
Alexandra Baudelot

There is a thread running throughout the choreographic and plastic work co-signed by Jennifer Lacey and Nadia Lauro, which offers piece after piece new unique artistic codes. Rooted in the bodies and the spaces in which they evolve, these codes toy with modes of representation. The spectator does not simply experience a remarkable encounter with choreographic materials, but is invited into a continuous dialogue with the dancers and performers. This interaction is played out well beyond artistic frames and is tied to the images and characters on stage, which have a strange capability to build their own fictions without being rooted in narration. The performing bodies are in themselves fictitious, displaying clothing signs and subjective poses drawn from familiar contexts. In Lacey's and Lauro's performances, these fictitious characters provide the narrative thread for the choreographic and performing processes, and emerge through an imagery that is fantasized yet real. They are constructed through artifacts that they test out directly, or in an ineffable manner, so that they can confront the artifice to better shape an experience of intimacy.

It is therefore clear why these artists use the stage and the space of the image as a backdrop for the mise-en-scène of their choreographic and scenographic processes: the stage, the black box, the picture frame, where everything has to be artificially recreated— where everything is contrived on the basis of spectacular conventions—seem better suited to recreate an artifice that induces the spectator to grasp reality. An artifice that, little by little, replaces personal experience by creating parallel worlds where self-construction remains just as active. Visual artifacts, such as those displayed by a Western culture keen on clichés and the presence of performers that embody a whole series of cultural archetypes, best reveal the hidden sides of intimate stories. They speak to, using the spectacular process, the need to invent forms that are not given as such but which open up spaces—a countless number in view of the freedom these visual devices entail and the fields they explore. More than any definition of gender or a movement unified by a common artistic history, the oeuvre of Lacey and Lauro is primarily based on an assemblage of codes specific to the realm of the two artists. In so doing, they blur the traditional conventions of spectacular economies, and, above all, create a language whose remarkably moving aspect reflects the constant mutation of our everyday environments—free of any artistic compromise.

$Shot (2000)[2] was the first collaboration between choreographer Jennifer Lacey and visual artist-scenographer Lauro. Later came *Châteaux of France* (2001–2004), *This Is an Epic* (2003), *The Sound of Flat Things (Manga)* (2004), *Diskreter Seitlicher Eingang—a Squatting Project* (2004–2005),[3] and *Mhmmmm* (2005). These pieces prompted a singular research in the field of contemporary choreography. The involvement of bodies, scenographic dispositifs, and objects sketch the outlines of a universe in which form, though seemingly dominant, recedes, giving way to a sensitive and organic dimension. The results are hybrid, multiform works that can be considered as much through the mode of the spectacle as that of the exhibition or the performance: a twofold reading that grasps the surface of the images that furnish our everyday environment while allowing it to be permeated by what stirs them on the inside. More than these visible elements—movements and physiques of the bodies, objects used to activate the space and the gestures of the dancers, contexts where choreographic dispositifs take place—it is the subterranean constructions, abstract forms materializing *via* the artistic object, that invariably take over.

Those bodies formatted to meet conventional choreographic language and ready-to-use sets, which easily obey the constraints of a decorative rhetoric, are thus expelled. The space, objects, and materials used by Lauro are not alibis meant to provide a functional and aesthetic minimum needed to gain recognition in accordance with a spectacular charter. On the contrary, they upset conventional modes of visibility and shift our stable perception of space and objects into a muddled and intimate perception. The bodies shaped by Lacey do not attempt to create a choreographic vocabulary that would express the world of the choreographer using accepted formulas. Instead, they explore a movement state that the dancers disseminate, each in their own way, using strong, culturally marked images as if they were catalogues of familiar figures and situations with which we cohabit daily. The images are drawn from a broad range of sources. Among others, sanitized porn stars (*$Shot, Châteaux of France*, and *The Sound of Flat Things (Manga)*); various Marie-Antoinettes, Fantômas, fairytale princes, and Jackie Kennedy-style transvestites (*Diskreter Seitlicher Eingang—a Squatting Project*); characters from Stanley Kubrick's *The Shining* and *The Thing* by John Carpenter (*This is an Epic*); mock witches from the Salem witch trials and the Japanese-inspired specter from Hideo Nakata's *The Ring* (*Mhmmmm*); and the unclassifiable, though vaguely identifiable, figures of two women wearing panties, hats, T-shirts, long socks, and clogs, like an outgrowth of an advertisement for Gap (*Châteaux of France*). These characters, who oscillate between the fantastic and the banal, stage their legitimate right to representation as an affirmation to appear beyond the frozen physical rigidity in which they are usually confined. Leaving image aside, they engage in actions that never substantiate their appearance, thus endowing them with a presence that verges on neutrality. They seek to invent choreographic forms that will define them differently than what is suggested by their external context: a place, a gesture for oneself or toward the other, a sentence—already lost as soon as uttered. These attempts succeed in marking traces that are ephemeral yet also persistent; traces that at first never seem to reach us. They follow their own, slow temporality, shaking off the dynamics of everyday life, a temporality rarely explored, rendered almost useless by the ineffectiveness it confers on the gestures and the places that frame them, and yet which results in strange possibilities of appropriation. The traces revealed by this temporality infiltrate us deeply. They join the flow of images stored in our memory; images that we had believed were deleted, but which in fact had stayed with us, dormant, in our perception of daily life, waiting to rematerialize later in new narratives.

Lacey and Lauro are interested in the experience of reception. If a vocabulary exists to define this type of experience, it at once incorporates images of characters, and different characteristics of places, actions, atmospheres, states, and sounds. Using this *corpus*, rather than developing a form or structure, they prefer to create permanent deformation: bodies, objects, and spaces take shape through mutual dissemination. These become places for experimentation in their own nature, rather than only vectors of a choreographic staging. Through constant mutation from the inside and by reconsidering what makes them materialize in a public space, and as an experiment with the audience, the forms activated by Jennifer Lacey and Nadia Lauro attempt to overflow their own frames of representation in order to grasp a new image in which to think and see the body differently—and, by extension, to seize the space, no longer as the setting for a performance, but as an environment in its own right. The shows, visual installations, performances, and series of drawings that the ensemble of pieces co-written by Lacey and Lauro create fit together in ways that create extensions of one artistic form reaching out to another. Turning their attention from the stage viewed frontally, the audience is invited to consider the nooks and crannies of the theatre, as well as other spaces from television to comic strips. The space of the body's representation is not envisaged in terms of a defined artistic frame. On the contrary, by parodying frames, the two artists assert the need for the body and its environment to be staged and observed from multiple angles so as to prevent it from being trapped in artistic definitions with strong historic and cultural connotations. They prefer to invent their own representational grids as frames suited to the reception and re-creation of images to test out the physical modalities of our time—via the experience of the dancer or performer—and the modalities of the environments that configure these experiences—via the artistic space. Consequently, Lacey and Lauro consider choreographic research no longer the prerogative of only the choreographer and the dancer, but also of the visual artist, the performer, and the sound artist, who all work so that the multiple voices of the body and its modes of representation can resonate together.

Let us recall that even though this approach has appeared in different currents of the history of Western modern and contemporary dance during the twentieth century, it has been greatly brought up to date in Europe since the mid-1990s, when a generation of new choreographers emerged who wished to revisit the founding principles of choreographic representation, its spectacular modalities, and its critical practices. The body and "its dance" are no longer the monopoly of choreographic conventions, but the result of constantly changing observations and reflections that expose the body to multiple relations within its cultural, social, political, and artistic environment. It is therefore less a matter of creating choreographic forms under the influence of artistic conditioning than of appropriating the signs of a period and creating interplay between the past and its artistic conventions, and the present and the emergence of new forms conceived in tune with a time. The experience of the gaze and of the body become predominant, bringing together different artistic practices, infiltrated spaces, and invented fictions. In a similar way to what Nadia Lauro and Jennifer Lacey are doing, new paths are traced to create other modes of corporal and visual reception—paths conceived as experimental foundations for a new politics to think the body, its place in a fictional or everyday environment, and its impact on the outside world. The recent evolution of choreographic forms appears as the consequence of this politics of the gaze, as it is rooted in corporal research and is able to introduce different systems of representation. These systems revolve around modes of thinking that are independent of the canons of the choreographic institution, canons that today still lead to categories like "dance" and "non-dance," when "dance" is not "danced" according to conventional choreography. Unconcerned by such absurd oppositions and even more absurd definitions, the forms of contemporary dance discussed here prefer to assert themselves as not being the prerogative of an authority's ownership. In fact, they constantly disturb the formal rules that attempt to define dance. Rather than a current, it would be more exact to talk about the singular aesthetics by which each choreographer creates her or his own structures and plastic dimensions, which manage to not establish the form of a "signature" that would make the works immediately identifiable. Choreographic art is not limited to the space of danced movement alone. It expresses a constant interaction between culture and the body, each time requiring the invention of a structure and a vocabulary that make it possible to actualize the many situations we are caught up in. These situations can be seen as founding experiences that continually re-signify the grammars of the choreographic genre. In this respect, Lacey and Lauro show us that dance is first and foremost a question of the body, languages, and frames. These are conveyed by images and artistic dispositifs that bring out, for each new project, different ways of considering the status of choreography itself. Lacey says: "Whatever the movements or the energy present in the pieces, the source is always the same, the bodies... Only the projects change, and with them the type of movement."[4] No effect of style or gender is sought out, only a constant exploration of the forms and dramaturgies to come.

Lacey tackles this question of gender using the body itself, through the vision she has of, among other things, sex and gender identities. For this American woman who lived in New York before coming to Paris in 2000, the concept of gender is not an academic specialty or a theoretical discourse. It is above all a modality of thinking and of becoming—a mode of "performativity" and of the "capability to act," to use Judith Butler's terminology—that makes it possible for the body to build its own identity-related gender beyond the man/woman binary. The space that Lacey explores is an "in-between" of genders, enabling movement from one pole to the other in order to throw a different light on these culturally defined bodies with the aim of offering a more intimate and singular vision of them. In other words, Lacey plays with her sexual identity and, in so doing, toys with representations of bodies and sexualities "traditionally" at work in dance history: sexualities supposed to personify femininity and masculinity and, through these two genders, to embody fictions that illustrate the "founding" impulses in the relations and narrations between men and women. Attraction, repulsion, confrontation, avoidance, the solitude of one without the other, mutual support, apotheosis through physical union, etc., are events that have long structured the dramaturgy and choreography of movements. They have been handed down directly from classical dance's great figures and narratives and have endured even after the explosion of contemporary dance in Europe during the 1970s, with choreographers creating singular choreographic vocabularies and structures still according to this binary relation between a man and a woman. Whether they are for or against this binary, it is always through the prism of this bond that bodies and movements are presented to us, establishing from the beginning a hierarchical and stereotyped relation between bodies and genders. Even if contemporary dance at the time attempted to establish on stage a new, more "democratic" type of body, far, as it was then said, from the aesthetic canons then imposed by classical and modern dance, it was nevertheless still linked to a universal, rather than a singular, vision of the body in which feminine or masculine qualities were attributed in a clearly legible way. It is therefore not through the impulse of these dancing bodies that the foundations of body representation were disturbed, but rather through a plastic and visual invention of danced movement, each choreographer inventing his own choreographic space and vocabulary. The next generation, which emerged in the mid-1990s—with choreographers like Boris Charmatz, Claudia Triozzi, Vera Mantero, Christian Rizzo, Myriam Gourfink, Jérôme Bel, Xavier Le Roy, La Ribot, Alain Buffard and Emmanuelle Huynh—tried on the contrary to denaturalize this stereotyped body by offering a series of strategies for the construction, deconstruction, and reconstruction of the body. The body is here approached as an instrument capable of considering its own field of representation differently, without affects or pathological relations to these patterns of bodies in motion. What is then left of the body? A putting into action, a corporeal yet diffused "capacity to act" that draws directly on the resources offered by cultural exchanges. This is why defining the different aesthetics and strategies of these choreographic works as a multidisciplinary act distorts its reading. Indeed, as these strategies materialize through ever-changing identities, they integrate the surrounding dynamic contexts so as to create different ways to represent the body in the cultural field, as well as other meanings through new artistic signs. These signs are created on the body and through the choreographic act, and should not be defined layer by layer like in an archaeological excavation in which the found disparate elements would be placed side by side in order to reconstruct an artistic enigma...

Through the act of representation, the bodies Lacey takes responsibility for, the dancers and performers with whom she works, freely appropriate these cultural signs, far from a passive definition of the sexes whose language—many times repeated and codified—offers no other possibility than a stereotyped representation of the body and therefore also of the choreographic. What Lacey shows is both an a-sexualization and a hyper-sexualization of the body. No causal link exists between the two, only self-inventing, contemporary fictions, since these fictions are drawn from the contemporary iconographic register, and then used to in turn reinvent themselves. These bodies develop fictions, visible on their surface, that instantly reveal their timelessness. They do not attempt to leave a mark on their time—just to uncoil the thread of a time that will repeat itself in loops, with the goal of appropriating their own performative gender. Thus embodied, they become palpable and visible to the spectator, and thus appear intelligible. This is the matter on which the choreographer works, an issue that goes beyond accepted genders. That is why, once again, choreographic form has little importance. The form tends toward a possible autonomy of the sexes and its fictional arborescences. It builds its own narrative logic by choosing to observe what sets the bodies in motion, which is what gathers them in a community based on the flows that link bodies together, rather than on shared utopias or ideologies. Jennifer Lacey and Nadia Lauro explore these territories like playgrounds, inventing their own rules to enable the audience to be active in relation to the artistic objects they offer. They draw a cartography in which the layers of experience of the body and its environments determine the experience of perception and representation.

[1] This text is excerpted from *Jennifer Lacey & Nadia Lauro. Dispositifs Chorégraphiques* written by Baudelot and published by Les Presses du réel in 2007.

[2] The musician and composer Zeena Parkins and dancer Erin Cornell also collaborated to *$Shot*.

[3] Literal translation: "Discreet side entrance—a squatting project."

[4] Jennifer Lacey, "Le chantier," interview by Laurent Goumarre, *France Culture*, 7 May 2005.

LOOSE ASSOCIATION:
EMMANUELLE HUYNH AND TRISHA BROWN[1]
Julie Perrin

Sparse Movements

Why put forward a parallel between Trisha Brown and Emmanuelle Huynh?[2] What kind of reduction will such a comparison lead to? Though looking at their respective work on release techniques enables us to trace common potentialities of movement and imagination, this in no way suffices to define the scope of an aesthetic, or even to wholly describe a movement style. From there, the paths these two artists have taken are as diverse as their gestural imaginations allow. Is it even possible to define, once and for all, Brown's style? The choreographer accustomed us throughout her career to move along a series of cycles that punctuated the evolution of her questionings. Therefore, we must instead consider her work as manifold form, if not of heterogeneity then of becoming, and irreducible to any rapid synthesis. But isn't this the very reason that Brown has had an influence that is so difficult to grasp? An influence that can express itself on many levels, and can concern only a moment or an aspect of Brown's work.[3]

When Huynh attends her first Brown performances in 1987, the company is in the middle of the Valiant Cycle, in other words, at a moment in which Brown has abandoned the fluid and undulating nature so characteristic of her earlier movement (starting with the Unstable Molecular Structures Cycle) in favor of creations built around the power [*puissance*] of bodies. The mischievous, sensual, quick, and elusive character, and the off-balance and swinging movements give way to a more geometric vocabulary in which the dancers seem to be like blocks propelled into the air, playing with counterbalances and abstract relations. There is thus a shift in the relationship with the audience: the spectators are no longer immediately drawn into the empathy of the continuous whirlwind produced by a "kinesthetic, outgoing, and flamboyant"[4] kind of dancing, as the choreographer describes it. Shifting from the unexpected and lively impulses a flow of barely fathomable movements springs from, Brown chooses to show clear forms that are outlined in the air, like the "flying warriors"[5] from *Newark*, as Huynh calls them. It is the gesture's point of impact—the effect of a determined and powerful decision—that is at the heart of this new approach to movement. The audience is most certainly impressed, but also in a way put at a distance by this power—the unknown of this virtuosity, the juxtaposition of events rather than their succession, the more interrupted rhythm and the colder abstraction that radiates from the dance.

Huynh's early pieces carry the mark of this more distant relationship with emotions, this sculptural character of bodies. One might say that her dance is far from the image of the supple and silky movement that one generally recalls of Brown's style. Nothing in it flows, gushes, or swerves. And yet, no exacerbated virtuosity, no aerial prowess characterizes these pieces either. The solos *Múa* (1995) and *Passage* (1997) take risks with arduous balances; the positions and intentions are never glorious or "valiant." Refusing impetus and fluidity of movement, these dances principally take the form of slowness punctuated by interruptions and stillness. For instance, *Passage* is structured by a repetition of the same sequence of simple movements done in different orientations. We see a succession of figures at a standstill, not frozen or petrified but rather self-possessed; one might say, "he looks composed": calm, concentration, and gravity. And a play of supporting movements and extensions unfolds on the ground, on a low level. Two hands under a thigh support a leg while the body, half-lying, half-sitting, resting on the pelvis, comes to a halt. Accelerations, rolls on the floor, and repeat again. There is something determined, simple, and inevitable in the development of this choreography: something that in the end reminds us of the Accumulations Cycle of Brown and the quality of interpretation that it demanded of the dancers.

By the middle of the 1990s, Huynh is not yet familiar with Brown's first cycles beyond a description in a 1990 publication.[6] She therefore knows nothing of the particular quality of this Accumulations Cycle, which has also been called "mathematical"[7] (1971-1976), in which the dance seems to be able to continuously unroll, without inflection or psychology or dramatization, leaving the dancers "almost like solid objects."[8] Nevertheless, the question of simplification and of stripping down is very much at the heart of the young choreographer's interrogations, like a response to the necessity of pursuing a refusal of expressivity, already present in *Momentum*,[9] like an echo of her interpretations of Cunningham and Cage in the 1980s. Ever since a workshop with Lance Gries in 1992, this set of problems gradually has pervaded her work.[10] They haunt her exchanges with Brown: the search for a simplicity defined less in terms of reduction than by going back to what is essential;[11] simplicity in its intrinsic power, like a form of purity that expresses itself outside of appearances or any extraordinary character;[12] the simplicity of movement that is sparse, rarified (rather than reduced, a term that refers to minimalism), and that makes room for silence, for stillness;[13] and finally, simplicity as the attempt to come back to movement only, to its performance in the least audacious or sophisticated manner possible, a simplicity that owes everything to bareness.[14] This interrogation also traverses the workshop given by Brown and Wil Swanson in Montpellier in July 1995, where what is often at stake is a "reduction to the essential" (Huynh's notebooks of the 8th and 9th of July 1995).[15] If such a theme obsesses Huynh in the 1990s, that is to say, in a context that was still very different from that of the 1970s in America, it is also in reaction to a certain kind of French dance that she denounces both for its spectacular aspect and its lyricism. This happens through a detour, a detour toward her origins so to speak: a Villa Médicis Hors les Murs grant enables her to go to Vietnam while she is making *Múa*. There she recognizes, and in a way renews, a body that perhaps bears this simplicity that she has been looking for: "(In Vietnam) I recognized a way to move the body that was at once nonchalant and discreet."[16]

Furthermore, when Christophe Wavelet makes a connection, in his critique of *Múa* in 1999, between the piece and the New York avantgarde, he acknowledges these references as what now shapes Huynh's artistic culture. "Closer to the *neutral doer* dear to the New York avantgarde in the 1960s than the character, the quality of expressivity that is played out in *Múa* is a nod in the direction of a desublimation of the dancing body and the spaces, symbolic and real, that it opens up for the benefit of each viewer."[17] Huynh also claims in retrospect, in 1998, with regard to *Múa*: "It is urgent to recognize the legacy of the artists of the Judson Church and I attempted to express a necessity in this stripping down and the reduction of effects."[18] In spite of the scarce documentation then available in French or even just accessible, and the near absence of video documents, a certain idea of *postmodern dance* took shape for Huynh. During her stay in New York in 1990, she was able to see the film *Man Walking Down the Side of a Building* (1970) from the Equipment Pieces Cycle at Lincoln Center. The workshop in Montpellier in 1995 allows her to first approach the notion of the "task," with which she will experiment further in 1996 when performing *Continuous Project – Altered Daily* by Yvonne Rainer, and Steve Paxton's *Satisfyin Lover*, recreated by the Quatuor Albrecht Knust, and then later, *Parades and Changes, Replays* by Anne Collod and Anna Halprin in 2009. She familiarizes herself with the attitude the task entails—detached, without affect, but also at times playful—and how the task has been an ever-recurrent theme throughout the period of *postmodern dance*, from its conception at the end of the 1950s with Anna Halprin in California, up to its metamorphosis for the stage and its multiple reinterpretations in New York City with the Judson Dance Theater. Here, the term "task" always signals a gap with regard to an average trend in the economy of danced movement and its methods of stage representation—a gap that can be measured in terms of increasing scarcity.

Commenting on her pieces *Distribution en cours* (2000) and *Bord, tentative pour corps, texts et tables* (2001), Huynh insists on the importance of the ideas of scarcity and a simplification of interpretation.

> I try to make it so that what happens is only what happens. I am absolutely not interested in seeing something get amplified, in the facial expression or in the movement, without there being a reason. All the work on sensations (postural yoga, Feldenkrais and Alexander methods, etc.) means that one is already engaged with a certain number of events. Leaning on a table, pushing it, pulling it, I feel like that's already a big event. Fundamental and simple movements, performed like the tasks that they are—the inversion of gravity, touching another person's skin—are maxi-events, to be protected from any parasites. [...] In *Distribution en cours*, the dismantling of the object is a sort of metaphor for it: it's the removal of layers, of strata, and the taking away of certain choreographic attitudes that require us to invade the empty space with exacerbation, to blow off steam energetically.[19]

Exposing performers as they are, entirely involved in the activity to be done, without emphasis—states of presence that are reserved or held back, rather than expansive. Other pieces show this. It is a calm and methodical quality of concentration (*Passage*); concentration necessary for the ordering of objects (*Distribution en cours, Numéro*[20]); necessary for the construction game with tables, conceived by visual artist Nicolas Floc'h, that the dancers tip over and move, whose tops they dismantle, that they stack to make a sculpture or to create a new stage design configuration (*Bord*). This is also an exploratory quality of concentration, in connection with the activity of discovering the materiality of the other the interstices that imply possible circulations: clearing a path between the bodies and the tables in *Bord* in order to test the materials and their resistance, as if to slide between the words of *Anachronismes* by Christophe Tarkos, pronounced with caution, while preserving intervals of silence, pronouncing all of the syllables distinctly. Decomposing, giving the audience time to see, resisting getting carried away, calmly persevering in one's idea. Might what is being outlined here also be a method of addressing others and of paying attention in a particular way?

When working on the piece *Le Grand Dehors, conte pour aujourd'hui* (2007), the writer François Bon and Huynh collaborated in text. A passage written in 2006 evokes this key question of simplicity:

> Returning to the simplest things of the body.
>
> Sitting, lying down, walking. Just turning one's head, standing up.
>
> Working on paths, lengths, runs, walks, explorations.
>
> Bringing everything to life: the hand can tempt the foot, it can make the foot want to move. A hip summons a shoulder. A knee has a life of its own.
>
> I am attached to things that I cannot see, things that I can only see when I am dancing.
>
> Ordinary movements: walking, sleeping, that can be seen as dances—that are dances. All you have to do is look at them as such.

Sleeping inhabitants of a town as one big nocturnal dance.

Running, walking, backing up, climbing: that's dance, that should be part of dance. Lots of time and many years before dance touches you in your ordinary gestures.

Before a gesture is dance. […]

It's the body that's going to find it. It's not my head that will find it. I'm waiting to be surprised by my body that will find it. For my body to find what it hasn't yet felt, what I haven't yet wanted, what I haven't yet seen. […]

And that changes the way of thinking, acting, behaving.

Sorting out, knowing why it happened. Try to send the world over to the side of other gestures. Dance is the place of the act. To fight for it to happen.

Dancing changes ways of thinking so much. […]

I have always started my work by emptying, emptying, emptying.[21]

This text says a lot: about the vocabulary implemented, about the ways of thinking about movement that can motivate a coordination, about stage crossings, about the slowing down of bodies and of viewing, about an increasing scarcity, about a research starting with the body, about a thought born from and through movement. In this overlapping of thinking and dancing, we find almost word for word one of the pursuits of Simone Forti, Brown's mentor,[22] who wrote: "I realized that we think differently when we are in motion. And this is the form of thinking I try to access."[23] "The body solves problems before the mind knows you had one,"[24] Brown would add. In the slowness and simplicity of Huynh's dance, what kind of thought, formed in the movement, shows on the surface? A space of thought also opens up for the viewer, in the silences or the pauses; in the interstices of the gestures, it slips in, wanders, or develops. It is an audacious aesthetic choice, that of contemporary art. Because there is a sort of risk and courage in presenting oneself in this way to the public: "Having the courage to not do. Just stand," answers Brown[25]— to abandon all excellence of the danced movement, to be simply there with nothing to hide—this is a "terrifying" quality of presence for the dancer who feels as if they were "put under a microscope."[26] She adds, "Simplicity is very hard to perform. You have to have the courage to be there when you are not concealed by a flurry of gorgeous actions. That kind of 'being there' makes my heart beat double just talking about it."[27] This speaks to the fear of the dancer when she takes the risk of becoming scarce, the risk of not being able to sufficiently captivate the audience's attention or satisfying expectations.

Between Presence and Absence

Simplicity produces a paradoxical interpretation, oscillating between presence and absence. Just being there is to appear fully, completely, yet without shining. Being there, present to oneself and one's action. To concentrate all of the attention, to become the object of focus and of an intensification of the gaze onto oneself and one's action. Just 'being there' is at the same time accepting to become the medium of thoughts that only the viewer has control over. The dancer consents to a sort of letting go of herself. Huynh's modality of being on stage perhaps lies at the heart of this paradox. Since *Múa*, a line of questioning runs across (almost all of) the works in her career, weaving this performance paradox: how to be visible and invisible? How to both appear and disappear in front of an audience? It is not a question of doing a magic trick (even though the choreographer played with such references in *Numéro*) but rather of working on the qualities of performing or weighing its paradoxes.

This haunting question finds echo in the work of Brown. Hasn't the American choreographer ceaselessly played at making her dancers disappear, or at disturbing the impression of a mastery of the visible that the stage procures? Whether one thinks of her dance experiences in offstage, unusual spaces where the dancer competes with the site (Joseph Schlichter in the New York architecture of *Man Walking Down the Side of a Building*, 1970), where the dancer disappears, camouflaged and still as a sculpture of fabric (the dancers suspended in the structure of *Floor of the Forest*, 1970), where dancers are invisible to passers-by (in *Roof Piece*, 1971), or drift away from the audience (the dancers on rafts in *Group Primary Accumulation*, 1973). Or whether one recalls different processes of erasure and disappearance onstage: the overlapping of one dance on top of another, as if it erodes or interrupts the unfolding of a dance (*Accumulation with Talking plus Watermotor*, 1979); certain instructions in *Set and Reset* (1983) that involve remaining on the edges of the stage and being invisible, for example, by lying down, exiting the stage, turning one's back – or doing secret movements, imperceptible to the viewer because they are so tiny (two little fingers that intertwine) or hidden behind another dancer. The choreographer has also choosen to go beyond the boundaries of the stage, like in *Glacial Decoy* (1979), a dance that extends into the wings. And choosen to strictly forbid the face-to-face, in her famous solo, back turned toward the audience, *If you couldn't see me* (1994).[28] And finally perturbed any attempt at grasping gestures in her cycle Unstable Molecular Structures in which movement escapes, deviates, and resists any controls on the way it is seen.

Huynh's strategies are different. Although they call for simplification in performing, like in the mathematic cycle of Brown, they also involve stage practices of covering up. Darkness is inserted between the viewer and what is on the stage, or, just the opposite, the light dazzles and blinds (*Múa*, with lighting by Yves Godin). Caty Olive's lighting is sporadic for *Distribution en cours*. The dancer disappears behind an enormous mobile sculpture, a sort of "combines" à la Rauschenberg, a quasi-grotesque conglomerate of disparate objects, piled up on a stand with wheels: the movement of the object has little to do with the solo that is going on and regularly obstructs the view, according to the principles of autonomy between dance and set design dear to Cunningham (*Nothing to Say About…*, 2000). Creating obscurity also means making the dancer disappear under a piece of cloth or paper. "We had the idea of making a piece in which everything would be covered up all the time."[29] After *Numéro* and *La Feuille* (2005), also conceived with Nicolas Floc'h, in which one or the other are hidden under a big leaf—becoming the creators of a surprising sculpture, shifting and bumpy—Huynh covers the dancers up under a big piece of cloth for *Le Grand Dehors*, and stretches a dance out into a panoramic space, which makes grasping the whole thing difficult, in *Distribution en cours*. Finally, the choreographer just simply empties the stage, as if to scoop out the presence of the dancers, while the soundtrack continues. This is the case in *Passage*, in which the stage is deserted for a period of time between two sequences of movement, and at the beginning of *A Vida Enorme/épisode 1* (2003).

From the 1960s in the United States to the 1990s in France (and more widely in Europe), one can observe the extension or reactivation of a question: that of the mode of a dancer's presence in front of an audience. How does one present his/her body to another? The stakes are those of the relationship to and consideration of the subject: dancer-subject and viewer-subject. In the middle of the 1960s, this question was formulated in a debate on narcissism and voyeurism, of which Brown appears to be, once more, the heir in a November 1994 conversation about her solo, *If you couldn't see me*.[30] Different processes are imagined for resisting the temptation to seduce and flatter the viewer, such as moving away from a traditional practice of the face-to-face situation: no longer facing the audience (not looking at them any more like in *Trio A* [1966] by Yvonne Rainer, or turning your back on them like in Brown's solo) is like taking away its role of mirror, tearing away the narcissism of the performer, and breaking up all alienating reciprocal identification. The narcissism-voyeurism couple appears then in the discourse as an indissociable equation. This is why, according to these artists, not seeing the audience does not amount to putting a form of voyeurism into place, even though actually, this enables the audience to see without being seen. Not seeing means undoing the mirror effect and the identification between audience and artist. It is the first step toward undermining the exhibitionistic and narcissistic nature of the gesture.

Although by the 1990s the terms of this interrogation have shifted, it is still a matter of thinking about the hold that a performer can have on a spectator. In the case of Huynh, this paradox of a performance between presence and absence attests to a need for questioning ways of being on stage. Her experience as a performer has given shape to this reflection, whether with regard to the traditional frontal arrangement of the stage (in particular, with Hervé Robbe[31]), or in her experiences of situations offstage, which have confronted her with the proximity of the viewer and multiple points of view (as in *Chambre. Étapes chorégraphiques en chambre d'hôtel* (1997-1999) by Catherine Contour). In addition are the improvisations in the context of exhibitions and collaborations with visual artists: these are all situations in which the performance must be thought of as in dialogue with another work of art, uncomfortable and difficult situations where the dancer takes the risk of being outdone by the power of another work. It is also about understanding the delicate equilibrium that will enable the viewer to find his place inside this back-and-forth between dance and visual artwork. Though it is more on stage that Huynh assumes, in this kind of withdrawal toward discreet performance, one cannot simply compare a presence on stage and a presence in the context of an exhibition. The tension at work in this contrast is perceptible throughout Huynh's career. It must be understood that along with what I have called the paradox of a performance between presence and absence, intensification and divestment, there is an entirely other way of being on stage that owns up to the pleasure and exhilaration of movement. Thus, *Tout contre* (1998), *A Vida Enorme, Heroes* (2005), *Futago (Monster Project)* (2008), *Cribles. Légende chorégraphique pour 1000 danseurs* (2009) and *Spiel* (2011) let the pleasure of expenditure burst forth. Huynh, like Brown, starting with the Unstable Molecular Structures Cycle and then the Musical cycle, seem to savor physical expenditure—which is what makes Brown say that at the end of *Watermotor* she felt like an American football player at the end of the game with his helmet falling down over his eyes.[32] This is the same expenditure that leaves the ten dancers in *Cribles* out of breath. Most often it is non-demonstrative expenditure, but it is nevertheless absolutely real. The performers are thoroughly pierced through by movement, leaving them in the state of alertness and receptiveness required for improvising, even though the dance is actually set. This state of paying attention to the present moment is what Huynh is looking for: to always dance as though one were improvising, "thinking about the form as improvisation."[33]

Huynh and Brown also seem to share a desire to fly. One famous anecdote recounts how Brown was sweeping the studio floor with a broom and, by propelling her body horizontally one meter above the floor, looking exactly like Anna Halprin taking flight. "I think that I dance because I would like to fly!" she says during the public encounters in Angers in January 2006. As for Huynh, she writes:

> To be hanging in space.
> Trying to make myself feel something other than what I know about myself and about the world. Dreams in which I dance-fly. A very simple dance. I'm lying on my stomach, I feel the speed of the air like when you put your head out the window and there's air. Dreams in which I'm not touching the ground. I take off, I do a dance.[34]

In the end it seems that the main reservation expressed by Huynh in regard to the work of the American choreographer concerns the quality of performance, or more precisely, the place of the performer in certain works. Even though Huynh is immediately passionate about this search for another type of dancing body and recognizes the contribution of release techniques in their capacity to lead one to rethink form and get back to sensations and gravity, some reluctance has emerged. Interviews with Huynh and Guillaume Bernardi attest to a concern about the place of the subject in performance and signal a gap in the direction taken by Brown's work. In the interview of February 26, 1997,[35] both evoked the consequences of the work of Susan Klein[36] on the body of Brown's dancers and what they call a "white dance." At that time (this will be later contradicted by the evolution of Brown's work), work on alignment and on movement initiated by the skeleton seemed to them to be a form of de-motivation of movement. In other words, if the performers reach perfection and efficiency in the accomplishment of a gesture, they no longer seem to be touched by what they are doing. The spectator then loses the sense of what motivates movement. "It's anatomically perfect. The dancers have integrated the technique and the release, but their dance has become white; the aspect of a voracity in doing things, the vitality of the impetus, has been erased. It's not a question of denouncing Susan Klein's technique, which has enabled the dancers to do unbelievable things, but of fully considering the uses of it in the different phases of the company. At the time we made these interviews, the dance had maybe lost the humor that characterized the previous period with pieces like *Newark*."[37] It remains true that this conception of the body, shaped by these alignment and release techniques and, in the case of some dancers, coupled with Eastern philosophies and practices (Zen, Tai-Chi), is not insignificant as far as the interpretative posture of the dancer is concerned. Eva Karczag, a dancer in the Brown Dance Company from 1979 to 1985 says: "One of the images that I use when

I'm dancing is that I want to be transparent in order to transmit the flow of energy that dance is. [...] I want to be entirely malleable, while at the same time knowing that I have a strong core. [...] I dissolve when I dance."[38] This outlines a form of erasure of the subject that removes one of the sides of the performance paradox previously defined. Huynh resists such a definition of the performer-subject: "being transparent" or "dissolved," acting to serve the "flow of energy that dance is." And though Brown herself steers clear of this, the question still preoccupies her. She explains that when she started, "in the early dances, when I subjected myself to a formal structure, what one saw was the dance and not the dancer."[39] Here the two choreographers debate a concern for the dancer as a person, as an individual whose very personality, colors and gives body to performance and gives meaning to dance. Also, at the time, Huynh committed herself to inventing a graduate level program for choreographic artists within the CNDC in Angers, and so all of these reflections came to inflect the training program that began in 2005.[40]

[1] This text is an excerpt from "Une filiation déliée," which constitutes the second part of the book *Histoire(s) et lectures: Trisha Brown / Emmanuelle Huynh*, eds. Emmanuelle Huynh, Denise Luccioni, Julie Perrin (Dijon: Les presses du réel, 2012). The book opens with a series of conversations between the two choreographers between 1992 and 2006. The essay explores the stakes of this encounter for Emmanuelle Huynh, bringing up the question of heritage, its relationship with history, and the cultural circulations in dance. Published with the authorization from CNDC – Angers, direction Robert Swinston

[2] Emmanuelle Huynh was born in 1963. Her career as a dancer started at the end of the 1980s (notably dancing for Odile Duboc, Hervé Robbe, and the Quatuor Albrecht Knust). She made her first choreographic piece in 1984. The passage that precedes this excerpt describes the importance of release techniques in Emmanuelle Huynh's career, as well as somatic methods that she discovered through workshops, starting in 1992, with Trisha Brown's dancers. These practices shaped a solidly grounded posture, with a tranquility characteristic of any work dealing with postural balance and proprioception.

[3] This excerpt reveals only part of the influence that Trisha Brown has had on the work of Emmanuelle Huynh.

[4] Marianne Goldberg, "Trisha Brown. All of the Person's Person Arriving. An interview by Marianne Goldberg," *The Drama Review* 30: 1 (Spring 1986): 160.

[5] In "Rencontres publiques avec Trisha Brown à Angers, 12-14 janvier 2006," *Histoire(s) et*

lectures: Trisha Brown / Emmanuelle Huynh (Dijon: Les presses du réel, 2012), 111-165.

[6] Lise Brunel and Trisha Brown, Trisha Brown. Collection "L'atelier des chorégraphes" (Montreuil: Bougé, 1987).

[7] In Hendel Teicher, ed., Trisha Brown: Dance and Art in Dialogue, 1961-2001 (Cambridge: The MIT Press, 2002).

[8] "The inexorably repeated sequences in Brown's early work were grounded and predictable to the point of making the dancers seem almost like solid objects," in Marianne Goldberg, "Trisha Brown," 157.

[9] Momentum, essai chorégraphique sur le balancement, co-created with José Besprosvany, is Emmanuelle Huynh's first piece, created in Brussels in 1984 when she was a student at the Mudra school (directed by Maurice Béjart) focusing on expressionist dance.

[10] The workshop was taken by Emmanuelle Huynh at the Théâtre contemporain de la danse in Paris: "Lance Gries clears the way for French dancers to find a corporeality that will completely change their physical imagination," Emmanuelle Huynh in Histoire(s) et lectures: Trisha Brown / Emmanuelle Huynh, 7.

[11] "Je nage quand je danse," Conversation, La Ferme du Buisson, Noisiel, 24 November 1992, trans. Denise Luccioni, in Histoire(s) et lectures: Trisha Brown / Emmanuelle Huynh, 27-31.

[12] "J'ai dû travailler très dur pour comprendre," Conversation, Montpellier, 10 July 1995, trans. Denise Luccioni, in Histoire(s) et lectures: Trisha Brown / Emmanuelle Huynh, 59-67.

[13] "Je ne prends rien à la légère," Conversation, New York, December 1994, trans. Denise Luccioni, in Histoire(s) et lectures: Trisha Brown / Emmanuelle Huynh, 45-58.

[14] "J'en restais là jusqu'à ce que je puisse avancer," Conversation, Bruxelles, 21 April 1998, trans. Denise Luccioni, in Histoire(s) et lectures: Trisha Brown / Emmanuelle Huynh, 68-79.

[15] Histoire(s) et lectures: Trisha Brown / Emmanuelle Huynh, 220-222.

[16] Emmanuelle Huynh, "Corps sous-exposé, corps sur-exposé," in Le Corps tabou, Internationale de l'Imaginaire 8 (1998), 9.

[17] Christophe Wavelet, "Expeausée: sur Múa d'Emmanuelle Huynh-Thanh-Loan," in Danse et Utopie (Paris: L'Harmattan, 1999), 191. The neutral doer corresponds to only one of the modes of engaging in activity practiced by the avantgarde. It must be distinguished, for example, from the effervescent body that Sally Banes describes. The expression neutral doer is used by Yvonne Rainer in the famous text "A Quasi Survey of Some 'Minimalist' Tendencies in the Quantitatively Minimal Dance Activity Midst the Plethora, or an Analysis of Trio A," in Gregory Battcock, Minimal Art: A Critical Anthology (New York: Dutton, 1968), 263-273.

[18] Emmanuelle Huynh, "Corps sous-exposé, corps sur-exposé," 143.

[19] Gérard Mayen, "Nous esquissons un en-commun possible. Entretien avec Emmanuelle Huynh," mouvement.net, 9 July 2001.

[20] This is a piece by and with Emmanuelle Huynh and Nicolas Floc'h that was created in 2002.

[21] François Bon, Emmanuelle Huynh, Le Grand Dehors, 2006. See full text: http://www.tierslivre.net/spip/spip.php?article379/

[22] Trisha Brown, interviews with Klaus Kertess, Early Works 1966-1979, DVD Artpix, 2004.

[23] Simone Forti, "Danse animée. Une pratique de l'improvisation en danse," 1996, trans. Agnès Benoit-Nader, in Simone Forti, Patricia Kuypers, Laurence Louppe, eds., Manuel en mouvement, Nouvelles de danse 44/45 (Fall-Winter 2000): 222.

[24] Trisha Brown, "How to make a modern dance when the sky's the limit," in Trisha Brown: Dance and Art in Dialogue, 290.

[25] "J'en restais là jusqu'à ce que je puisse avancer," Conversation.

[26] Trisha Brown, interviews with Klaus Kertess, *Early Works*.

[27] Trisha Brown, in Marianne Goldberg, "Trisha Brown," 170.

[28] "Tout ce que je vis me transforme," Conversation, Grenoble, 23 November 1994, trans. Denise Luccioni, in *Histoire(s) et lectures: Trisha Brown / Emmanuelle Huynh*, 32-44.

[29] Emmanuelle Huynh, unpublished interviews with the author, July-September, 2008, CNDC Angers.

[30] "Tout ce que je vis me transforme," in *Histoire(s) et lectures: Trisha Brown / Emmanuelle Huynh*.

[31] Huynh danced with Hervé Robbe (Le Marietta Secret Company) from 1990 to 1995.

[32] Trisha Brown, interviews with Klaus Kertess, *Early Works*.

[33] "Je ne prends rien à la légère," in *Histoire(s) et lectures: Trisha Brown / Emmanuelle Huynh*.

[34] François Bon, Emmanuelle Huynh, *Le Grand Dehors*.

[35] Guillaume Bernardi is a stage director and assistant to Trisha Brown for *L'Orfeo* (1998). Conversation with Guillaume Bernardi, "Parler à la sensibilité de Trisha," New York, 26 February 1997, in *Histoire(s) et lectures: Trisha Brown / Emmanuelle Huynh*, 98-101.

[36] The Susan Klein technique (http://www.kleintechnique.com) was taught within the Trisha Brown Dance Company from the 1980s onward by Diane Madden and others. It insists on an awareness of posture and an alignment of the bones, and mobilizes the deep muscles in order to develop the potential of the dancer with a consciousness of her anatomical reality.

[37] Emmanuelle Huynh, unpublished interviews with the author, July-September, 2008, CNDC Angers.

[38] In Aileen Crow, "Une entrevue avec Eva Karczag," in *Nouvelles de danse* 46/47 (Spring-Summer 2001): 56-66.

[39] Brown, in Marianne Goldberg, "Trisha Brown," 160.

[40] Emmanuelle Huynh directed the CNDC in Angers and its graduate school from 2004 to 2012.

A DANCE THAT IS[1]
Mårten Spångberg

1. Any set of signs can be engaged in a process of translation. Signs are weak entities involved in strong relations. The letter L means L and nothing more—perhaps "left" but that's another story all together—but is given orientation, or says meaning through its relations.

Objects are different: objects cannot be translated. They can be described and organized, introduced into semiotic systems, but objects are not signs. Signs are also objects but as objects they are not signs.

2. Dance understood in respect of culturally coded systems introduces dance to semiotics, to meaning production, to signification, to translation. Since the early 90s performativity has been firmly attached to semiotics, haunted by a somewhat naïve reading of the post-structural dictum that language is all there is, thus forgetting the self-corruptive tone of voice resonating through "How To Do Things With Words."

3. Semiotics is like currency: exchangeable. If Peggy Phelan and others had issues with performance and archive in the 90s—how performance ontologically speaking could not not be an implicit critique to reproduction based economies—the problem today is rather what could possibly escape semio-capitalism. A dance whose starting point is signification and meaning production does certainly not imply a critique of anything at all, or if it does, such critique has turned into a "modest proposal"—not a full frontal assault [however impossible but nevertheless] but a benevolent or even cheerful affirmation of the already possible. Dance understood as semiotics, or that wants to be understood as, necessarily sells out its specificity. It becomes one among others and no longer a No-Manifesto.

4. If dance is made semiotics there must exist, so to say, a master key. A tool or diagram with which all dance can be deciphered and

understood. Such a tool has often carried the name reason. Ballet has often been understood, or suffered under the burden to be the master key. This is not just a matter of obligatory ballet class, or how dance critique tendentially fall into ballet lingua, or how Jonathan Burrows use to say, "In dance there is ballet and the rest, and those two seems always to be in opposition, or a mutual threat" (it might now be exactly what JB said but I like it), but all over the place from the performer to the spectator, from studio to showtime, from the magazine to the encyclopedia. Never mind that dance without competition is the art form most firmly attached to technical ability. Technique is obviously neither good nor bad, but homogenization certainly is.

5. If there is a master key this implies—as far as my competence concerning such keys—that it can easily master all other possibilities. Like language, if I know French it's a piece of cake to understand Italian, and if I know Latin I know it all etc. Learn ballet, the Latin of European dance and you'll be fine. Yet, evidently as we know from Stravinsky the moment you *know* your counterpoint you are so trapped, and still how tired am I not of ballet dancers vainly talking about unlearning, and further more trained or untrained is not an issue. Our current economical regime makes anything and anyone special and money on that. How was that worn phrase now "Perform or Else" and save me from "The Grammar of The Multitude."

6. If dance on the other hand is understood as an object, i.e. as a passage, or connected to trace (help), memory (double help) or presence/absence (triple freakin help), or as inscribed into the regime of performativity with its sleazy psychoanalytical sidekick. If dance is an object it's not a matter of translation, it's not a matter of what it means or produces, it—the dance—is exactly nothing other than that. We shouldn't go into *whatness* but then what the fuck, dance is, concerning *whatness*—the condition of being an existent thing apart from whatever may be known or stated about that thing.

7. If dance is an object, i.e. if each dance is a more or less autonomous object and not translatable, each dance must be given the opportunity to develop or enjoy itself. If dance is an object there can be no master key, or at least the master signifier is just that: master —it's a dance but that means short of nothing and everything, but from there on each dance must be approached as a singular, an entity that produces its own existence and can enjoy itself without the help of humans, language, or signification. To paraphrase Ian Bogost, to make dance, or to engage in dancing is not a matter of language or writing, it's a particular kind of carpenting.

8. If dance is an object there can be no master technique but each dance—which might or not be repeatable—must necessitate its own practicing, its own address. A dance can be classified as a dance, yes as an object—it's not a stone but each stone is an object and itself not translatable. And the stone is at the same time complex as it is composed by phosphor, calcium, etc., and those are in their turn composed by and so on.

However dances can be classified as much as stones and can be divided into smaller particles—but the regimes of representation that organizes classification can and must be other than the regimes of representation of each individual object and its being in the world.

Obviously, an object is also for itself in the world and it forms relations with other objects including humans, however those relations are never translatable into something human. Similarly, a dance is an object, and it is in the world as much as a stone, a cigarette, a waterfall, a scent, or a premonition. We must let dances have and enjoy their own existence, only then can they offer us interesting problems. The dance I want to dance is one that minds its own business, not one that I know what it means already before I start it up. The dance I want to experience is one that needs no anthropocentric back up, that is not *like* anything else but simply itself and enjoying it, a dance whose starting point is not relations or negotiation.

9. If each dance is itself distinct, each dance must ask for its own practice. It is no longer a classical "what" asking for essence and situating something in relations with and organized through some correlational master plan, it's a what that asks for an autonomy, not from something else but for itself and as such. Said in other words, it's only when we allow a dance to be as alien as it wants that it can exit the domains of the possible, the economic territory of imagination, creativity and enter potentiality, produce some sort of breach.

Ballet is a practice, equally good as any other, but it has been turned into a semiotics, a fundament of cultural code by dominant discourse, you know it. Nevertheless, if ballet has developed a kind of inner logic it is still possible to approach it as an object. And, again—if dance is a set of autonomous objects that cannot be translated each dance must be practiced as itself and as such, and the practice however ordinary it might seems must be autonomous, distinct, and finite. Dance is not a technique, or set of techniques, that has application but a cluster of practices that can and must not be forced to merge into a make-believe semiotics, whatever their names are: release, Limon, BMC, Forsythe whatever it was called, hang out technique of the early 21st century, occupy, and so on.

10. A semiotic system can only issue possibility. Objects carry the possibility of event. Something whose meaning we are already familiar with is not about to surprise us in any respect, or if it does at best as a "modest proposal," or criticality, or, in other words: re-active change, change already prepared, rehearsed and packaged. Objects *are* not events but as they are not translatable they carry the possibility of an emergence of active change, a change with, so to say, nor departure point or arrival—a change in itself and such.

11. Dance is a cluster of practices and practicings. It is not a semiotic but an object—it cannot be translated but only practiced—and each dance must be practiced as an autonomous existence, thus in no way subject to difference but always confronted as a particularity.

12. Dance is something we practice. To practice implies not to recognize but to allow for something to withdraw, to skip out of semiotics and cultural code, into a radical foreign, allowed to be alien. However, although not engaged in recognition, practice is not hope for the best, wait for the accident, or dance to the end of life (although it always is, too). It is harder than that because it implies exactly loosing oneself, and that can only be done through rigor, however a different rigor than one practiced by semiotics.

[1] This text was first published on Spangbergianism in 2012:
http://spangbergianism.wordpress.com/2012/09/15/a-dance-that-is/15

STEAL, DUPLICATE, UNMASK, STRETCH, CONNECT, INTOXICATE A DANCE-IMAGE[1]

From *Hexentanz (Witch Dance)* by Mary Wigman (film, 1930)
to *Écran somnambule* by Latifa Laâbissi (2012)
Isabelle Launay

The development of a dance work sometimes takes mischievous turns. Under the influence of what we shall call here, for lack of a better alternative, the historical gestural subconscious, going back to an earlier piece may take a detour via a different work. And, when this occurs, which forms of oblivion, untimely migrations, unexpected moments, deformed masks, and unsuspected overdetermination can a dance from the past be reactivated in accordance with? There are indeed some re-creations of dance pieces that reveal completely unexpected aesthetic potentials and political impacts, while illuminating a part of unknown history.[2] The revival of Mary Wigman's *Hexentanz* by Latifa Laâbissi in *Écran somnambule* is one of these. What is it that she documents as much as she produces in aesthetic terms? What kind of history, at once discontinuous and transnational, recomposing the geographic regions and chronologies stated by historiography, does she invite us to tell? And at what price? More precisely, what modalities does this French artist of Moroccan origin—a dancer and choreographer who trained at the Cunningham studio, a performer for numerous French artists (Jean-Claude Gallotta, Georges Appaix, and Loïc Touzé, among others), and *a priori* miles from the aesthetic and political issues that concerned Mary Wigman at the end of the 1920s in Germany—see in the few minutes of this film? The film is as much of an aesthetic shock as a resource, since it possesses critical potential for the production of a reproduction that is polysemic, fascinating and hypnotic, sardonic and monstrous, an obsessive fear, and illustrative of the contemporary unease of the minority.

In the context of France, the expressionist dance that arrived from Germany (*Audruckstanz*) experienced a crisis or rupture in the transmission of its experience.[3] Whereas before the war it had been received partly with interest and partly repugnance, during the post-war period, set against the landscape dominated by the neo-classicism of Serge Lifar, it was rejected outright since it had come from France's old enemy Germany. This repression repeated what had taken place in Germany when the heritage of Weimar was rejected from the intellectual and artistic scene for having been involved in the excesses of the National Socialists. Then, during the 1970s and '80s, it suffered a second rejection due to the appeal of young artists in the American choreographic scene, in particular that of Merce Cunningham and Alwin Nikolaïs—and then again in the '90s, under postmodern dance's influence on the new generation. It was only in the wake of the increasing success of Pina Bausch, from the early '80s on, that choreographic art from Germany began to receive recognition, and even then more in its relation to the work of Kurt Jooss, which differs from expressionist dance in many respects. In spite of the sustained efforts and recognition of a few artists influenced by this current, expressionist dance in France was unable to find neither performers nor a large public.[4]

Thus, for expressionist dance to achieve a new vitality, three conditions were required: first, that the oblivion it had fallen into could be considered a virtue, with confidence placed in the power [*puissance*] of art's memory traces; second, that stealing ideas or even an entire work from an author could be interpreted as necessary for the other and trust placed in the reasons underlying such an act; and third, for copying to be appreciated as a form of artistic work and creative transfer, even in the art of elaborating toxic figures. We'll come back to that. Like various twentieth-century choreographic works, the *Witch Dance* can be appreciated through the cinema medium. In using films as reference, dancers immediately transform the history of cinema into a depository of dance archives, movement scores, and a vast repository of attitudes and behaviors. The history of dance is thus partly mixed up with that of the cinema to which it is linked, and in so doing transforms cinema into a technique of the body. From this standpoint, in the choreographic field it is possible to develop Walter Benjamin's notion that modernity requires a new kind of relation to the past, and that the tradition of continual experience should be replaced by the appropriation of a citation that has already occurred.[5] This lineage-free citation is paradoxical: it is as much a place where memory is exercised (there is indeed a sort of return) as it is a place of an impossible transmission (since it is no longer linked to the continuity of a body-to-body experience): in other terms, it is made *in spite of everything*.

Possessing one's dance

First, let us recall a few elements. The *Witch Dance* was created in 1926 (following a first version in 1914), and it was the fourth solo in a cycle of eight titled *Visions* created between 1925 and 1928. An extract from the dance was filmed four years after its creation, in 1930, as part of a promotional film called *Mary Wigman tanzt*. The career of Mary Wigman, who was then aged 44, was then, from various points of view, on the rise: as an artist, her first group pieces in Germany were well received, and her status as a soloist was boosted internationally by her tours in the United States; as a teacher, her school in Dresden had several hundred professional and amateur students, employed new teachers (notably Hanya Holm), and other schools would soon open; in the political field, she was made head of the association *The Dance Community* in 1928 and she made clear the divergence between her association and the one run by Rudolf Laban.[6] In this context, the *Witch Dance* can be considered a manifesto for expressionist dance: an artistic, pedagogical, political, and feminist manifesto.[7]

With regard to others performing her works, Wigman adopted a radical position: she refused to teach her solos to other dancers or to form a repertoire of works that could be re-created. Instead, she encouraged conditions that would allow anyone to develop their own dances, leading to the founding of the school of expressionist dance. In fact, as far as I am aware, none of Wigman's solos were ever danced by someone other than herself during her lifetime. Moreover, distrustful of methods of transcription, she did not think that her dances could be subjected to the analytical work of notation that could be reinterpreted by another dancer, so it seems that no scores of any of Wigman's solos were created during her lifetime. This attitude was underlain by two ideas: on one hand, Wigman made sure that she would not have to grieve for her past dances, "I would never have wanted to dance the dances of my youth [...] their place has been taken by different and more important things in the different seasons of my life."[8] On the other hand, and more importantly, she had developed a conception of dance—especially in relation to the *Witch Dance*—characterized by possession. Danced works were for her as much a question of being possessed by an inner impulse, conveyed by visions, as it was to possess and master the impact of that impulse. For Wigman, ecstasy was the keystone of her work, and this defined her not as a "professional dancer" but as a "dancing being" who experiences the moment "when awareness of things ceases."[9] For Wigman, who described herself as a "fanatic of the present, in love with the instant,"[10] the creative moment exists within a sort of eclipse of perceptive consciousness, allowing her to be "a thousand times exalted by dying and being reborn to life."[11] It is not insignificant that Wigman would often prefer to use the term dancer in her writings to that of performer or interpreter. In this state of ecstasy, a dance is not interpreted, nor is it organized on the level of a choreographic score: it is lived and experienced. The work thus finds itself suspended   between   choreographic/legislative   power   and performative/executive power. It becomes a *Tanzdrama*, a danced drama, the drama of a work tested by the powers of a corporeality that consumes it as it consumes itself. This "absolute dance" is organized by means of an ecstatic form of conduct in a dialectics between Wigman the choreographer and Wigman the dancer.[12]

It is understood that whereas "the work will disappear at a rate dependent on its excellence and the quality of its performance,"[13] it only has meaning through its promises of unconscious recollection, faculties opposed by the memory-screen that prevents the working of the imagination. This ideology of possession organized the ecstasy of this dancer, who constantly felt threatened each time she went into a trance by the loss of her self-control, though she nevertheless always came out victorious: "As soon as the curtain rose [again], it was necessary, and I wanted it so, to be present and acknowledge the audience. Once again I had succeeded!"[14] The rapture of her self-sacrifice, and the kinesthetic and existential vertigo she experienced were thus salvaged through the blessing of the applause showered upon Wigman as she stood on the stage in all her power. No one could recreate this incommunicable interior need, doomed to disappear. Wigman never gave an encore of her dances. Her expressionist dance was based on the possibilities offered by a unique and unforgettable event, each of which inscribed the name of the artist, who was inseparable from her work, into dance history while her dances were destined to disappear. Mary Wigman's creation was thus founded on a necessary amnesia and a prohibition placed on the circulation of her works. The possessed creator was the possessor of her creation. All that remains of the *Witch Dance* is a film lasting 100 seconds,[15] a few notes and photographs of Wigman, articles in the press, and, above all, the retrospective account of her creative process and its visionary foundation that was published much later, in 1963, in *Le Langage de la danse*.

1ˢᵗ moment. Steal-duplicate-unmask: Phasmes (2001)

In this context, Laâbissi's "capture" of the *Witch Dance* is first and foremost a critical act, an act of disobedience. When she appropriated this dance, which had become almost untouchable, she did not ask permission to do so from the Mary Wigman Society or work with the support of the former pupils legitimately able to offer it. Instead, she taught herself the dance alone. *Phasmes* (2001) consists of three solos in which Latifa Laâbissi copied the work of Mary Wigman, Valeska Gert, and Dore Hoyer as seen in three successive films. For *Witch Dance*, the bare stage was set out to suggest the humble nature of research. The poor quality and discontinuous images of the *Witch Dance*, of which the last few seconds are an addition in close-up, are presented to the public just as they are. Nothing stresses the character of aura conferred on the old black-and-white films by our fascination with what is remote from us. The films are presented using the most domestic of formats, either a VHS or DVD played on a television screen before the audience. There is no mention in the program of the provenance of these copies, which have most likely been pirated from sources of varying legality that circulate among a network of art lovers and artists, who use all means and materials available to produce their work, as the occasion offers.

The films are not simply played once but repeated several times. Thus the source material has a sort of rehearsal value, like a study tool for the dancer who imitates what the bodies are doing in the picture. In art, and particularly in dance, artists tend to copy others in order to avoid the risk of imitating themselves—assuming that it is more dangerous to copy oneself than others. It all resides in the way a gesture is recreated in the new environment. Laâbissi's attitude is neither one of a melancholia caused by the demise of a moment of unforgettable dance that needs to be resuscitated, nor of a fanatical desire to attain an ideal. The production does not, therefore, turn the dance into a farewell, or a tribute, or, even less, a choreographic tomb. Instead, it develops a dialogue and an encounter between the images and their duplication.

Facing the public from the center and back of the stage, in the vast space of a studio lit up like the space of the audience, Laâbissi (or Annabelle Pulcini) is seated like Wigman's witch, wearing a warm-up suit, her face bare and her hair tied behind her head. She performs Wigman's dance three times in a row accompanied live by a percussionist playing the score transcribed for drums.[16] The audience watches the rehearsal of a dancer who repeatedly runs through the movements: she is brightly lit, unlike the dark restricted space that Wigman occupied, as though stripped of the spatial envelope that both threatened and protected her. The dancer-duplicator presents variously productive constructions of new relationships with time and space. Wigman's contradictory dialogue with space is here transferred into a direct dialogue with the sound space. The solo is transformed into a duet. The performance of the percussionist on the stage (who is invisible in the film) harmonizes with that of the dancer. They are aware of each other's performance in order to ensure that the beats and their resonance, of which the choreography is composed, are in perfect unison. Here the synchronization of the pair's percussive movements, with which the breathing of each is coordinated, attains visibility. Whereas in the film the poor synchronization of the sound track with her movements gives Wigman the appearance of a witch-conductor, who solicits, controls, and dismisses the sound world she conjures up, Laâbissi's version presents a game of reciprocal control between the percussive beats of the musician and the movements of the dancer. Lastly, when the television screen is turned toward us after the looped projection, the audience is invited to study the disparity, with astonishment, between the two performances, one in images and the other live. In using the film as a ready-made, and in simulating Wigman's dance, Laâbissi is emptying out the images of their original content. She also exploits the intrinsically subversive aspect of the act of imitation: an imitator exposes what we all believe is inimitable and unique about us, and leaves us unmasked, challenging our narcissistic inclination to consider ourselves exceptional, and making public the manner in which we act (the way we look, touch, communicate, stand, sit, etc.). The mere fact of the imitation frees the audience's captured attention and the mesmerizing Medusa influence produced by a film that has become a totem of the history of modern dance. This deconstruction through imitation consequently defuses Wigman's Medusa trap and, in doing so, repeats, in its own way, the aesthetic and political debate that pitted the cabaret artist Valeska Gert against Mary Wigman. The following is the critique and caricature that Gert made of Wigman, mocking the serious side of expressionist dance in general and targeting the *Witch Dance* in particular: "Suddenly we were confronted by visions that could have come straight from the imagination of a devotee of chapbooks. [Wigman] slithered on the floor disguised as a chimneysweep, to the sound of the rolling of pea-filled drums, using movements like devils from the service stairs that in any variety show would be considered a mediocre performance."[17] Skilful in her use of criticism in her own choreographic work, Gert wanted to deflate both the tone and the scenario of the tragi-pathetic appeal of an "interior need" aimed at organic growth, i.e. the growth of the motif as a principle of composition.

Given that *Phasme* certainly no longer suggests the self-portrait and manifesto of a modern dancer as a witch at grips with the context and issues of the 1920s, why did Latifa Laâbissi feel the need to return to this instance of the German expressionist avantgarde? On one hand, she had a wish to experience these dances that had not been included in her training, being in many respects the opposite of the aesthetic, technical, pedagogical, and political choices of American abstraction. She also wished to have the experience of teaching herself, as if it were necessary in order to leave behind the imitative process inherent in any dance course, to throw herself into an even more demanding replication, which examines and makes a display of even the act of looking. On the other hand, she had the desire to allow herself to do it without having obtained permission. As a result, the project was met with resistance: how could she claim that she was interpreting *Hexentanz* by Mary Wigman? Wasn't this setting up a deceptive act? The dancer showed the tactics of the poor, who, lacking a part of their history, are led to revisit it using the means at hand. Furthermore, although she never referred to them, in France, Latifa Laâbissi's Moroccan origins gave her copy an important cultural slant. Wasn't this Arab dancer-witch imitating a German dancer who made a political compromise with the cultural policy of the Third Reich,[18] as recent work by historians in France has demonstrated? Upon closer examination, it seems *Phasme* permeated with a degree of political irony, attacking from behind both the unquestioned and unconditional approval given to the expressionist avantgarde ("Who does she think she is?") and the politically correct rejection of expressionist dances of the 1920s and '30s by offended leftists ("How on earth is it possible to dance Wigman's dances today?").

2nd moment. Stretch-connect:
Écran somnambule (2009, first and second version) in Rebutoh

In April 2009, Latifa Laâbissi invited by Boris Charmatz to take part in the opening event *Étrangler le temps* for the new Dancing Museum in Rennes. Along with the dancer Dominique Brun, she performed a second, experimental version of her copy of the *Witch Dance* under the title *Écran somnambule*.[19] In this version, she gave a slower but exact performance of Wigman's film score. However it was with a presentation she gave, which lasted 32 minutes (that is to say, sixteen times slower than the film), several months later, as part of the *Rebutoh* event at the Dancing Museum, that the dance achieved an unexpected historical perspective by condensing and reversing the direction of expressionist dance's migration in France by making a detour to Japan and revisiting butoh. Although these two versions are still not fully perfected, particularly with regard to the difficult timing and the type of face make-up (entirely in white) and costume (dark green crushed velvet), what does this echo of *Hexentanz* reveal? In other words, isn't this witch concealing another? The stretching of time, the pleats and folds of the skin of a body huddled up on the floor, the whitened face, the fragility of the movements, the work on the metamorphosis of an enigmatic figure: are they all not suggestive of a work close to butoh, which was discovered in France in 1978? Butoh was itself strongly influenced by expressionist dance from the 1920s. Doesn't *Écran somnambule* bring back unexpected memories of a series of witches conjured up by butoh practitioners Carlotta Ikeda and Yoko Ashikawa in particular? Who's films Latifa Laâbissi has also seen? In fact, in *Hitogata* (*Human Shape*, 1976) Tatsumi Hijikata, entirely supported by Yoko Ashikawa's grotesque metamorphoses, reproduced several motifs identical to those in Wigman's dance in a similarly explosive dynamic. Were they blurred citations or a subconscious, though mostly overdetermined, recollection? Latifa Laâbissi's "rebutoh" astonishingly condenses, against the grain, the aesthetic migration of expressionist dance from Germany to Japan from the 1920s on, where it was metabolized during the 1960s and 70s by butoh, and then returned to France during the '80s, where today it is once again present. It is as though expressionist dance, with the aesthetic of conflict by which it is characterized, needed to pass through its simulation and then its Japanese fantasies in order to discover a new place of expression in the 2010s.[20] This summary of a history of dance migration is a deterritorialization that reveals the extent to which dance is able to assimilate ideological, cultural, and identity issues.

3rd moment. Intoxicate the copy: Écran somnambule (2012)

Freed from this butoh-related context, *Écran somnambule* undergoes a final development phase in order for its duplication to become a separate piece in itself. Each element of the film is at once integrated and altered, in short, metabolized. The choreography, music, costume, mask, and lighting have all been recreated. The music was initially recorded so that it could be remixed by Olivier Renouf. The tempo was not slowed down but stretched, dilated, thus allowing it to maintain its pitch, its relation with the sound environment, and enabling the dance to preserve its relation with the suddenness of the movements that strike the floor. The music is like a long muted chord given new life by cymbal strikes. Thus resonance and continual vibration—both sonic and gestural—are the themes of this version, or, more precisely, the resonance of the resonances of *Hexentanz*. This seated dance loosens the cinematic suspense of Wigman's dance, copied in its every gesture and intensifying the tension. The movement follows a permanent continuum broken by the stresses necessary for the "original" impacts that Latifa Laâbissi wanted to preserve with their full force. The effect is all the more surprising as the abrupt and rapid ruptures have their origin in a much lower physical tonicity, such as a spider slowly weaving its web that suddenly throws out a net over invisible prey. The surprise jolts the audience out of the hypnotic state into which it has been induced. By distending time and deploying vibration, Latifa Laâbissi both rarifies and intensifies the contrasts.

Additionally, the dilation of time allows us to view the dance quite differently: our attention, which was caught in the internal tensions and concentric dynamic of Mary Wigman, can here wander from one part of the dancer's body to another and observe the subtlety of the micro-tension of the forearms, the hands, the relationship between the hands and face, the toes and ankles. In this extreme slowness, and having been liberated from Wigman's choreographic net, the dance follows the kinesthetic events that organize the perception of the dancer and take on the semblance of an instantaneous composition. The relation to the choreographic order is thus undermined by the constant metamorphosis of perception. On the other hand, our gaze can also follow the curves in space, the lines slowly etched, and the diagonals that emerge and then fade away at the same slow rate. As in the film, the light is focused on the figure, thereby making the surrounding space disappear, strengthening the dramatic power, and holding the audience's attention captive despite the extreme slowness. It simply offers variations in intensity every fifteen minutes, a simple dramaturgical device that refocuses our attention. The sculptural and plastic dimensions of the figure are formed before our eyes rather than forcefully planted right in front of us. By shifting the simultaneously fascinating and repugnant frontal view of the figure, what is exposed is a play of twisting, the independence and dissociation of her movements. We are able to see into the recesses and reliefs of the sculpture, to slide our gaze over the surfaces, to imagine the hidden faces of the limbs, to appreciate the transformation of a shape, and to fix on one bodily zone and then abandon it for another. We also have the time to associate images, to lose ourselves in an imaginative excess that was previously concentrated into just a few seconds. Whereas the attention of the audience was immediately captured by the shocks and pauses of Wigman's witch, here it is tested by a figure that is both asthenic and powerful, and that displays all its plasticity.

Moreover, the carapace-like costume devised by stage designer Nadia Lauro, made to imitate snakeskin, intensifies the protective aspect of Wigman's shimmering dress. And while it has those same sparkling qualities (another essential notion of Wigman's aesthetic link to vibration), it reinforces them through an effect characteristic of a creature as it molts, slowly separating itself from a first body (Wigman's as much as that of an animal). Lastly, Nadia Lauro decided to not recreate Wigman's mask but produce Latifa Laâbissi's by following the Wigman process, namely taking a cast from the dancer's face. However, whereas the Wigman mask emphasized the fiendish traits of the dancer in the same way as Noh masks, leaving no doubt that she is in fact wearing a mask, the mask worn by Latifa Laâbissi is almost imperceptible and helps to smooth over her features. As a counterpoint to the animal nature of the costume, the face with closed eyes seems inert, creating another source of tension in the contrast between a dead face and a living body. Whereas Wigman's creature was compact, caught in a crossplay of contradictory yet also harmonized tensions, Laâbissi's is instead marked by the heterogeneity of its flesh and tonicity of the different parts of its body.

In both cases, the figure created is one of "otherness": other than Reason, other than the discursive knowledge of the Enlightenment; knowledges that are literate, rich, masculine, white. But the dark, asthenic, and powerful figure with the reptile skin is endowed with a forceful sense of enigma originating in other sources. It is no longer a question of dominating the audience's attention by imposing the authority to communicate of a complex figure. This *Écran somnambule* has more to do with the hypnotic register, all the more so because it rests on the art of the exact copy: the art of copying exactly and the art of creating "toxic figures"[21]—with a double meaning and on several levels. Cinema and dance infect one another here with their respective strengths: this figure is effectively "intoxicated" with cinematic images, copied pretty much exactly, but it also inoculates them with a counter-virus because, conflicting with certain aesthetic and political aspects of Wigman's piece. Furthermore, in freeing Wigman from her portrait as Medusa and deconstructing it, its effects are subverted. Far from being hypnotized, our gaze wanders, rambles and dozes, opening onto the potential of the anarchic scenes of our fears and waking dreams.

---

[1] A French version of this text is forthcoming in *Scripter, Documenter. Mémoires et transmissions des œuvres performatives et chorégraphiques contemporaines*, ed. Anne Bénichou (Dijon: Les Presses du réel, 2014).

2 On this perspective, see André Lepecki, "The Body as Archive: Will to Re-enact and the Afterlives of Dances," *Dance Research Journal* 42:2 (Winter 2010) and Mark Franko, "Reproduction, reconstruction et par-delà," *Degrés, Le texte spectaculaire* 63 (Fall 1990). For a broader examination of dance practices and history, see Ramsay Burt, "Memory, Repetition and Critical Intervention, the Politics of Historical Reference in Recent European Dance Performance," *Performance Research* 8:2 (2001); Marina Nordera and Susanne Franco, *Ricordanze, Memoria in movimento e coregrafie della storia* (Turin: UTET, 2010); and Isabelle Launay and Sylviane Pagès, *Mémoires et histoire en danse* (Paris: L'Harmattan, 2010).

3 On this, see Susanne Franco, "*Ausdruckstanz*: traditions, translations, transmissions," in *Discourses, Keywords in Dance Research*, eds. Susanne Franco and Marina Nordera (London: Routledge, 2007); Isabelle Launay, "Poétiques de l'extase, mémoire et oubli en danse dans l'Allemagne des années 20," in *Destruction, Création, Rythme, l'expressionnisme, une esthétique du conflit*, ed. Georges Bloess (Paris: L'Harmattan, 2009).

4 Françoise and Dominique Dupuy were influenced by Hans Weidt, and Jacqueline Robinson and Karin Waehner by Wigman in particular.

5 See Hannah Arendt, *Vies politiques* [Walter Benjamin] (Paris: Gallimard, 1974).

6 For an analysis of this context, see Laure Guilbert, *Danser avec le IIIe Reich* (Paris: Complexe, 2000).

7 For greater detail, see Isabelle Launay, "Portrait de danseuse en sorcière," *Théâtre Public* 154-55 (2000): /http://www.danse.univ-paris8.fr/; and Mary Anne Santos Newhall, *Mary Wigman* (London: Routledge, 2009), 106-11.

8 Mary Wigman, *Die Sprache des Tanzes* (Munich: Ernst Battenberg Verlag, 1963); *Le Langage de la danse*, trans. Jacqueline Robinson (Paris: Chiron, 1986), 20.

9 Mary Wigman, Conference in Zurich, 1949, in *The Mary Wigman Book: Her Writings*, ed. and trans. Walter Sorrell (Middletown: Wesleyan University Press, 1975), 166.

10 Wigman, *Le Langage de la danse*, 13.

11 Wigman, *Le Langage de la danse*, 13.

12 On Wigman's creative process, see Isabelle Launay, *A la recherche d'une danse moderne, Rudolf Laban et Mary Wigman* (Paris: Chiron, 1996), 211-23. http://www.danse.univ-paris8.fr

13 Wigman, *Le Langage de la danse,* 20.

14 Wigman, *Le Langage de la danse*, 41.

15 Unnamed producer, music by H. Hasting and W. Goetze.

16 The musician is Henri Bertrand Lesguiller, also known as "Cookie."

17 Valeska Gert, *Der Querschnitt*, May 1926, trans. Gabler, in Claudia Gabler, *Mouvement et montage de gestes dans les danses de Gert*, DEA dissertation under the direction of Isabelle Launay, Département Danse, Paris 8, 2000.

18 See Laure Guilbert, *Danser avec le IIIe Reich*.

19 See "Le corps de Wigman est un médium, entretien avec Dominique Brun," *Repères, Cahier de danse* 30 (November 2012).

20 See Sylviane Pagès, "Résurgence, transfert et voyages d'un geste expressionniste: une historiographie discontinue et transnationale. Le Bûto entre le Japon, la France et l'Allemagne," in *Mémoires et histoire en danse*, 373-84.

21 This is the title of a research session organized by Laâbissi in 2013-2014 at the Laboratoires d'Aubervilliers.

DEAR N[1]
Jenn Joy

1 December 2013

Dear N,

Last night Julie's rehearsal followed me into dreams, voices echoing in my sleep: *there are other worlds... worlds in which recognition is not the only barometer of brilliance or human worth... there are other worlds... dreams in which failure is feasible even worth striving for... there are other worlds.*[2] A requiem intoned against the buzz of a tattoo needle as two performers in black mesh hoods drag each other by the ankles around a star pattern of florescent lights splayed out on the floor. This retracing of Lovett/Codagnone's *WEIGHTED* (2010) by Julie Tolentino as part of her research for *The Sky Remains the Same*[3] trusts the performer's body as its own complex archive of movement, gesture, emotion, image. Expansive and intimate like sky touching skin, history (ours, theirs, and that of the work) meet in the quiet community of the studio. An encounter with a world as image, difficult to narrate precisely, but deeply felt.

This new iteration of *WEIGHTED* enacts a complicated duet between dance and image. Not only as the dancers lie together in stillness or in the careful slowness of their movements, but in the qualities of temporal and spatial condensation that I sense glittering along the edges of vision. Such a precarious choreography opens toward a meditation on and mediation of image as always conditioned by movement. Speaking of the image, what he refers to as "the distinct" something approaching the sacred, Jean-Luc Nancy writes of a participatory seizure that happens when we encounter image as "force—the energy, pressure, or intensity."[4] Approaching and receding like a cautious lover: "The image floats, in sum, at the whim of the swells, mirroring the sun, poised over the abyss, soaked by the sea, but also shimmering with the very thing that threatens it and bears it up at the same time. Such is intimacy, simultaneously threatening and captivating from out of the distance into which it withdraws."[5] More submarine than chthonic, the image relies on an ambivalent play of seduction.

To be touched, seized, seduced these acts breech the safe perimeters of viewing to demand a different quality of attention. In these moments of condensation our own tremulous archive coincides with what moves, as so many images opening to time. Attempting to make sense of this temporal conflation, Giorgio Agamben returns to an archaic essay "On the Art of Dancing and Choreography" that locates the peculiar art of dance in the uncanny moment of its arrest: "to dance through phantasmata [...] This necessitates that at each *tempo* you appear as if you had seen Medusa's head."[6]

Admittedly, I read this and thought of Hélène Cixous's gorgeous laughing Medusa, which is not at all what Agamben or da Piacenza had in mind. Yet, N, don't you find this a strange moment in the text, an evocation of fierce feminine beauty in proximity to ghosts? Again, dance offers itself to writing and to image as interruption and arrest, this time not only for the witness but also as an imperative for the dancer. Within this interstice memory and imagination collide "as a pause that is not immobile but simultaneously charged with memory and dynamic energy."[7] Agamben's description returns me to Maria Hassabi's dances that embody such exquisite tension of image and its accompanying phantoms. Here image acts as a point of departure but then transforms into something quite else severing our too easy recognition of the iconic to reveal less stable, shaking, tears along the edges of what is seen.

This image from *Solo*:[8]

Maria begins lying on her back under the carpet off to the side of the space; white noise, footsteps, cars passing, horns, audience conversations fill the space. She lies still long after we enter. Slowly propping up one knee, she pauses, then rolls over, then pauses, then climbs out from under the carpet. She pauses. Now splayed out on the carpet, her leg catches on the fabric. She rises to roll up the carpet and it becomes less surface skin and closer to a collaborator in her spatial negotiation. Now perpendicular she arches her back and her head disappears. This distended figure pauses, again. The duet with carpet continues—falling, leaning, wrapping. Later standing against the back wall, she appears almost camouflaged staring out over the crumpled carpet. Yet it seems to call her and as the lights dim she carries it to the edge of the stage before returning to the wall.

And this from *SoloShow*:

Maria sits on the edge of the platform in stillness as I enter the theater. Dressed in creamy beige pants and translucent tank top, her skin seems almost indistinguishable from the fabric. Spotlights illuminate half of the platform so that it almost disappears into the dark. She uncrosses her leg and turns away from me, one leg propped on the platform with one arm resting and the other draped off the edge. She moves her arm from knee and places it behind as she leans back. Her tendons strain as her neck extends. The poses are long, almost too long, almost long enough to lose me. Yet this never happens, I remain entranced. Her chest lifts and lowers with each breath as the sound, a crush of white noise cut with fragments of conversation and an occasional song lyric, fills the space. She continues for almost an hour carefully exchanging positions, executing a choreography of excruciating transition across the platform.

And this from *SHOW*:[9]

Waiting. Still waiting. Time amplified by the intense heat from the pile of stage lights. Waiting. Still waiting. A subtle entrance as Maria and Hristoula Harakas walk into the space among the audience dressed in gray with long black hair. A duet doubled, at least: Maria with Hristoula, Maria with me, Hristoula with someone else, and now you and I writing to remember.

Over coffee last month we spoke of another philosophic seduction. For Alain Badiou dance acts as a "thought-body" as a "metaphor for thought."[10] Yet I want to hold onto the deeply material, physical, desiring bodies of the dancers and audience and not allow our seduction to end only in metaphor. *SHOW* renders such a gorgeous intimacy drawn out through a subtle positioning and repositioning in the space marked by a tremulous intensity of extreme presence and virtuosic groundedness. What is more seductive than to witness these machinations of attraction, energetic or erotic, even as performed?

Maria speaks of dance as a mode of language and of communication that exists only when the audience is present. She is not concerned with duration, but rather with details or intensities of heat, light, proximity. The choreography evolves from the delicate articulation of distance between Maria and Hristoula, and between the individuals composing the audience. When she stretches her arm behind me, she establishes a trajectory through space. Yet, she rarely reveals these patterns, instead secretly shifts from one encounter to the next. And she waits, as we waited in the beginning, for me to acknowledge our relation before she moves toward the next.

SHOW might appear very quiet; at moments Maria and Hristoula almost disappear into the audience or into the dimming lights. And yet, the trembling sweating sensitivity of each moment articulates the subtle violence of togetherness and this is the paradox of *SHOW*— as imperative and as title. There is no illusion of theatricality. I feel the heat of the lights and the relief as they dim. I move with her in this "space of consciousness," of desire, of attention. It is an intimately precarious mode of address that touches choreography as desire.

Desire—the distance between what we imagine and where we stand now. Anne Carson reminds me that "desire is poised on an axis of paradox, absence and presence its poles, love and hate its motive energies." Once captured desire disappears. Poof! "Who ever desires what is not gone? No one."[11] Does desire only inspire a cruel kind of optimism as Lauren Berlant writes?[12] Or is this concatenation of temporality a romantic if nihilistic anachronism as Masha Tupitsyn concedes: "Everyone is out of joint, not just you or time. Everyone breaks your heart. Falls short of what could be. Again and again."[13] Perhaps. And yet, I think these arrested phantasmata might conspire differently, inciting an alternative temporal frame and dancing desire's distantiation.

Always Maria is dancing, with Hristoula, with Robert, or alone; "breathing and trembling are my movements," she reminds me. Her work explicitly stages a precarious mode of address, one that acknowledges my complicity as witness and asks me to participate (and not only during the performance but in thinking about it as well). Writing of this precarious relation, Judith Butler points to the constructed quality of such tremulousness attention. We do not decide to be addressed, but are called, invited, placed in relation, one to the other. Often the conditions of our relation, dare I call them shadows, imperatives, or ghosts are never so visible. Yet I sense in her work an impulse toward their revelation.

And finally *PREMIERE*:[14]

Maria, Hristoula, Andros Zins-Browne, Biba Bell, Robert Steijn wait for us in stillness and silence as we walk across the stage. Gray footprints in dust trace our passage across the stage illuminated by two walls hung with theatrical lights. *PREMIERE* choreographs temperature and electric vision, amplified by the buzz of the lights and the accidental bursting smoke of an overheated bulb. In the beginning none of the dancers move. Turned away from us, they pose—standing, reclining, sitting—distinct levels in faded shades of denim with finely detailed multiple collars. Then Biba's foot slides slowly, extending her lunge. Incremental almost incidental movements follow. Slowly, carefully Maria turns toward us and then away. The precision of her movements is heightened by the sound of shoes sticking to the floor and the darkening stains of sweat appearing on her clothes.

Such minute attention to the suspended duration of dance casts an alienated distance between the dancers. Then as Maria turns, I see her catch Robert's gaze or Hristoula's and in the space of a blink or trembling tear, longing dissolves into tenuous correspondence.

The accumulating intensities of light and heat interrogate the conditions of *PREMIERE*, revealing constant illumination not as an enlightened ideal but as a blinding almost violent saturation. Maria's perceptual apparatus returns me to a quite different piece by DD Dorvillier that even in its inverse proposition addresses a similar precariousness of the visible. So language—as dance and as writing—must approach that which wants to remain illegible. "What haunts are not the dead but the gaps left within us by the secrets of others" intone Abraham and Torok.[15] To choreograph this secret even melancholic aporia, we must experience dance against vision as proximity and heat something more explicitly phenomenological, intensely somatic and disorientating; or at least this is how I experience "the dark part" of DD's *Nottthing is Importanttt* (2007).[16]

Seated in almost complete darkness, vision becomes transfigured and fleeting within the dense humid dark. I hear the dancers breathing as they fall, run, and slide behind and in front of me, sense their movements from the air moving in the confined space, see flashes of limbs as an occasional light flickers, yet mostly I sit in blackness interrupted only briefly by faint luminescence. Both light and sound—an eerie compressed instrumental rising and falling—seem without an identifiable source, emitted from a series of hidden bulbs and speakers hanging above me. My inability to see the dancers' bodies, but only to intermittently smell and hear them makes me more aware of my own limbs rubbing against the other audience members, cramped from sitting on the floor. The partial exposure of the dancer's bodies exhibited in suspended moments of undress in the opening scene of the dance becomes paradoxically a total reveal in this final section; not one of taunting nudity, rather a revelation of perceptual illegibility cast in chiaroscuro shadows. No longer discretely separate, the audience and the performers participate in this obscure disfiguring of choreography through discomforting physical contingencies, shifts in energy and attention, and rising temperature. Together we encounter a strategic dismantling of vision and representation so that we are never certain of what we are actually looking at; we must wait for ghosts.

There is so much we have still to discuss...
Sending love until we meet,

jenn

[1] Fragments of this current text draw from "30 December 2012. Dearest Maria" commissioned for the American Realness catalog in January 2013. Related reflections on Hassabi's work also appear in "Tremulous Histories" included in the anthology *Body/Archive* to be published by Dance Advance, Philadelphia.

[2] The words spoken in *WEIGHTED* are all collected quotes from Arundhati Roy.

[3] Julie Tolentino's residency and open rehearsal series *The Sky Remains the Same* happened at the New Museum, New York, NY, 11–24 November 2013 as part of the exhibition *Performance Archiving Performance* curated by Travis Chamberlain, 6 November 2013 – 12 January 2014.

[4] Jean-Luc Nancy, *The Ground of the Image*, trans. Jeff Fort (New York: Fordham, [2003] 2005), 2.

[5] Nancy, *The Ground of the Image*, 13.

[6] Giorgio Agamben, *Nymphs,* trans. Amanda Minervini (London: Seagull Books, [2007] 2013), 7; italics in original. This quote is da Piacenza cited in Agamben.

[7] Agamben, *Nymphs*, 10.

[8] *Solo* premiered September 29-October 4, 2009 at Performance Space 122 in partnership with PERFORMA 09. The piece was conceived as part of a diptych with *SoloShow*, a performance that premiered November 12–15, 2009 at Performance Space 122 in partnership with Crossing the Line. Both pieces feature lighting by Joe Levasseur, clothing by ThreeAsFour, dramaturgy by Marcos Rosales and Scott Lyall, sound score by James Lo, set design by Scott Lyall and Hassabi.

[9] *SHOW* was performed at American Realness on 10 January 2013, Abrons Theater, New York, NY. *SHOW* is directed by Maria Hassabi; performed by Hristoula Harakas, Maria Hassabi; sound design by Alex Waterman; lighting and set design by Maria Hassabi, Joe Levasseur, Scott Lyall; styling by threeASFOUR; dramaturgy by Scott Lyall, Marcos Rosales.

[10] Alain Badiou, *Handbook of Inaesthetics*, trans. Alberto Toscano (Stanford: Stanford University Press, [1998] 2005), 70.

[11] Anne Carson, *Eros: The Bittersweet* (Champaign: Dalkey Archive Press, [1986] 1998), 11.

[12] Lauren Berlant, *Cruel Optimism* (Durham: Duke University Press, 2011).

[13] Masha Tupitsyn, *Love Dog* (Los Angeles: Penny-Ante Editions, 2013), 74.

[14] *PREMIERE* opened at the Kitchen, New York, NY on 6 November 2013 as part of PERFORMA 2013. *PREMIERE* is directed by Maria Hassabi; performed by Biba Bell, Andros Zins-Browne, Hristoula Harakas, Robert Steijn and Hassabi; sound design by Alex Waterman; dramaturgy by Scott Lyall, Marcos Rosales.

[15] This quote by Nicolas Abraham and Maria Torok serves as the epigraph for Gail Scott, *The Obituary* (New York: Nightboat Books, 2012).

[16] *Nottting is Importanttt* premiered at The Kitchen, New York, NY on 8 February 2007. Choreographed and directed by DD Dorvillier; music and sound installation by Zeena Parkins; lighting design by Thomas Dunn; sound installation design by Doug Henderson; performed by Danielle Goldman, Martin Lanz Landazuri, Alejandra Martorell, Andrea Maurer, Paul Neuninger, Mina Nishimura, Peter Sciscioli, Otto Ramstad, Elizabeth Ward.

III.
SPACES THINGS WORLDS

MANIFESTO FOR A DANCING MUSEUM[1]
Boris Charmatz

Manifesto for
a National Choreographic Center.

I am not losing my temper, I simply wish to propose removing the word "Center," then the word "Choreographic," then the word "National"!

The word "Center" in National Choreographic Center is the result of an impressive public policy which has proved that the center could be plural and multiply elsewhere than in the capital of France. And in order for this impetus to remain, a further emancipation must be expressed today: the question of center and decentralization would then give way to a space where such issues would continue to surface only in traces.

The search for the "center"... For a dancer, this word resonates physically first of all. Not so long ago, the dancer, when he was training, was systematically told to "find his center." But today, it is generally acknowledged that the body has no center, and he doesn't miss it. The body of modern times has no need for a center, because that absent center, the core which would enable one to feel reassured, isn't there, has ceased to be there. For in the void of a body expropriated of its center, there is room for dance.

This is why one can also erase the word "choreographic," in order to approach it from another angle. Dance certainly includes a properly choreographic dimension, but it also happily overflows beyond this framework. Dance is much broader than what is simply choreographic: its territory must enlarge if we wish to see the overly enclosed space open up, in which it still stands in our society. The space of a National Choreographic Center must expand well beyond that which is simply choreographic. It should even be possible to transfer the direction of such an institution to a dancer (and not only to the choreographers)! A dancer is both more, and less, than a choreographer: he is someone who works under the direction of other choreographers, who also supports more than just his own work, and who knows that his body is worked upon by the work of many others, the body of his parents, the body of his teachers, the entire body of society. And if he sometimes is the interpreter of a choreographic script, a dancer can also be just anybody, because almost everybody has tried, at one time or another. I propose erasing "Choreographic" because a National Choreographic Center is much more than a space that enables a choreographer's art to flourish. Beyond the supporting of dance companies, one must also think outside the choreographer-interpreter-company framework in order to create a richer symbolic content... Everybody then, the ones who practice, the believers, the artists, the non-believers, the outcasts of the world of art, wrongly believed to be excluded from it, the others, all the others, who do not yet know where the Choreographic Centers are to be found, could discover there a place to activate their imagination. What makes a dance should go well beyond the restricted circle of those who structure it in everyday life, and open itself up to an anthropological dimension that joyfully explodes the limits induced by the strictly choreographic field.

And then the "National" isn't sufficient anymore either. The mental space of a far-reaching action must be at least locaglobalregioneuropeinternationabretontranscontinensouth. Universal and distinctive.

Also, on the façade, one could simply write:

a dancing museum

I therefore propose to transform a National Choreographic Center into a Dancing Museum.

Seriously.

Seriously and joyfully.

I propose mixing all the tasks normally associated with a National Choreographic Center and shaking them together inside a framework that would be both ancient and modern, humorous and antiquated, dusty and stimulating, a Museum with no equivalent in the world. I would like to put into effect a transfiguration which would give a meaning to the tasks which have been fashioned in the course of this institution's history. Every activity that takes place would be reviewed through a different prism, a prism that would be able to combine in one single movement the patrimonial and the spectacular, research and creation, education and fun, openness to singular artists and the desire to produce a collective work. It seems to me that the designation "Museum, Dancing Museum" could function like a door flung wide open to culture and the art of dancing that we will not change into a sanctuary.

A new National Choreographic Center project cannot today be content with merely developing and enhancing the systems that were established during the course of its development. If one wishes the National Choreographic Center of Rennes and Brittany be the matrix of an infinitely larger diffusion of dance, and to play more than ever its part locally, to become a pole of international stature, it seems to me that its global policies must be carried by an artistic project which would give shape to all of its activities. The city of Rennes and the region of Brittany possess both the conditions and the energy necessary to produce a symbolic vehicle that will transport everybody, the artists, the audiences, the amateurs, the professionals, the teachers, the pupils, the spectators, the students, the politicians, the visitors, the tourists, the research workers, the journalists, the citizens, everyone above and beyond those who are usually on board. And they also have the dynamism so that such a vehicle can fulfill all the tasks of a Choreographic Center while taking a radical, new and unusual direction.

There are few museums of dance. Very few indeed around the world.

"There are in France one hundred and eighteen museums of the wooden clog, but not one museum of slavery." I often think of that remark once heard on the radio... There isn't a real museum of dance either, in this country. Dance and its actors are often defined in opposition to the arts that are said to be perennial, lasting, static, for which the museum would be the favorite place. But today if one wants to stop obscuring the historical space, culture and choreographic heritage, even the most contemporary, then it is time to see, to make visible and bring alive the moving bodies of a culture which largely remains to be invented. And if one wishes the choreographic tradition to pursue the new technological trends and truly embrace the trans-media space of the contemporary world, then it seems to me that under the designation of "Museum" the artists will be able to have fun and create freely.

For we are in an exciting era in which museography is opening itself up to ways of thinking and technologies which are enabling something completely different to emerge rather than simply having exhibitions of remnants, faded costumes, models of stage settings, and rare photographs of productions.

We are at a time in history where a museum can be alive and inhabited as much as a theatre, can include a virtual space, and offer a contact with dance that can be at the same time practical, esthetic and spectacular...

We are at a time in history where a museum in no way excludes precarious movements, nor nomadic, ephemeral, instantaneous ones.

We are at a time in history where a museum can modify BOTH preconceived ideas about museums AND one's ideas about dance. Because we haven't the slightest intention of creating a dead museum, it will be a living museum of dance. The dead will have their place, but among the living. It will be held by the living, brandished at arm's length.

In order to do so, we must first of all forget the image of a traditional museum, because our space is firstly a mental one. The strength of a museum of dance consists to a large extent in the fact that it does not yet exist. That it doesn't yet have a suitable place..., that the spirit of the place emerges before the place..., that everything remains to be done, and that the daily life of this construction site makes room for every audacious idea and every eccentricity.

First of all, a museum can "take place" every Saturday.

(A national choreographic center is also run like one runs a cabaret, a ball or a dance floor. Or also like one holds a siege. One can hold it against wind and tide because one is upheld by some kind of faith.)

The museum would comprise of and include the spectacle, because to our way of thinking, the museum contains the dance studio, the theatre, the bar, the school, the exhibition, the library. This itinerant museum will be the Trojan horse within a radical expansion of the normal NCC's dance "production." The collective building of a future Dancing Museum aims at transforming an institution into a symbolic space of epic proportions: one must imagine a policy of provocative diffusion that will meet the need to radically expand the number of people concerned. The Museum will not be content with merely "programming" events, but will be a means of breathing life into a place, an audience, an adventure, and will be- come a place where one can go, like in the case of a museum, without knowing in advance the day's program. An unlikely place for the workshop meeting, the dance hall, the show; initiation in the strongest sense of the word.

To not cut the matter short, ten commandments:

a micro-museum

but a real one. It fully embraces its museum tasks and maintains a balance between its various functions of conservation, creation, research, exhibition, diffusion, raising of public awareness, mediation, without neglecting any of them. Such interdependence is what justifies the creation of a museal structure.

a museum of artists

researchers, collectors, curators exhibition commissioners participate in the life of the museum, but above all it is essentially artists who invent it by creating works. It is therefore an artistic project initiated by Boris Charmatz, but produced by numerous artists.

an eccentric museum

it intends to be an introduction, an appetizer, a place for enhancing public awareness of dance and choreographic culture in the broadest sense, of the history of the body and its representations. However, it is not centered exclusively on choreographic art: it does not seek to establish a taxonomy of dance, its goal is not to offer a settled definition of the subject. Its ideal isn't to give an exhaustive representation either of the different dances performed around the world. It wishes to stimulate the desire for knowledge.

an incorporated museum

it can only develop provided that it is built by the bodies moving through it, those of the public, the artists, but also of the museum employees (attendants, technicians, admin staff, etc.), who bring the works to life, even becoming actors themselves.

a provocative museum

it approaches dance and its history through a resolutely contemporary vision. It spends time questioning the ingenuous knowledge everyone has about dancing. It induces unlikely links, confrontations between worlds usually poles apart from one another. It questions the accepted conventions that circulate about dance... and therefore elsewhere in society.

a transgressive museum

it fully acknowledges the fact that its activity does not limit itself to the quest for and the representation of the "authentic" object; it encourages artists and visitors to make works their own, it stimulates plagiarism. Artistic creation and the visitor's experience are at the core of its action. Being a place of life, a social space for controversy, a place for talking and interpretation, it is not only a space for accumulation and representation.

a permeable museum

it defends the principle according to which an openness to a broader concept of dance means allowing other movements to influence us, to leave behind a fixed identity. To open up to difference.

a museum of complex temporalities

it deals with both the ephemeral and the perennial, the experimental and the patrimonial. Active, reactive, mobile, it is a viral museum which can be grafted onto other places, can spread dance in places where it was not expected. It is also a museum with a program evolving with the rhythm of seasons, able to relocate to beaches in the summer period or to propose a winter University...

a cooperative museum

it is independent, but works in connection with a network of partners, cooperates with institutions linked to dance (contemporary, classic and traditional, scholarly and popular), to museums, to art centers and galleries, to research centers and universities, and it in no way sets itself against them. It builds deep relationships with individuals, whether they be artists of international fame like Mikhail Baryshnikov, Steve Paxton, William Forsythe, or passionate amateurs.

an immediate museum

it exists as soon as the first gesture has been performed.

[1] Boris Charmatz, "Manifesto for a Dancing Museum," first published in 2009, http://www.borischarmatz.org/en/lire/manifesto-dancing-museum/

EMAILS 2009-2010[1]
Jérôme Bel & Boris Charmatz

Jérôme Bel: I just learned that Merce is dying.

Boris Charmatz: Shit. What are you thinking about?

JB: I start crying when I think I wouldn't be who I am if he hadn't done what he did.

BC: So maybe we should talk about death. […] I can't help thinking that Merce isn't a choreographer of death, that one can't stop thinking, writing, dancing while he dies, if he dies. Because he is not the choreographer of interruption and drama, but, on the contrary, the artist of shoots, eyes open on what moves daily, again, always, uncovered. I believe that having a moment of silence and of stillness isn't appropriate, even though I am not sure either how to go on knowing this, that "Merce is dying." In David Vaughan's book,[2] on page 155, there is a photo that I call "Merce's death." I don't have the book with me, but it is a photograph of *Place* (1966); he is wrapped up in transparent plastic and looks as if he is collapsing. But, of course, the moment after, the page after, he is on the wall, upright and thinking, before bodies get back to moving on the following pages, full of colors and dazzling spaces, without lingering on that strange moment. What are you thinking about? Are your pieces—and the relation to other works that your pieces draw, from Susanne Linke to the dances that the dancer-witnesses evoke in your recent solos— also a way to try to ward off fate? Do you consciously or unconsciously want to bring with you the culture that made you who you are?

JB: I sometimes think that art is for preparing yourself for the last five minutes before you die. It's as if, as a spectator, art enabled us to do a rehearsal of this final moment, and learn to know what to do and think in that ultimate moment. […] Merce, you're quite right, is the choreographer of the present, that's all that's involved: no past, no future. In one of the solos you mention, *Cédric Andrieux* (2009),[3] Cédric Andrieux, who danced for eight years in Merce's company, talks at a certain moment about how after shows Merce never gave the slightest note or correction. I couldn't believe my ears! Most choreographers and directors try to improve the show by continuing to "direct" the dancers and actors after the performances. Okay, you dance in your pieces, and I wonder incidentally how you manage. This, all the same, is the lucky thing with the "perfoming arts," that, from one night to the next, you can change things in the show… Well, no! For Merce, what had happened had taken place and there was no further talk about it. I found that wonderful: no judgment! Which comes from "Cage's thinking," hailing from zen. It's zen applied to dance. Whatever the case, I learnt that, barely a month ago, Merce had made certain provisions about the future of his oeuvre after his death. Namely that the company would make a world tour lasting two years and that the dancers would carry on being paid during the third year for re-training purposes if that's what they wanted. This is quite simply admirable. He was consistent right to the end.

In fact I've always known that what I could do in my work was only possible because of the work of certain colleagues and predecessors. There's no Jérôme Bel essence, there's just a construction of this subject, and this construction is first of all made, for me, in theatres.

So the solos of the "witness-dancers," who evoke their professional experience, are, for me, attempts to try and understand how certain dance praxes can constitute the subject of the spectator. It is evident that what dancers recount is what I would like to recount, but they have a legitimacy that I can't lay claim to: I haven't danced at the Paris Opéra like Véronique Doisneau, nor have I practiced royal Thai dance like Pichet Klunchun, nor danced with Merce Cunningham like Cédric Andrieux, nor with Pina Bausch like Lutz Förster. They act as spokespeople to the spectator that I was at those dances. Talking like this, I sound like a choreographer of the past... Brrrrr. Or else that my work in these past years has consisted solely in trying to shed light on the incomprehensible things that have happened to me, sitting in the darkness with a few hundred other spectators looking at the lit stage.

Does the "Dancing Museum"[4] project that you're setting up in Rennes stem from a similar desire? What's it about exactly?

BC: By the word "museum," a lot of people actually understand "mausoleum," or even "old people's home"... as if, in the final analysis, it wasn't necessarily the museum space that made people afraid, but death, quite simply death, and, in the case we're dealing with, the death of living art, of contemporary dance, and of dancers themselves. What do you hear, first of all, when you utter the words "dancing museum"?

JB: I should tell you that I felt slightly the same thing the first time I heard about the "Dancing Museum." What bothers me is probably the notion of place, and that heaviness that is always associated with the museum, not to mention the "curators"... But once over that impression, there is a novel idea there and I'd like you to explain the challenges to me.

BC: The Dancing Museum is above all a way of going forward. Of prospecting, inventing, and drawing a future. Above all, it involves an openness, the openness of a mental space, even if the architectural issue, in the traditional sense, is also raised. But when you're a dancer, it's obvious that the body is the main museum space. Learnt dances exist in the body, as well as taught gestures and seen performances. The body is also made up of gestures that we would greatly like to forget, but don't manage to. The body is made up of an infinity of gestures performed and received that construct it on a daily basis and—though its landscape may well be ruined or incomplete—it is THE medium of its culture and the art that goes with it. In this sense, the body thought of as a museum is not only a body that leans in an almost archaeological way on what supports it, the experiences that are its foundation, the readings that have marked it, and the identities that fix it: it is also the untidy mass that makes it possible to react and invent the actions and postures of today and tomorrow. In the absence of any pre-existing and pre-determined collection, and within this idea of a body constructed to be porous to what is coming, there is the essence of a project that is not content with selecting, from the past, the right gestures to be saved and promoted.

Although there are one or two museums of dance in the world—in particular in Cuba and Stockholm—I think that this project is based on the fantasy that such a museum does not yet exist, and even that it is impossible to realize at the risk of killing off any dance that crosses its threshold. I have realized that the word "museum," for many people, was synonymous with old people's homes, and I think that an experimental "museum of dance" must tackle this notion of old people's homes in order to promote a time, another time than that of the school and the theatre.

JB: This is a very, very... expanded conception of the museum. The equation (Dancing Museum = body) seems brilliant to me. But what will this new analogy produce?

BC: You know, one of the first projects we are launching, this autumn, is an "Expo zéro."[5] This is an exhibition project with no works: no photos, no sculptures, no installations, no videos. Zero things, no stable object. But artists, areas occupied by gestures, projects, bodies, stories, dances that everyone can imagine as they like. Ten personalities (artists, architects, archivists, researchers) will be hosted in residence in the new dance space in Rennes, called Le Garage. After this residency, they will present to visitors their subjective and utopian visions of what a "Dancing Museum" might be. I would really like this to be both an actual exhibition to be imagined in these empty places, and a think tank about what this museum project is. Through analysis, description, performances, movements, and the ideas that each "artist-guide" will develop with visitors, we shall attempt an important stage of what this Dancing Museum might produce. When the Bocal (2002-2004) nomadic and temporary school project started, I knew what was motivating me, but I did not know what this would "produce." Today, I reckon that this project has pushed me to write,[6] and that the "bocalists" have quite brilliant careers as artists and teachers. The educational terrain has considerably evolved, through numerous projects, including this one. With this Dancing Museum project, we are launching a three-year site, and I hope that a lot of people will be able to take part in the reflection and the action, including yourself!

————

JB: Merce died.

BC: Yes. Strangely, even though he was very old, and that nothing about him and his work calls for suffering and mourning, it is devastating. […] Somebody said: philosophy is there. Philosophy. Not relics. Not treasures, even alive. Not heritage. Or then yes: heritage. Go for the heritage. *But we are the heritage.*

Might you want to continue our exchange? Write what comes to you... Or: I would like to know how you work with Cédric and what difference there is—if any—in the work with him, in relation to the other dancers with whom you collaborated for those solos?

JB: Yes, I'm quite happy to pursue our conversation, with pleasure. Reading you is very interesting for me. I react:

1) "Expo zéro, zero things, no stable object."

I'd like to know what the system for the exhibition is. Is it a museum exhibition, from 10 am to 6 pm? Or rather, as in theatres, from 8 pm to 10 pm? I'm very curious, because for several years now I've failed to find a solution to the London Tate Modern's demand for an exhibition of dance. I also wanted to put on an "exhibition of dance" when I was invited to the Lyon Contemporary Art Biennale in 2007. I wanted to "expose dances" by you, Raimund Hoghe, La Ribot, Xavier Le Roy, Eva Meyer-Keller, Jonathan Burrows and Jan Ritsema,

William Forsythe, Claudia Triozzi, and Myriam Gourfink. But I never managed to find an adequate connection between the museum framework and dance: the scope of the work day during the three months that the exhibition would have lasted (dancers' exhaustion + size of budget), visitors' time-frame and dance time-frames, etc. Perhaps Expo zéro could meet that demand? I can't wait to visit it. We must try and solve this problem: dance is starting to be recognized as art. In the end it's as if you had to enter the museum to be legitimized! As a result, pressure to exhibit is growing: I was recently contacted by New York's MoMA, because they've just opened a "Media and Performance Art"[7] department. The model of that museum—which, it seems to me, though I'm not sure, was the first to exhibit not only the fine arts, but also architecture, film, and design—is now interested in dance. The first exhibition put on by this department, this spring, was incidentally devoted to Simone Forti and Yvonne Rainer. In tandem, I have recently noted a growing interest from certain visual artists in spectacle/performance/events. And there's also my former colleague, and still my friend, Tino Sehgal, who is producing remarkable work with his "scenographic situations" where neither objects, nor photographs, nor films are produced. The "visual" work consists in a performative event, a real physical and verbal action, carried out by living people (museum security guards, or gallery owners, or anonymous people taken on for the occasion) in the exhibition spaces.

Tell me how the presentation of the exhibition happens? This is perhaps the key to the problem. Earlier you were saying: "To promote a time, another time than that of the school or the theatre." I imagine that this exhibition is the emblem of this. Do you think it's important to find other ways of showing and/or practicing dance? Do you think the theatre isn't sufficient?

2) *Cédric Andrieux*, Merce Cunningham, "we are the heritage."

Cédric is part of Merce's legacy—he is the closest to it. And I'll say closer than Merce himself, because Cédric is the incarnation of certain Merce dances and even at times of Merce's body, when he dances his roles in the old pieces. By being extreme, one might say that I, too, am Merce's patrimony because I was at a dozen performances of his dances, during which I had different experiences that I can talk about today. So I am also the recipient of the work, and I can therefore partly transmit it by the simple fact of describing my own experience, as any spectator of a Merce show can do. By that I mean that I'm capable of orally (and gesturally!) describing my subjective experience as a spectator. I can recount what I've seen, experienced, and thought in order to transmit it to interlocutors. I think this type of oral transmission is extremely important. There are shows that I "know" without ever having seen them. I remember that at the time I was a student at the National Contemporary Dance Center in Angers (CNDC) I described to my fellow students certain scenes from Pina Bausch's shows *Walzer* (1982) and *Nelken* (1982), which I had just discovered at Avignon. Like the hilarious scene where Mechthild Grossmann endlessly repeats in her husky voice: "Another little glass of wine and a cigarette before going home... another little glass of wine and a cigarette before going home...oooooooooo noooooooooo? Another little glass of wine and a cigarette before going home..." Or the scene where Dominique Mercy, in *Nelken*, screams at the audience: "So, what do you want to see? What do you want to see? Eh? Grand jetés? Okay, grand jetés. Here they are! And now? What do you want to see? Tours en l'air?" and so on.

I find this transmission that eludes all control incredibly rich. When I started to put on my own shows, I constantly thought about that: whatever spectators were seeing on stage, they had to be able to tell their friends. So it was important that what I was showing could be easily described so that it could spread outside the theatre.

It's possible that this is one of the reasons why I haven't used dance in my shows. It is actually much harder to describe a dance with words than a simple action like: the four performers come on stage naked,[8] the first one writes on the black wall at the back of the theatre in white chalk, "STRAVINSKY IGOR," then starts humming the music of *The Rite of Spring*; the second, carrying a light bulb at the end of a wire to light up the stage, writes in her turn, "THOMAS EDISON," and so on. And this: he stretches the skin of his testicles, pulls it up towards his pubis in order to hide his penis, and it looks like a pair of underpants on him.

With *Cédric Andrieux*, the issue involves transmitting this "patrimony" or, let's rather put it this way, the intensities of works that have been decisive for me. Directing Cédric so that these questions, this knowledge, and this experience are shared. I have trouble comparing the work undertaken with Cédric and that with Véronique Doisneau at the Paris Opéra, or with Pichet Klunchun in Bangkok. Cédric is, first and foremost, a "workhorse." The fact is I don't like virtuosity very much, because of its alienating and competitive character. However, there is a virtuosity there combined with a power to work that amazes me. Incidentally, it was the same thing with Véronique. These dancers are also highly perfected machines with an impressive know-how. So my work with dancers like Véronique and Cédric consists in skirting around their mechanisms and their expertise in order to introduce doubt, questioning, and subjectivity.

My position is a bit ambiguous. I can enjoy myself as a spectator of virtuosity, although it seems to me politically unacceptable, but I cannot re-enact that fatal scenario, because that virtuosity usually comes from the part of a dancer's work that I regard as alienating— infinite repetition of the same movement, and competition—not mentioning the ideology that underpins that practice. I use these historical materials (classical dance, modern dance) and I use them for my project: alienation verses emancipation. I try to emancipate these dancers from what tends to reduce them to functions, and turn them into subjects, and I try to remove them from that status of dancing objects that prevails in the type of "artistic" education they have received as well as in their practices. When Cédric started working with Merce, he didn't understand what was at stake in that work. He had come out of a traditional alienating kind of teaching (the National Conservatory) and was probably not trained to understand a project such as Merce's. He could of course do the dances, but he couldn't understand their artistic challenges. So he misinterpreted things, and that made him unhappy as long as he stayed in the company. Cédric needed time to understand that Merce's dance is an emancipating project for him, whereas he himself often experienced it as subjecting.

The thing that interests me most today—for the last four years, in fact—is transmitting knowledge—what you perhaps call "patrimony"—that seems to me to be relevant, and it's possible that the Museum (the MoMA or the MDLD—Dancing Museum) is another possible mediation for dance.

BC: For Expo zero, we'll be opening from 11am to 8pm, but the show only lasts for a weekend, preceded by a week of work in residence. This plan will be the same at Rennes, Saint-Nazaire, and Singapore. There's nothing stopping the exhibition from lasting for longer periods, but we're testing it like this to start with. Contemporary art museums are possible work places, needless to say, but, at the same time, we have to invent our own symbolic spaces and not be content with invitations from already existing places. I want to see contemporary art through the prism of a museum of dance, to understand how dance can unfold differently: the range of contemporary issues, political, social, and aesthetic, can also be outlined by and for dance, understood in the broadest sense. Seeing what the museum can do to dance, including negatively, the horror of the museum (old people's home, hospital, cemetery, aesthetic closure…), and seeing what dance can do to the museum, by imagining a new type of museology, collection, and mental space for dance.

[1] These fragments are excerpted from the book of the same title published at Les presses du réel in 2013.

[2] David Vaughan, *Merce Cunningham: 50 Years of Dance* (New York: Aperture, 1997).

[3] Jérôme Bel has created a series of solos where the title of the work is the name of the dancer who performs it and for/with whom the solo was created. The work, its content, and its performer merge in this latter's civil identity.

[4] The Dancing Museum is a project that Boris Charmatz put forward for his nomination as director of the Centre chorégraphique national de Rennes et de Bretagne. This project is associated with a manifesto, *Manifeste pour un Musée de la danse*. The opening of the Dancing Museum took place in April 2009, in particular on 27 April 2009, from 7 pm to 7 am, at Le Garage in Rennes. Titled "Strangling Time," it consisted of an all-night program of dance pieces, performances, a concert, dance classes, traditional Breton dance, where each of these practices and works were slowed down.

[5] Expo zéro is a Dancing Museum project that took place in September 2009 at Le Garage in Rennes. A virtual visit and the exhibition catalogue can be seen at: expozero.museedeladanse.org.

[6] Following the Bocal project (2002-2004), Boris Charmatz published *Je suis une école. Expérimentation, art, pédagogie* (Paris: Prairies ordinaries, 2009).

[7] In 2009, the Museum of Modern Art in New York opened a "Media and Performance Art" department run by Sabine Breitweiser. Within it, the "performance" program has included, in spring 2009, Performance 1 – Tehching Hsieh (May to June 2009), Performance 2 – Simone Forti (March 2009), and Performance 3 – Trio A by Yvonne Rainer (March 2009). In January 2011, Performance 11 was devoted to the work of Trisha Brown under the title: "On Line/Trisha Brown Dance Company." In 2012, Bel was part of the Some Sweet Day series curated by Ralph Lemon; in the fall of 2013, Charmatz and the Musée de la danse presented a series of events there titled Three Collective Gestures.

[8] What follows describe the actions in the performance *Jérôme Bel* (1995) by Jérôme Bel.

MUSEUM ARTIFACT ACT[1]
Mark Franko

What do we await from dance with/in the museum? Is there, has there ever been—since dance in the museum is not a new phenomenon—such a thing as a museum-dance? How do dance and the museum "communicate"? I take this term from Derrida's *Signature Event Context* (1972) where he interrogated the meaning of communication in the context of visual and performative instances of expression. "[W]hat is transmitted, communicated," he wrote, "does not involve phenomena of meaning or signification." "Communication," he continued, "designates nonsemantic movements [...]." "[O]ne can, for instance, *communicate a movement* or [...] a tremor [*ébranlement*], a shock, a displacement of force can be communicated—that is, propagated, transmitted."[2] In this theoretical light, what tremor or shock does dance communicate to the museum? And, how does the museum absorb this displacement of force? And, why does the museum want to? If Derrida criticized speech act theory (Austin) in light of eighteenth-century ideas of the origin of language (Condillac) do we not find ourselves here today in a comparable situation—perhaps that of art-act theory—in which we seek to understand some continuity or points of contact between the old pedagogical and didactic as well as documentary project of the museum in the context of the lively phenomenal—perhaps even shocking or traumatic—presence of contemporary dance?[3]

This is one starting point. Another can be drawn from a few examples. The phenomenon whereby a particular site is articulated by the movement performed within it or wherein movement takes on a specific dimension and meaning by virtue of the site in which it is performed is, I think, quite well known although worthy of further exploration. Bringing a museum to life through performance assumes a hidden life in the collection and makes of the collection an environment, which criticism of the museum has long reproached museums for lacking. Quite literally, movement brings life to the collection, restores life to the objects that have been severed from their original physical and cultural locations. It happened with Donya Feuer's *Dances for a Museum* (1963) staged in the Historiska Museet in Stockholm. In this work, Feuer used the rune stones of the museum to reflect on pre-bourgeois aspects of contemporary Swedish society. In a work I did at the Getty Antiquity Museum in Santa Monica, *Operratics* (1995), I used the dancer's proximity to statuary to reflect dance in relation to expressive demands placed on the body by the projection of theatricality. Something is communicated between the artifact and the act in both cases that exceeds theatrical heightening and becomes an exchange of qualities. This can also be the case in much site specific work, but when the museum is the site a historical component communicates with liveness.

Consider now Michael Clark's *Who's Zoo?* produced in 2012 at the Whitney Biennial.[4] A very large fourth floor gallery space of the Whitney Museum in New York City was redesigned to look and feel like a performance studio. The audience sat on the floor along one wall during the forty-minute show. As they were not scattered throughout the space, but assembled in a line at one end of it, they maintained the mutual anonymity characteristic of a theater audience. The space marked out for dancing was quite wide although not comparably deep, and two entranceways framed the back wall symmetrically to act as wings for the performers. A laser-like lavender line cut horizontally across the back wall joining the two entranceways. The walls were white, the dance floor was black; a lighting grid in the ceiling rendered the technical lighting apparatus unobtrusive as in most theaters while providing the capability of professional lighting effects. Apart from the challenge of crowd management briefly imposed on the museum staff I was unaware of being in a museum. I do not have the time to enter into further details about the piece itself except to note that the title and the choreography suggested that the dancers were animals in a zoo, implying a critique of museum culture that would make the dancer the colonized group on display. This seemed underlined by the use of untrained performers alongside professional dancers and the pairing of dancers in costumes that identify them as two or three of a kind. Clark evokes the ethnographic past of the museum. As Mieke Bal points out the critique of the museum is motivated chiefly from the ethnographic perspective and *Who's Zoo?* seems to present dance knowingly as a museum artifact by pairing dancers as creatures in a sort of Noah's ark.[5] But, it does so in a space that is trying very hard *not* to be museal. Clark seems to be forcing the museum to be that which it no longer wants to be.

If the museum is, historically at least, as Tony Bennett reminds us, a rational and scientific project that documents and explains material and visual culture, the presence of danced performance in its galleries points to the intrusion of the oral into the sphere of visual and material culture.[6] This could also be viewed from the perspective of time. The museum, in Foucault's terms, is "a sort of perpetual and indefinite accumulation of time in an immobile place"[7] whereas dance "spends" time, "takes" time, in a way that simulates the presence of being. As William Forsythe has said:

> I am inclined to believe that because we are bodies and possess perceptive mechanisms we also have time. I suspect our ability to construct time is predicated on the manner in which the body integrates its perceptions and upon the action necessary to generate these perceptions.[8]

The experience of time for Forsythe would be impossible without the lived body (as he points out, the body's actions generate perceptions) and hence it becomes clear why dance is often considered as purely durational whereas the museum is considered static despite

253

its imposition of a choreographic path on the visitor. How, then, does what I am calling, following Derrida, the presence of being, 'communicate' (in the sense of create an opening onto) with a guided itinerary through the display of a time past, organized to a didactic end with space as a metaphor for historical time? And, how does the presence of being communicate with the performativity of the image? If, as with *Who's Zoo?* the spatial and display qualities of museality are institutionally and curatorially resisted then any such communication between these two ideologies of image and act is aesthetically, critically, and historically evacuated from the encounter.

At the other end of the spectrum indicated by Clark's work at the Whitney we could locate Boris Charmatz's project: Musée de la danse. In taking over the Centre chorégraphique national de Rennes et de Bretagne, Charmatz proposed to eliminate the terms "Center," "choreographic" and "national," replacing them with the title: Musée de la danse.[9] In his *Manifesto for a Museum of the Dance* Charmatz makes the following important claims:

> We are at a time in history where a museum can be alive and inhabited as much as a theatre, can include a virtual space, and offer a contact with dance that can be at the same time practical, aesthetic and spectacular...
>
> We are at a time in history where a museum in no way excludes precarious movements, nor nomadic, ephemeral, instantaneous ones.
>
> We are at a time in history where a museum can modify BOTH preconceived ideas about museums AND one's ideas about dance.[10]

Implicit in Charmatz's discourse is that dance contains within itself the universal conditions of its own possibility to transform poverty into wealth. The most nomadic, ephemeral and instantaneous gesture has the power to create its own space—to become a museum in its own right—indeed, to institute its own space no longer as one of guided tours, behavior regulation and initiation into citizenship, but of auto-didacticism: a space in which one can experiment, research, learn, and freely experience with one's own body. Dance in the presupposed space of the museum becomes by virtue of this collocation an emancipatory procedure. This is practically the reverse of Paul Valéry's comment that when faced with the vast accumulation of objects, "he [Man] is impoverished by the very excess of his wealth."[11] Adorno saw Valéry's comment as a critical of the museum's "false wealth" embodied in its accumulation of artifacts.[12] The wealth of museum collections is productive of extreme poverty whereas the poverty of dance is productive of extreme wealth.

Clark and Charmatz, therefore, are extreme examples; the first stops short at the simple fact of a performance in a museum space; the second enters into a utopian vision of dance as a museum inspired in part by Jacques Rancière's *Le maître ignorant*. "La force d'un musée de la danse," specifies Charmatz, "réside en grande partie dans le fait qu'il n'en existe pas encore." Charmatz belongs to a critical tradition that sees the museum as a utopian project:

> A refuge for things and people—literally, a building dedicated to the muses and the arts they inspire, a space in which to muse, to be inspired—the museum puts people and things into a relationship quite unlike anything encountered in the world outside.[13]

The Museum of Dance in Rennes is, as I understand it, *not* a museum properly speaking —Charmatz points out himself that such a thing does not yet exist—but a reconceptualization of the choreographic center, a place traditionally dedicated to dancer training and choreographic experimentation. As Charmatz develops the idea in his book *"Je suis une école." Expérimentation, art, pédagogie*[14] the difference between this and a conventional Centre chorégraphique in France is that the dancer him or herself takes over their own education. Behind the Musée de la danse project is an earlier one—*Bocal*—which is the subject of *Je suis une école.* In what looks like a pilot project for *Musée de la danse* the dancer becomes an auto-didact: the line between experimentation, historiography, and creation is being breached:

> Our theories smell, our practices can hurt, our ideas for classes are classes themselves, our classes are performances, our performances are our daily, slippery exercises.[15]

This project has obvious connections to the issue of education generally, and to dance pedagogy and training in France in particular. A sense of the contemporary dancer as autodidact emerges from recent debates in France over dance technique and from the interventions of Charmatz in that debate. This project, inasmuch as it does underlie Charmatz's conception of the museum in relation to dance, also derives in part from the 1999 statement of the so-called signatories of August 20th. The open letter the signatories signed expressed discontent with the situation of contemporary choreography and state sponsorship of dance. The object of this statement was the recently created Centre national de la danse and the signatories witnessed an "increasing divide between the logic of institutional structures and artistic dynamics."[16] One finds in this letter a critique of the pedagogy of dance in France aimed at the young professional contemporary dancer:

> It is a training that has not bothered to give to dancers the tools of critical analysis, which would allow them to choose their movement practice, nor a capacious cultural and aesthetic history that would enable them to situate their work in an expanded field.[17]

In "*Je suis une école*" Charmatz emphasizes this point above all. Here one can reconstruct the trajectory whereby the pedagogical issue of dancer training encounters the idea of what a dance museum might be. The transformative potential of the museum for dance in Charmatz's view resides paradoxically in its very educational project, although that project must itself be radically reinvented by dance itself. One way Charmatz has proposed this choreographically is, as Noémie Solomon has analyzed it, to "strangle time." In the first project of the Musée de la danse, *Préfiguration* (2009), Charmatz staged a whole night of performance works that were slowed down. As Solomon notes:

> By performing a radical slowing down of movement, the event might be seen as an attempt to press together the apparently contradictory terms of dance and the museum until their respective codes, techniques, and concerns become attached in a knot...[18]

As Forsythe also pointed out, movement is the instrument of time as experience: its actions generate the perceptions necessary to the experience of time itself.

This transfer of the contents of the museum or—let us say, the archive—into dance and the body is also characteristic of the tendency in contemporary dance toward historical reenactment, which has had some relationship to curatorial practice, but which also exists autonomously. There has been talk of late of the body as an archive. How is the body a museum? What would a museum of choreography look like? The two questions seem related as reenactments collect and exhibit dance's past by and through "corporeal research."[19] This is the term used by Fabian Barba in discussing his presentation of Mary Wigman's 1930–31 US tour.

I would like to conclude with a few words about this phenomenon.

It seems to me that despite quite a bit of disparate activity, a common trait of dance reenactments is the refusal to impersonate a previous artist. This is significant in dance where the artist's work to be reenacted is in most cases inseparable from the body of that artist, especially in the tradition of modernism. What comes out of this particular refusal to impersonate the predecessor in conjunction with various methodologies for theatrical distancing and a rejection of all convictions about repeatability is, paradoxically, a sensibility for the objective nature of choreography as such. That is to say, the implication of much contemporary reenactment in the dance field is that past choreography exists in potential space, and can be recovered through specific spatial or even display practices. As Forsythe has written about "choreographic objects": "Could it be conceivable that the ideas now seen as bound to a sentient expression are indeed able to exist in another durable, intelligible state?"[20] If the objectality of choreography still remains to some degree elusive, it is nonetheless true that there is a movement afoot to uncover its materiality rather than its ephemerality. And, in respect to this project, which is barely beginning, the concept of the museum, if not its physical and cultural reality, is crucial.

[1] This essay was first published in Irene Brandenburg, Nicole Haitzinger, Claudia Jeschke, eds., *Tanz & Archiv: ForschungsReisen*, Heft 5: *Mobile Notate* (Munich: epodium, 2013): 94-103.
[2] Jacques Derrida, "Signature Event Context," in *Margins of Philosophy* (Chicago: University of Chicago Press [1972] 1982), 307.
[3] Of course, something has also changed in Derrida's questioning of communication as a "homogeneous field". "When we say that writing *extends* the field and powers of a locutionary or gestural communication, are we not presupposing a kind of *homogeneous* space of communication? The range of the voice or of gesture certainly appears to encounter a factual limit here, an empirical boundary in the form of space and time; and writing, within the same time, within the same space, manages to loosen the limits, to open the *same field* to a much greater range" (Derrida, "Writing and Telecommunication," in *Margins of Philosophy*, 311). Digital culture, it seems, has given gesture, vocality, and other visual signs the same disseminatory scope as writing. The question of communication remains an open one with less factual and empirical limits than previously thought.
[4] *Who's Zoo?* was produced at the Whitney Biennial, March 14-April 8, 2012, with music by

Jason Buckle and Jarvis Cocker, lighting design by Charles Atlas, and costumes by Stevie Stewart and Michael Clark.

[5] "The very distinction between ethnographic and art museums is itself an ideological fallacy that sustains what it should critically examine." Mieke Bal, "The Discourse of the Museum," *Thinking About Exhibitions*, eds. Reesa Greenberg, Bruce W. Ferguson and Sandy Narine (London: Routledge 1996), 205. See also Bal's discussion of the relation between the artifact and the art work, 206.

[6] See Tony Bennett, *The Birth of the Museum: History, Theory, Politics* (London: Routledge, 1995).

[7] Michel Foucault, "Of Other Spaces" (1986), cited in Bennett, *The Birth of the Museum*, 1.

[8] William Forsythe and Markus Weisbeck, eds., *Suspense* (Zürich: J. R. P. Ringier, 2008), 50.

[9] Boris Charmatz, *Manifesto for a Dancing Museum*, http://www.borischarmatz.org/en/lire/manifesto-dancing-museum/, 2.

[10] Charmatz, *Manifesto*, 2-3.

[11] Paul Valéry, "Le problème des musées," in *Pièces sur l'art* (Paris: Gallimard 1934), 97; cited in Daniel Sherman, "Quatremère/Benjamin/Marx: Arts Museums, Aura, and Commodity Fetishism," in *Museum Culture. Histories, Discourses, Spectacles*, eds. Daniel Sherman and Irit Rogoff (Minneapolis: University of Minnesota Press, 1994), 124.

[12] Theodor W. Adorno, "Valéry Proust Museum," in *Prisms* (Cambridge: The MIT Press, 1988), 177.

[13] Barbara Kirshenblatt-Gimblett, "The Museum – A Refuge for Utopian Thought," http://www.nyu.edu/classes/bkg/web/museutopia.pdf (23.05.2013), 1.

[14] Charmatz, "Je suis une école." *Expérimentation, art, pédagogie* (Paris: Les Prairies Ordinaires 2009).

[15] Charmatz, "Je suis une école," 7. "Nos théories sentent, nos pratiques peuvent blesser, nos idées de cours sont des cours, nos cours sont nos performances, nos performances sont nos exercices quotidiens et glissants."

[16] "Les Signataires du 20 août: Lettre ouverte à Dominique Wallon et aux danseurs contemporains," in *Mouvement* 3–4 (1999–2000): 1. This document can be found on the website of the Dance Department of Paris 8: http://www.danse.univ-paris8.fr/chercheur_bibliographie.php?cc_id=4&ch_id=6. "[L]'écart qui se creuse entre la logique des structures institutionnelles et les dynamiques artistiques."

[17] "Les Signataires du 20 août: Lettre ouverte à Dominique Wallon," 4. "C'est une formation qui ne s'est pas souciée de donner aux danseurs les outils d'analyse critique leur permettant de comprendre et de choisir leur pratique du mouvement, ni une culture historique et esthétique large leur permettant de situer leurs travaux dans un champ élargi."

[18] Noémie Solomon, *Unworking the Dance Subject: Contemporary French Choreographic Experiments on the European Stage*, Ph.D. Dissertation, Performance Studies, New York University 2012, 220.

[19] Fabian Barba, "Research into Corporeality," *Dance Research Journal* 43:1 (2011): 82–89.

[20] William Forsythe, "Choreographic Objects," in *Suspense*, 7.

PERFORMATIVE PRACTICES / CRITICAL BODIES # 2:
WHAT MAKES DANCE[1]
Céline Roux

In the field of French choreography, the decade of 1993–2003 was a space-time favorable to the emergence of performative practices. These practices operated as a critical counter-force to a system that no longer fulfilled its creators' desires. The consequences of this period are still present within the creative and choreographic fields today, in the processes of creation, of presentation, of reception—in what Hans-Robert Jauss calls "the expectation horizon"[2]—and, most importantly, in the critical practices of the dancing body and all things choreographic. Consequently, Xavier Le Roy played on the expectation horizon when he proposed a recreation of the *Rite of Spring* (2007). In this, Le Roy did not present a historical revival of Nijinsky's original creation—as several dozens of choreographers have done before him—but invoked Stravinsky's musical score and presented a solo based on the music itself and the figure of the conductor. In this manner, he succeeded in creating a twofold reflexive shift. On the one hand, a shift in the space of the theater and space of the performance: the audience in their seats became the musicians, while on the stage, Le Roy took the place of the conductor himself. On the other hand, he established a change in the content of what makes dance and what makes choreography by assigning these modalities to the presence and movements of the conductor.

As of 2004, the choreographic artists at the origin of this conception of the dancing body and the unframing of the choreographic have achieved high visibility in the institutional field. Certain periods and connections fostered this development in the French world: 1993–97 was a period of confidentiality for the new choreographic practice, when new modes of production and distribution emerged; 1997–2000 was a period of questioning and recognition, particularly as a result of the actions led by Les Signataires du 20 Août. It was a time for different commitments and a political positioning that opened up new fields of work and drew attention to evolving choreographic aesthetics and the need for dance policy. 2000–2003 was a good period when temporary coalitions of artists, as well as connections between artists and researchers, were created, leading to a form of assertion that brought about the start of accessions into the institutional system and gave rise to the emergence of new places for the choreographic.

This nascent movement began to enlarge in 2004. Early instances of expansion concerned the academy and those institutions that maintain the traditional values of French choreography. In 2004, the Ballet of the Opéra de Lyon commissioned Christian Rizzo to create a performance for seven dancers, *Ni fleurs, ni Ford mustang* (2004), and in the same year, Jérôme Bel was invited by the Paris Opéra to give an "interpretation" of the *sujet* Véronique Doisneau.[3] He presented an autobiographical work called *Véronique Doisneau* (2004) that greatly diverged from the customary productions staged by the institution. Defined by Jerôme Bel as "cooperative," the piece grew out of a partnership between Bel and Doisneau, that is to say a cooperation between the choreographer and the Paris Opéra, and between a new form of creation and an emblematic figure of the French choreographic tradition. The three weeks during which *Morceau* (2000)—a project initiated by Loïc Touzé at the Théâtre de la Bastille and co-produced with the Centre National de la Danse—ran at the beginning of 2005 represented the start of an evolution in the dance community that involved the integration and assimilation of these new practices. Since then, the trend has grown stronger and performative projects are now part of almost every institutional program and festival. This mutation of the choreographic field has also brought about changes to learning processes and heralding renewal in the training of contemporary dancers within the classroom and the manner in which transmission occurs. In 2004, Emmanuelle Huynh was appointed director of the Centre National de Danse Contemporaine in Angers and appointed a teaching committee that in its initial year included the choreographers and dancers Loïc Touzé, Anne-Karine Lescop, and Sophie Lessard, the visual artist Daniel Perrier, and the university lecturer Isabelle Launay. The purpose of this pedagogical committee, renewed each year, was to reflect on the changes taking place in the field of dance. At the same time, the training course *Essais*, a project designed to encourage research in contemporary dance by young artists, whether French or foreign, and to foster trans-disciplinary practices, was implemented. A new period of change began in 2008, with, in particular, the search by the Centres Chorégraphiques Nationaux for new directions. In spring of that year, Boris Charmatz took over as director of the Centre Chorégraphique National de Rennes et de Bretagne from Catherine Diverrès. And in the same year, Myriam Gourfink succeeded Susan Buirge as artistic director of the Centre de Recherche et de Composition Chorégraphiques de la Fondation Royaumont, upon which she proposed a new professional course entitled *Transforme*.

In this changing choreographic environment, this essay attempts to outline a contextual reflection on the dancing body, its image, and its usage across these practices that present critical connections between history, culture, and autobiographical paths. It is about the construction of reflective and reflexive thinking processes that suggest new ways of being in the world. Starting from the dancing body and "what makes dance," it considers the disparity created by the performative practices between dancing corporeality and choreographic writing, raising the issue of what makes a work of dance and, by extension, what is at work in these artistic projects. [...]

The questions at stake here, at the beginning of the twenty-first century, will be contemplated in a global contextualization that extends beyond the field of aesthetics. These choreographic practices have developed a resistance to the dominant economic and political order and globalization, and a necessary resistance to productivity. New modes of production have been introduced, not new to their forms—as they already existed in the field of the visual arts and in postmodern experimentations in the choreographic field, particularly in America—but in terms of the institutional value that they have acquired within the choreographic field, and in relation to the context they engage with, i.e. a context that is the consequence of the position of contemporary dance—and not, as was the case in America in the 1960s and '70s, as a rupture with modern dance on the one hand, and with the Cunningham dancing body on the other. These new modes of production brought about a shift in the understanding of the notion of the work of art and, for a while, disturbed the expectation horizons of the community: it is not a question of an "outside of" or a negation, but of a reconsideration of what makes dance and of what makes the choreographic. The performative attitude tends to propose a critical comparison between the different coveted materials performative dance creates visible artistic potential from. The artistic relationship with the spectator becomes more important than the production itself. The experience of the audience lies at the heart of this new questioning, and they are active in triggering the artistic relationship. They are constantly required to reconsider their expectation horizons and to reevaluate their habits in order to be perceptively touched by the here and now.

Beyond the choreotype

In a society invaded by the mass culture of the body, the performative act is an insertion within the social fabric. Within the choreographic field, the performative attitude is faced by the challenge that a body dancing on stage is just one more image to be seen and consumed. In order to be able to keep its critical potential and elaborate a reflexive approach within the system, rather than simply excluding itself as postmodern dance did for a while (voluntarily abandoning the theater and the scenic space following an Artaudian idea of art), it is necessary to develop strategies against becoming a signifier of consumption. Exposing nonproductive and underexposed bodies is part of this requirement. For Emmanuelle Chérel and Daniel Perrier, "[these practices] are more offensive than the propositions of the '60s, and more impure than American 'postmodern dance.' Boris Charmatz summed up this artistic philosophy in the following way: 'manhandle the quest for an ideal body' in order to find a 'critical impact'."[4] The idea is to bring self-reflexivity to Yvonne Rainer's famous "NO manifesto" of 1965: "NO to spectacle no to virtuosity no to transformations and magic and make-believe no to the glamour and transcendency of the star image no to the heroic no to the anti-heroic no to trash imagery no to involvement of performer or spectator no to style no to camp no to seduction of spectator by the wiles of the performer no to eccentricity no to moving or being moved."[5]

This resistance to the quest for an ideal body is realized through questioning the choreotypes and the fetish of technique.[6] Desublimation is activated as a transgressive process as much for the artist as for the spectator. Through desublimation, performative practices challenge composition and physical presence, either through under-exposure, over-exposure, or disfiguration: under-exposure in *Con for fleuves* (1999) by Boris Charmatz and *Mùa* (1994) by Emmanuelle Huynh; over-exposure in *Self Portrait Camouflage* (2006) by Latifa Laâbissi; sexual disfiguration in *Good Boy* (1998) by Alain Buffard, in which the donning of several pairs of briefs disfigures the very place where sexual identity is marked, and the disfiguration of human corporeality in *Self Unfinished* (1998), in which Xavier Le Roy experiments with the human body's legibility and illegibility. Each of these works enacts principles of interference with the signs and encryption of the materials used.

The issue at stake with the dancing body is off-kilter projection, which tends to recreate a point of imbalance, eliminating any dimension of fascination, fantasy, or projection from an idealized body. This is one of the concerns dealt with in *Véronique Doisneau* (2004) by Jérôme Bel, which examined an ideal, fascinating, and trained body. With regard to this project, Bel stated that "Véronique Doisneau is not a character, she is herself. She is not a fiction, but a type of documentary on a real person, as it happens she is a dancer at the Paris Opera, therefore this is what we are talking about. [...] Everyone has a particular story. There is no fascination for Véronique Doisneau. She understood the concept and played the game. That is the most important thing. What she actually says many other dancers could have said; it would have been different, but it would have had the same value for me. With Véronique Doisneau, I wouldn't have wanted to reproduce the fetishisation of a so-called excellence, a dominant ideology in the realm of Ballet. What I was interested in was her work as a dancer, so, since she is an artist, my approach to her is artistic. However, before being an artist, she is also a citizen and a social being, which is why this work has a political and social dimension."[7]

This reflexive position and objectification of the act of dance necessarily raises a self-reflexive question on the "dancing" process and its significance in a society of spectacle that, in its own way, consumes bodies. The first necessary action is to bring a halt to the fetishisation of the technique that displays a virtuosic body and to propose a critical reading of gestural codes, recognizing the influence of the French choreographic tradition. As Gerald Siegmund has emphasized, everybody seems agree on one point: "Eliminating the fetish of technique makes it possible for a non-marked body to join in."[8] This approach takes shape through the re-appropriation and exhibition of a choreographic history by reactivating works, through citations and by playing on references, and by choreographic artists organizing workshops, whether derived from a process of creation or from a working technique created by the choreographer who is involved in the history and evolution of the dancing body. Performative dance evolved by being stripped down to its essence, projecting artistic creation as a counterpoint to, on one hand, the consumer society and its myths, and, on the other, the French choreographic tradition.

This reduction to the bare bones of corporeality in dance can also be seen first and foremost in the presence of the body and its potential metamorphoses. With *Self Unfinished* (1998), Xavier Le Roy offered a work in which the human body is considered as a series of processes or transformations rather than as a fixed state. He questioned how it functions and looked into various physical poses and sequences that examine elementary concepts of the body and its potential by referencing images of the body and human figure. He thus gave the body a mutability in which it shifted between something hybrid, an object, and something monstrous, creating zones of indistinguishability and generating a disturbed perception of the human body. The creation of such zones opens new spaces and makes it possible for the spectator to become active, even reactive, with regard to what is proposed. In multiplying the different physical forms he adopted, Le Roy was seen in turn by the audience as a spider, a decapitated chicken, a headless double torso that mixes masculinity and femininity, and a body made of rock. However, the public was aware that the names they attribute to these forms are only metaphoric comparisons that are not completely appropriate, and that they even deform the meaning of the reality of the mutating body.

Performative practices consistently establish a dialogue between the body of society and the body of the subject in an increased awareness of the present moment. In *Self Portrait Camouflage* (2006), Latifa Laâbissi presents an unimaginable and horrifying body, shifting the codes and expectation horizons of nudity and the display of the grotesque—in a reference to German expressionism and

Valeska Gert—while also displacing codes of interpretation and discourse registers within a contextual and political work. Definitions shift, multiply, and depart from their etymological meaning in order to become the place of expression for experience, the place of the problematization of the practice by practice itself. When asked for a definition of the word "dance," Loïc Touzé answered: "For me, dance is a domain that cuts across a field of experience that confronted me. It could easily have been something other than dance, but that is where my personal history led me, and from there I made the choice to make this domain the one where I could work. It matched my artistic sensibility, and I found that what was interesting was that it was possible to combine corporal, physical, and intellectual experience with the human experience of encounters, geographical experience, and a form of experience that seeks to invent a language and to modulate our relationship to our environment and space. It intersects with lots of the things that interest me in what I wish to approach and understand."[9] As with many definitions and experiences that have a common vector: the body is a place for a critical discourse.

Therefore, performative practices are restating the conditions of existence for the basics of dance by distancing them from the ideas—which remain widely established and communicated—of harmony, balance, and symmetry—and even of dissymmetry and organized chaos, which are instrumental to the exhibition of a trained body. Performative practices are restating the conditions for interpretation and how the dancing body and its language is put into action. They suggest a body that is present, aware of its environment, and critical of its own history; they are very far from presenting a trained body that interprets a discourse and a form outside of itself. Performative practices thus present the conditions of validity for danced movement in a critical re-appropriation of the history of its own field.

What makes a work: The critical dimension

Let us consider the challenge posed to the "*doxa* of the inspection reports" denounced by Les Signataires du 20 août in their open letter to Dominique Wallon and to contemporary dancers (*Lettre ouverte à Dominique Wallon et aux danseurs contemporains*):

> Thus, an ideal choreographic piece has first to be "composed" according to the doxa of the evaluation reports, often shared by the press. But composition is held as a dogma, a normative given (which totally disregards the complex history of the notion of composition in contemporary dance and its criticism). A piece should be "mastered, finished, rigorously built," able to present an "appealing occupation of the stage," without however being "too formal, too direct, too assiduous" as it would run the risk of becoming a simple "exercise in composition." A contemporary choreographic piece should therefore present "exceptional images," a "carefully designed [even sophisticated] setting," and lighting to bring out the best in the dancers' moving bodies. In addition, It must be supported by "sublime performers" endowed with a "real dancer's physique" who are able to display their technical prowess in "beautiful moments of virtuosity." It should also be in "harmony with the audience," "without pretention," so as to share "something in common" with them. Something that is "reserved for the initiates," an experience, a performance, a happening where "nothing much" would take place, would therefore be more the work of a "researcher" than of a "choreographer."[10]

Here performative practices raise the question of composition and writing, and hence of choreographic language and its double potential for "making a work" and "being at work" in the here and now, while refusing to consider the work as some form of obligation.

Many of these choreographers demanding a shift in the outlook of the choreographic world have already had careers as dancers in pieces that came out of Bagnolet[11] and are the result of the creation of the Centres Chorégraphiques Nationaux, whose purpose was the creation of a specific vocabulary and whose interest was directed to a certain sophistication of gesture—not on a questioning of the modalities of choreography itself. In this way, they have contributed to the creation of the founding works in the new French dance, or *"danse d'auteur."* Thus, these choreographic artists are members of the generation that considers the space of the stage and the traditional modalities of a production with a critical eye, not necessarily rejecting them or adopting an antagonistic viewpoint, but accepting the different potential they have to offer. The subject under debate is how to turn the scenic space into a playground that allows for the entire choreographic experience to be, on one hand, a space that reflects on its own existence, and, on the other, a space for a reflexive discourse on the world. The choreographic plays on this gap, distance, and distortion between discourse and its enactment.

The choreographic therefore works on the gap that often underlies the interplay between presentation and representation, i.e., the activation of a heightened sensitivity in the presence of the here and now, while maintaining full awareness of the images of the body directly exposed by a real body. It is in no way a question of transposing experiences from outside the theater or offstage into the place of the show or onto the stage, but rather of conceiving of a critical presence within this real and symbolic space. Performative practices restate the conditions of representation by engaging the principles of presentation developed in the thought of Jean-François Lyotard and the American postmodernists, and by including them in the initial frame of representation. "Closure of representation if representing means presenting something while being absent—but representation still, if representing is presenting anyway, presenting what is unpresentable, representing in the sense of making for someone re-presentations, re-monstrances, re-monstration."[12]

For *Self Portrait Camouflage* (2006), Latifa Laâbissi brings into play a use of discourse and its critical impact. In regards to the piece, she tells the following story: "Between the first World Fair in 1855 and the Colonial Exhibition in 1937, France successively presented eleven national events, providing occasions for the public to praise the splendors of its colonial Empire. Men, women, and children provided curious attractions. In 2006, Marianne, in her own way, still investigates these haunted zones of the Republic's universal values. But don't worry, between cannibal and wahine this is a perfect case of integration..."[13] The encoding associated with a dramaturgical work entails confusion and ambiguity when discerning between fiction and reality, between a personal trajectory and the exposition of the political game. The performative, choreographic work creates a distance between the imaginary and reality, science and science fiction, identity and alterity, the present and duration, personal and political, which results in the consideration of art as action rather than a work; art as an active relation, not as an object to be seen.

Performative practices reconsider the conditions of the choreographic by questioning its value and its processes, and by including other processes of construction and enunciation. To do so, these practices are prepared to put choreographic composition to the test in a way that goes beyond the presence of the body or that simply filters it through other formats: In what way does the choreographic make work about the fundamental relation between time and space? Talking about *Habiter* (2004), a choreographic project that presents a solo in an everyday domestic space, Latifa Laâbissi explains:

> To my mind, there is nothing interesting in seeing this project live. These dances, performed in an apartment, were of course seen by the people who live there, but it is a project that is

really meant to be recorded in images, whether photographic or film. That's how I conceived the project and I very quickly thought—at least as far as I am concerned—that there was nothing of interest in the live dimension of the project, either in its performance, or in its reception. The reception needs to be distanced from its support, it needs something in between, like a relay. [...] I sent the first version of *Habiter* on DVD to people I had not necessarily met, and who decided for themselves under what conditions they wanted to watch it: during their lunch break, while eating a sandwich, with friends they had invited to watch it with. And I liked the fact that I did not have a hand in that, and was very much interested in the fact that it could go around in a totally different way.[14]

In this case, performative practice laid down the conditions of existence for the notion of work by jointly exhibiting the "doing"—that is to say, the processes, the protocols, etc.—and the work itself in the same time-space.

In this way, performative practices initiate new uses and new spaces for a dancing body in metamorphosis and for a choreographic object in mutation. It is a matter of establishing codes and shifting them so that their dimensions of recycling and reappropriation can be viewed positively. It is about exposing critical thought on the constructed body and the construction of its representation. The choreographic is thus interested in the image of the body in direct relation to its discourse and its work.

[1] This essay is part of a series of essays and articles begun by the author in 2007 titled *Pratiques performatives / Corps critiques*. The articles are numbered in order of creation. They are autonomous, do not refer to each other, and each addresses a different context. This article is a shortened version of an essay published as "Ce qui fait danse: de la plasticité à la performance," *La Part de l'œil* 24 (2009): 112-23.
[2] Hans-Robert Jauss, *Pour une esthétique de la réception* (Paris: Gallimard, 1978).

[3] In the hierarchy of the Paris Opéra, a *sujet* corresponds to the third, mid-level echelon and performs corps de ballet and soloist roles.

[4] Emmanuelle Chérel and Daniel Perrier, "Parler la danse," *Revues les langages de la danse* (Nantes: erban and Lieu Unique, 13-16 November 2006), 1.

[5] Yvonne Rainer, *Work 1961-1973* (New York: New York University Press, 1974), 51.

[6] For more on the question of the "choreotype," see Christophe Wavelet, "Ici et maintenant. Coalitions temporaries," *Mouvement* 2 (1998): 18-21. "The choreotype is to dance what the stereotype is to language."

[7] Jérôme Bel in an interview with Agnès Irzine, "Le traité du sujet / Jérôme Bel / Véronique Doisneau / Brigitte Lefèbre," in *Danser* 236 (October 2004): 23-24.

[8] Gerald Siegmund, "Partager l'absence," in *Être ensemble. Figures de la communauté en danse depuis le XXème siècle*, ed. Claire Rousier (Pantin: Centre national de la danse, 2003), 332.

[9] Loïc Touzé in an interview with the author, 1 August 2003.

[10] L'Association des Signataires du 20 août, "Lettre ouverte à Dominique Wallon et aux danseurs contemporains," in *Mouvement* 7 (February/March 2000): 9.

[11] Created in 1969, the Concours chorégraphique international de Bagnolet was instrumental in the emergence of a Nouvelle danse française, or the French contemporary dance of the late 1970s and 1980s.

[12] Jean-François Lyotard, *Des dispositifs pulsionnels* (Paris: 10/18, 1973), 7-8.

[13] Latifa Laâbissi, conversation with the author. Marianne refers to the national emblem and figure of the French republic.

[14] Unpublished interview with Latifa Laâbissi, February 2006.

DISOBEDIENCE AND DIY[1]

Laurent Goumarre

To begin with: a story. At the Festival Les Intranquilles last May in Lyon, Guy Walter, director of the Villa Gillet, asked choreographers Alain Buffard and Claudia Triozzi to make works based on the figure of Pinocchio, Collodi's puppet. And it was perhaps in this commission made to two choreographers, emblematic figures of the renewal of dance such as it has evolved since the late 1990s, which has been referred to as the "young generation," "emerging forms," "conceptual dance," and even "non-dance"—recognition of this semantic dematerialization is enough to indicate the extent of the suspicion this dance/performance practice has been subjected to—in short, it was perhaps with this commission that today something of another history of the link between puppetry and dance may come to pass. At the risk of reading too much into it, something can be distinguished in the fact that the reason Guy Walter gave for his commission was that Pinocchio is simultaneously a figure of disobedience and the product of a do-it-yourself [*bricolage*] methodology. At the risk of over interpreting, we can point out the stakes and the parallels with this deceptive form of dance: disobedience and DIY.

Of course, the choreographers were not expected to be literal or to provide an illustration of Collodi's story, nor most importantly to bring the living body face-to-face with the wooden puppet. It is not the contrast between the mechanical and the living that is of interest; it is not the mannequin as an anti-realist interpretative model for use by the dancer/actor—typical of the 1920–30s—that is to be celebrated; there would be no staging of the umpteenth mise-en-abyme of the interpreter and his effigy, the umpteenth discourse on artificiality, doppelgangers, depersonalization, monsters, parody, the subject-object relationship, the essence of representation, and so on... Whereas Josef Nadj is still continuing his work, in which puppets systematically appear, to the extent of conceiving his next piece as a new stage in the dancer/marionette identification, taking on the existence of the puppet in an attempt to experience another human condition; and whereas Karine Saporta gave doubles to the performers of *Á propos Andrei Roublev* (2003) in the form of puppets in a brief gestural choreography that imitates robots; in short, whereas still today, here and there on the dance stage, we see the presence of puppets infect choreographic composition and bodily states, we understand that Triozzi's dance/performance *Pinocchio* (in the end, Buffard declined the invitation) forcefully flies in the face of these practices, or rather it ignores them and makes a show of disobedience. There is no trace of the puppet in her piece, not even the metaphor of one. The choreographer does not take up a position with regard to an effigy but instead shifts the theme to the rough fabrication of a piece. The result is an uncompleted "thing" with—I've been told, and I'm ready to believe it—an inconclusive attempt at video, and live telephone calls made to Italy to ask random anonymous correspondents what they thought of Roberto Benigni's *Pinocchio*. With uninteresting replies, the piece smacks of a fiasco, and Triozzi has seemingly created less of a show than something simply cobbled together: in short, she made a promise and has not delivered. It is not a defeat, but a disappointing result easily predictable for anyone able to read the warning included in the program: "What we should say when..." "Breed an animal with the prerogative to make promises..." (Friedrich Nietzsche) "The puppet (Pinocchio) is a 'reliable,' 'regular,' 'necessary' being that is answerable for his own future, in the words of Nietzsche – An ambivalent figure of the possible and the impossible on both sides of the promise. In any case, without the promise, perhaps nothing will happen. *Promise me*." (Claudia Triozzi and Alain Buffard)

Taking the puppet as a theme is no longer a matter of dealing with the contrast of a living and an artificial body but is more a loosely concocted practice of danced representation: the spectacle of its failure, the displacement of its expectations. *Pinocchio*, or the adventures of an undisciplined dance, makes its questioning and (telephonic) calls the subject of the performance. Just like the puppet who, having hardly even been modeled by his father, "opened the door and dashed out into the street," running through the world refusing to stop and listen to "those who knew more than him," Triozzi's debacle is the manifested symptom of a deceptive dance that actively circumvents any demands that an audience might make, and therefore appears as a stage show developed along the lines of an interrupted journey. As the puppet "not yet finished but already with no respect for your father," *Pinocchio* is a pronouncement using an essentially unfinished dance—to paraphrase a solo work by Xavier Le Roy—that does not believe in the merits of the perfect gesture, a quality of movement, written compositions, or pieces folded onto a supposed knowledge of identity. The dances are unfinished because the dream of a flawless, glorious body materialized, or turned into a metaphor, by the skillful mechanical nature of the automaton, and then of the robot—the progressive avatars of the marionette—is over. We knew that this belief in a perfect, reproducible body, particularly in the context of a one-dimensional dance as it began to be reproduced in the 1980s, was rejected by Xavier Le Roy in the first part of his solo *Self Unfinished* (1998). Reminder: Xavier Le Roy moves on the stage like a robot, breaking down every exaggeratedly stiff movement of his torso, arms, and legs into parts, to an accompaniment of mechanistic sounds. Apart from the slightly comic effect, there is nothing: the choreographer employs an over-used and overly familiar style that stimulates nothing except the recognition of a cliché. A body miming a mechanical device, that is to say a scientific application of Bergson's notion: "the attitudes, gestures, and movements of the human body are laughable in exact proportion as that body reminds us of a mere machine."[2] Imitating a robot has no meaning. The stereotyped sequence does not lead to anything, builds nothing, and comes to an end amid total indifference when Xavier Le Roy interrupts what we could call his skit to move on to something else, leaving the spectators with their laughter and their expectations of some form of development or conclusion, the expected unfolding of a dramaturgy. It is precisely the debacle of the sequence and the couldn't-care-less attitude of the performer/choreographer that indicates that the modernist dream of the robot-body and the modern era are over, and that now the fantasy of an efficient technical body belongs to the kitsch side of a science-fiction B-movie. What the comical opening of Xavier Le Roy's piece shows us is the failure of a whole system of progressive thought turned into spectacle by an obsolete style. Xavier Le Roy's body, stated as "self unfinished," begins by visiting this destruction of the Futurist dream of man's identification with the machine, while, at the same time, this start to his performance admits its disillusioned discursive dimension. Is it really necessary to point out yet again that dance is not based on either the imitation of an action, or the supposed reproduction of an ideal, perfectible body to be achieved, but on the production of an event?

In less than ten years, dance stages have become a place where composite figures are created: a repressed polymorphic body with changing identities for Xavier Le Roy, who metamorphoses into a phallus or a four-legged monster; the optical bodies with ludicrous anatomies of Saskia Höbling (*Exposition corps*, 2003) and Maria Donata d'Urso, under the direction of the visual artist Laurent Goldring, and Estelle Héritier (*Optiks*, 2002); figures that stand out against a background of digital screens for the Japanese collective Dum Type (*Memorandum*, 1999); the curious body covered in Lacroix boots that Christian Rizzo places in front of the light on a podium (*Et pourquoi pas: "bodymakers", "falbalas", "bazaar", etc, etc... ?*, 2001);

or bodies swollen by prostheses performed in Alain Buffard (*INtime/EXtime*, 1999) and Benoît Lachambre (*Not to Know*, 2001). The list is long—and could be followed by the parade of the Incroyables that opens Vera Mantero's *Poésie et Sauvagerie*—long enough to understand that this dance, non-dance one might say, calls to mind the anti-establishment nature of the avantgarde scene of the 1910s and '20s, which featured processions of puppets, masks, and wax bodies (see the excellent analysis by Didier Plassart in *L'Acteur en effigie*[3]). Aside from the differences in strategy, both cases entail the element of a rupture, of questioning the validity of the codes pertaining to choreography and performance. The dance that began at the end of the 1990s is less a writing of movement, the elaboration of a stylistic vocabulary, than the performative advent of infra-choreographic bodies. The dancer's body no longer performs a spectacle; it becomes the place, the condition, and the statement of the performance. As it is tautological, it does not need to be involved in an economy of movement/efficiency, it does not need to invest the space, or to annex the stage. Thanks to its presence, it often lies down (Xavier Le Roy, *Self Unfinished*), takes account of and adapts to the horizontality of the stage (La Ribot, *Still Distinguished*; Raimund Hoghe, *Another Dream*), and underlines the stage's flatness to the extent of letting itself be absorbed in a movement of transubstantiation (Gilles Jobin, *The Moebius Strip*, 2001, and *Underconstruction*, 2002). It is through this flattening of the body to match the flatness of the stage, when the stage floor is understood as a two-dimensional effigy of the dancer, that dance at the end of the 1990s found its real scope: a stasis, a halt. When Claudia Triozzi places her body at the center of a delirious machine—the DIY concoction of a hair dryer, a sausage dispenser, a system of shoe rings, and sponges on a table-football rod—when she mechanically fills up some bowls with earth and places them on a conveyer belt that systematically throws them on the ground (*Park*, 1998), it is not so much to figure womankind as domestic cleaning machines, household puppets defined by repetitive house chores, as it is to experiment with a non-productive but instrumentalized body using a prosthetic device based a priori on a logic of productivity. This puppet-body takes a position of passive disobedience to external requirements, and this disobedience becomes the motivation for a dance that rejects the expectations others have for it. Therefore, Triozzi's static and mechanical presence establishes a kind of resistant dance in the current flow of the choreographic and, more broadly, cultural production. I am not talking here of a metaphorical body, but of a presence that makes a performance of its own conditions of enunciation.

The dances of Buffard, Le Roy, Triozzi, etc., no longer use metaphor, imitation, or visible manipulation; thus their shifted relationship to puppets cannot be read in a confrontation with an effigy of their own bodies. What we are observing is the gradual shift of representation toward a performative aesthetic, which, using the language of linguistics, might be defined as "a statement that simultaneously constitutes the act that it refers to." La Ribot, a choreographer-performer who tapes pieces of wood to her body to the point of preventing all movement, as if she were a half-flesh, half-wooden puppet (*Chair*, 2000; one of the seven stations of the piece *Still Distinguished*), is an act; her presence is a choreographic act. Dance-performance is seen here as an action used to stop movement and exhaust choreographic form. Do-it-yourself, poorly assembled creatures, like awkward Pinocchios, La Ribot and Claudia Triozzi do not present paralyzed bodies and dehumanized movements that offer a discourse on failing humanity or something of that nature. There is no failure in these puppet dispositifs, slowed down to immobility, repetition with an absence of unfolding dramaturgy, to the point of the total erasure of subjective indicators, specifically the systematic disappearance of faces during recent pieces: with the use of furry hoods by Jennifer Lacey and Nadia Lauro (*This Is an Epic*, 2003), full-face helmets by Christian Rizzo (*Et pourquoi pas...*; *Skull*Cult*, 2002), animal masks by Michèle Murray (*Vladivostok*, 2003) and Benoît Lachambre (*Not to Know*, 2001), trousers worn upside-down on the head by Boris Charmatz (*Con Fort Fleuve*, 1999), ossicle wigs by Claudia Triozzi (*The Family Tree*, 2002), green wigs by La Ribot (*Another Bloody Mary*, 2000), and blond ones by the queer interpreters of *Dispositifs 3.1* (2001) by Alain Buffard.

Didier Plassart knows about this, "historians and theoreticians of performance willingly recognize the filiation that links performance art to the theatrical experiments of the 1910s and '20s," but he is mistaken when he nuances this parallel by saying that "a distance has developed with respect to the poetics of effigy, puppet identification, and mechanization specific to the historical avantgardes [since], in spite of these efforts, performance remains first, even in its excesses, the place for an epiphany of the individual and his biological body."[4] If this last remark finds justification in body art, it is invalidated by the treatment of dance-performance, which radically resists any temptation to indulge in an exalted, indeed incantatory, staging of the human body. It is exactly the contrary that is at work here – in the dispositifs that privilege the effacement of the individual, in the disappearance behind the walls, the masks of Christian Rizzo (*Avant un mois je serai revenu et nous irons ensemble en matinée, tu sais, voir la comédie où je t'ai promis de te conduire*, 2002), and in the darkness of the pieces by Raimund Hoghe.

"Perfo-dance" is the actualization of this disappearance, particularly when it performs/transforms the modernist dreams of technological progress: puppet, automaton, robot, cyber body, etc. The young Belgian choreographer Cindy Van Acker connects her body to computerized electric stimulators that hijack her movements, thus creating a dancing body that goes beyond its corporeal form. A grafted, connected, computerized body: *Corps 00.00* is the title of the work given by the choreographer. For her, dance becomes the exhibited practice of a real body providing the basis for another body that outdoes it. Worked on by technology, her body does not seek to be repaired by medical prosthetic devices, nor does it desire a higher level of performance. On the contrary, invaded by artificial stimuli, the body becomes the spectacle of its distortion: it is outdone and doubled. Contractions, involuntary dislocations, and external impulses interfere as much as contribute to the danced movement; Van Acker's choreography deceives the integrity of the movement and of the body. The choreographic act shows a floating body with an impossible outline: a real body with its ghost double; as a host for an invasive technology, it does not close itself but exhibits its openness. Shot through by the machine, its limits become extended, which does not mean the body makes a gain in power [puissance], precision, or speed—a modernist dream if any—it means that it experiments with mutation and visible manipulation. Thus the technological aspect creates a choreography of open bodies, and of controlled, constrained, and involuntary movements—of internal rhythms and external gestures. Dance becomes the actualization of the ghostly sensation of an additional body, virtual though visual, rather than visceral. The body is coupled in such a way that it puts into motion its disobedient ghost. Their interaction results in a choreography of the formless, a DIY job, something like a presence.

[1] "Désobéissance et bricolage" first appeared in Objet-Danse, *Alternatives Théâtrales* 80 (2003): 18-21.

[2] Henri Bergson, *Laughter: An Essay on the Meaning of the Comic*, trans. Cloudesley Brereton and Fred Rothwell (Rockville: Arc Manor, 2008 [1900]), 21.

[3] Didier Plassart, *L'Acteur en effigie. Figure de l'homme artificiel dans le théâtre des avant-gardes historiques* (Lausanne: L'Âge d'Homme, 1992).

[4] Didier Plassart, *L'Acteur en effigie*, 348.

EXPANDED DANCE[1]
Chantal Pontbriand

> Dance on myriad backs a season,
> Billows' backs and billows' treason –
> We need dances that are new!
> Let us dance in myriad manners,
> Freedom write on *our* art's banners,
> Our *science* shall be gay!
> —Nietzsche, *The Gay Science*[2]

What is the body, and what is dance? In what way is dance linked to the body, or the body to dance?

The multitude of questions stemming from the body today begs a renewed definition of dance. Dance no longer appears as linked to a genre, a well-defined code aiming at producing a performance by means of the body—or bodies—present. The dance performance is traditionally a representational art form. Dance represents something, someone, a being of some description. As representation, dance presents something other than itself; it re-presents. Classical, or even modern dance makes the body into a place of passage, a place of transit for figures of representation, figures that exist as signs, characters, emotions, attitudes—signs of storytelling, a narrative. The narrative underpins the dance. These issues are linked through the relation of an art with its material. The material is at the behest of a certain conception of art, or concepts within art. Seen as a sign, the body-material has an illustrative meaning conferred upon it that is subordinated to the narrative, or to the narrating that underpins dance.

Postmodern dance, since Merce Cunningham, aimed at uncoupling the body from the narrative, the sign from the narration. In Cunningham's work, we witnessed the birth of nonnarrative, in some sense abstract performance, where all the elements of the performance—music, choreography, the set, even the props—function independently from one another. We find ourselves more than ever in an era of juxtaposition, collage, and randomness. This conception of the performance brings with it a conception of the world that moves away from Western logos. The world is no longer seen as something to be traversed, supported by a conception of linear, one-dimensional, or even a progressive or idealized history. Cunningham's dance teaches us to appreciate the world as a process, a site of encounter and juxtaposition, a site of alternation. In this world potentialities, rather than finitudes, are expressed—the world is infinite.

Conceiving performance as a site of arrangements that express potentialities brings to mind the concept of "ease" developed by Giorgio Agamben. Very much in the spirit of Nietzsche, Agamben stresses the need to cultivate this space of ease between individuals, as bearing a potential for freedom between beings. He discusses the notion in his work *The Coming Community*, where he redefines the concepts of community and individuality through what he refers to as "whatever singularity."[3] This concept brings out the idea that the individual is linked to the community through being nondescript—providing both difference (individuality) and a common link (community). In Agamben's thought, individuals are linked to the community, the surrounding world, through difference, the nondescript, which is at once what distinguishes and links them. The recognition of the nondescript is, as he writes, "the political task of our generation."[4]

This conception of dance performance opens the way toward a conception of the body that is no longer that of a body-object, or even a body-subject, instrumentalized either by some preestablished narrative, or even by the expressiveness of the ego staging itself. The body becomes, in the very abstraction of what is put forth, *presence*, and no longer re-presence. The body is no longer *representative*, but is exhibited as such, as an exhibited body. Performance becomes at the same time exhibition, a shared presence with the other bodies present—the bodies of dancers and non-dancers (audience members) alike. One wonders if the dancers' bodies actually are, in this particular case, cast-member bodies, given how active are they in putting together the performance and what here becomes dance. Dance becomes copresence; dancers and non-dancers exist in a relation of copresence, where the narrative is in constant renewal. Dance is a process rather than an accomplished act. Gestures join together in distinct figures, whose pattern is not, however, predetermined. The necessity of the moment and the flux of intensities create a sequence that can be repeated, turned back upon itself, or spring forward toward something else. "In the movement of those who dance, the absence of purpose moves forward, the lack of means becomes a means, the pure possibility of moving, all-encompassing politics."[5]

Dance is a site of motion with the other, a site of being-together; it enables the emergence of the body-world, which is articulated with the other through dance. True dance is constantly running up against its own limits: the body is in extension, touching the extreme limit of itself, to the point of giddy exhilaration. In this exhilaration, it touches the unknown, the unfinished, its own unfinished being. In dance, the body carries out the exploration of its own incompleteness, its own lack, in a multitude of patterns. In this very movement, the body is in expansion, touching what lies beyond its possibilities.

Contemporary dance allows us to see beyond dance and the body. It offers us a multitude of possible approaches to that other of oneself, the other as such. It shows the body's unexplored registers. Contemporary dance can no longer be described in terms of genres or codes; the gestures are not codified, and there is frequent recourse to improvisation. Which makes it possible to go beyond the finite body, the body-limit, exposing the unknown, bringing it to the surface, exteriorizing it, pulling it outward. Dance is the language of the body, beyond words, expressing a form of thought that belongs to it alone and is not subordinated to logos. A material possession, the body expresses a virtuality—what is invisible in the body rendered visible by gesture, by presence itself. An enactment of thought; "pure," nonnarrative, presence.

But what is pure presence—the presence that can be experienced only through contact with the other, the audience member, and is "hybridized" through this very contact? Presence is contact, the experience of touching "with"; for there can be no touch in the absence of this "with," this other. Presence is what touches, what strikes the imagination of the other, what impresses the other through generated intensity.

Contemporary dance generates revelatory intensities by pushing back the limits of dance and of the body. What are these limits (if indeed there are limits)? One might think of the limits of the body—if not indeed the mind—of what has already occurred, as thought. The body's limits of speed and slowness, its mechanical limits, its members, its motor capacities, the limits imposed by contact—proximity to or distance from the other, or both—limits of the self, of each of us in our own bodies, the limits of bodies together, the limits of the sexes, the limits of the senses. Limits of the clothed body, and those of the naked body. And then there is an ecology of the body to consider, its environment, the limits of the institutions that provide a framework for dance (schools, genres, theaters, stages), the limits of the other arts (music, visual arts, literature)—coming into contact with dance. The limits of the world itself, the geographic, political, anthropological world.

Exploring and testing these limits: contemporary dance is extreme dance, moving toward the extreme, pushing back borders, expanding its territory. Contemporary dance is dance that stretches outward, that has expanded. "Expanded dance," like expanded cinema—a concept put forth by Gene Youngblood in relation to film in 1970—pushes back the borders of art, opening up toward the possible:

> When we say expanded cinema we actually mean expanded consciousness. Expanded cinema does not mean computer films,

video phosphors, atomic light, or spherical projections. Expanded cinema isn't a movie at all: like life it's a process of becoming, man's ongoing historical drive to manifest his consciousness outside of his mind, in front of his eyes. One can no longer specialize in a single discipline and hope truthfully to express a clear picture of its relationship in the environment. This is especially true in the case of the intermedia network of cinema and television, which now functions as nothing less than the nervous system of mankind.[6]

This movement that has shaken the world since the 1960s and which initially took hold in Europe, North America, and Japan, is now spreading to—or rather welling up in—Africa, South America, Australia, and Asia. Numerous choreographers now work on all continents, multiplying territories and approaches to dance, establishing a "nervous system of mankind." What is both surprising and seductive in this vast movement is that everyone exposes his or her own body—a body forged in contact with the other, in contact with its own ecology, made up of history, geography, culture and hybridization, a globally active mixture, which produces, to use Agamben's term, "proper singularities," for which dance serves as a pointer. In an essay on dance, Alain Badiou writes:

> Dance is like a poem uninscribed, or untraced. And dance is also like a dance without dance, a dance undanced. What is stated here is the substractive dimension of thought. Every genuine instance of thinking is substracted from the knowledge in which it is constituted. Dance is a metaphor for thought precisely as much as it indicates, by means of the body, that a thought, in the form of its eventual surge, is subtracted from every preexistence of knowledge.[7]

Why is dance so uncommonly able to reveal what distinguishes one individual from another today, or what defines the specificity of being in our contemporary era? What makes dance a process of learning freedom? How does it bring out the "beauty" of each and everyone, their difference and their uniqueness? How does it ensure that the community is enhanced, rather than leveled and neutralized as it naturally tends to be under the effect of the social institutions that govern us? The political task of dance is revealed in its ability to awaken conscience and to cultivate individual and collective freedom. Youngblood writes:

> The mass public insists on entertainment over art in order to escape an unnatural way of life in which interior realities are not compatible with exterior realities. Freedom, says [Norman O.] Brown, is fusion. Life becomes art when there's no difference between what we are and what we do. Art is a synergetic attempt at closing the gap between what *is* and what ought to be.[8]

Extreme dance explores and ensures the means necessary for its full potential to emerge; it enables the space that exists between what we are and what we will be to spring forth. In that respect, extreme dance finds common ground with what Youngblood fleshed out in *Expanded Cinema*.

Why might it be argued that the practice of dance today is more extreme, or more expanded, than that which preceded it? One might cite several factors: that of nudity, for instance, which is dealt with in many performances. Badiou assigns considerable importance to the concept of nudity in dance:

> Dance as a metaphor for thought, presents thought to us as *devoid of relation to naything other than itself*, in the nudity of its emergence. Dance is a thinking without relation, the

thinking that relates nothing, that puts nothing in relation. We could also say that it is pure conflagration of thought, because it repudiates all of thought's ornaments. Whether the fact that dance is (or tends to be) the exhibition of *chaste* nakedness, the nakedness prior to the ornament, the nakedness that does not derive from the divestment of ornaments but is, on the contrary, as it is given before all ornament—as the event is given "before" the name.[9]

The appearance of nudity in so many performances over the past several years seems to suggest that dance has attained one of its "extremities," not shrinking back from exploring it in many different ways, as seen in the work of Boris Charmatz, Gilles Jobin, La Ribot, Benoît Lachambre, or Sasha Waltz. Why now more than ever, if not because it has become a self-reflexive site of thought, an "unadorned" laboratory of pure thought? In contrast to the codified bodies that contemporary culture is so wont to offer up and impose upon us.

Dance is extreme, too, in its contemporary critique of the theatrical site as institution. More and more innovators within the new generation are seeking to "deterritorialize" dance—to use Gilles Deleuze's expression. Which means changing the parameters, framework, structures, modes of presentation, or even the modes of interaction with the public, opening it up to the imagination and the hybridity of sites and space. The theatrical site has been modified in its very structure: the proscenium arch or "Italian-style" stage—an authoritarian concept, and the legacy of a class-based system of social and political hierarchy—is manipulated in various ways. Or it is simply abandoned, in order to develop a form of dance installation where the audience is invited to mingle with the dancers. Or, in still other instances, all institutional and theatrical space is abandoned, and the dance takes place in the usual sites of everyday life: malls, museums, the street, and so on.

The distinction between performance and nonperformance falls to the wayside, laying bare the process of the elaboration of the work itself. These moments of gestation are accorded special privilege between artists, who consider them among the high points of artistic life, on the same level as a fully finished performance. At other times, the audience is invited to watch, and even to partake in the development of the performance, which becomes, once again, no less important in its moment of elaboration than in its moment of presentation as performance. Dance also functions like a laboratory of creation and thought when several artists come together within a single artistic experience, which, here again, may or may not culminate in a conclusive performance. One need only think of William Forsythe's experiments with other choreographers, musicians, and playwrights; or of the encounters organized by Anne Teresa De Keersmaeker between her company, Rosas, and others, including Ictus or Aka Moon in music, or Tg Stan in theater. These encounters have resulted in performances where the studio-laboratory is seemingly opened to the audience. The processes of improvisation, structuration, and exchange within the jointly developed activities remain visible right to the end—the moment of public presentation—and, revealing the processes at work, lead the spectators into lines of thought specific to dance. A factor of temporality plays a strong role in this regard: the audience is plunged into the time of creation; in other words, into the time of the elaboration of the ideas and concepts that are called upon to produce meaning. Audience members are transported from territory to territory, the rhythm of things allowing them to feel the advent of thought in their very bodies. This sudden awareness takes place both individually and collectively. The theatrical device is the site of a gathering of consciences, the site of an opening toward a potential world, forever awaiting redefinition.

Lynda Gaudreau's works open contemporary dance to new creative processes in still a different way. Among other things,

Gaudreau questions the traditional notion of authorship—the other extremity of dance as institution. She invites other artists to contribute certain aspects to her works. Here, invitation prompts exchange, giving and establishing different relationships between artists. Themes related to quotation and authorship arise; the authority of meaning is questioned. Where does meaning come from, and how is it articulated? Is there a specific site for the attribution of meaning? These interrogations are fundamental in the era of the Internet and growing cultural hybridization due to globalization. They tie back in with ongoing reflections on carrying out transplants between bodies (animal and human), transgenics (questions of authenticity, property, identity), or regarding techniques (mechanical or cybernetic) of image reproductibility and transformation, which also impacts the human realm.[10]

Christine De Smedt also delves into such themes of individuality and collectivity in her work *9x9* (2000). Nine dancers train nine other people, chosen according to various criteria of age or occupation in different cities around the world. The "performance" corresponds to a certain number of parameters, but the expressed content changes in keeping with the individuals who take part and the groups that come together. De Smedt thereby questions the political processes at work in the groups as well as in our contemporary societies. Her research is similar to that which, particularly over the past decade, explores new forms of civil society and new manners of perceiving democracy.

Aside from dance, we have to acknowledge the existence of multiple bodily-artistic practices in a variety of fields. The visual arts have produced a large number of works, particularly since the 1960s—above all through Conceptual art, body art, happenings, performance, video, and film—that investigate research on the body. Bruce Nauman, Vito Acconci, Dan Graham, Chris Burden, and Peter Campus—to mention only a few—form a band of artists who inquire into bodily practices, the representation of the body, its staging, and its relationship to the other, using the image to question how the body is filtered through representation, its relationship to space and to the viewer in real situations. These investigations are being carried out today in photography, video, film, sculpture, and drawing, in such a way that a very large portion of artistic practices also constitute "corporal" practices; that is, they question the very identity of the physical, social, familial, biological, ethnic, sculptural, virtual, political, gendered, material, and immaterial body.

Video and film provide us with possibilities for exploring the body by reproducing it via the image, transferring modalities of the imaginary in a created or recreated space-time continuum. This research has exponential value, for there is no end to exploring the multiple combinations that the body/image association brings to the surface of consciousness. Film-based choreography in movies and video-art practices has much to teach us about the way in which the body—or bodily presence—narrativizes in itself the meaning of a cinematographic or videographic work. The treatment of the body, of bodies, bears meaning outward. Certain works stand out as exemplary: those of artists such as Gary Hill or Bill Viola, or of filmmakers such as Claire Denis, Atom Egoyan, Philippe Grandrieux, David Lynch, Abderrahmane Sissako, or Tsai Ming-liang. A filmography around concepts of the body and gestures still remains to be drawn up in order to trace the evolution of extreme dance in the history of cinema—putting us on track of the likes of Michelangelo Antonioni, Robert Bresson, John Cassevetes, Carl Dreyer, Buster Keaton, and others.

Extreme dance is also to be found in sound-based and music practices. Not only do sound and music accompany dance, but they prompt it; they bear it within themselves. The body can be seen here as a thermometer of sound, a mediator or pointer. The body is itself an instrument of percussion: the body speaks via the sound it produces or mediates. Numerous sound and music creators today are interested in these bodily potentials, which are well served by electronics, enabling numerous previously unheard-of sites for research[11].

Finally, it is important to situate within the field of extreme dance all the bodily practices currently being researched in other fields that are not necessarily artistic and that have to do with everyday life or specialized institutes, in order to see how they keep with the body's "thinking"—biotechnologies and genetics, bio-computer research, environmental ecology, architecture, urbanism, leisure, sports, medicine, psychotherapy, the social practice of dance and its integration into mainstream forms such as pop music, mass cinema, food, agriculture, cuisine, even violence. These practices as a whole and the policies and research that stem from them can be taken into consideration to understand the way the body thinks, its limits, and the scope of dance right up and into its extremities.

These several examples give an idea of the repercussions that extreme dance can have on our ways of thinking and apprehending the world of today and tomorrow. In that sense, it is indeed a laboratory of thought whose specificity lies in its capacity to focus research on the body as an instrument directly linked to a mode of thought not mediated by logos or technical knowledge. ("Every genuine instance of thinking is subtracted from the knowledge in which it is constituted."[12]) Although it is informed by it, the work on the body, or on the basis of the body, enables us to invent new attitudes of thought, new schemes, taking account of inventive and creative ("deregulated") approaches. More than ever, dance becomes a tool for developing consciousness and a means for networking sensitivities globally in an era where borders fluctuate and become more permeable—whether these borders are artistic, corporal, identity based, geographic, or even political.

[1] This essay was first published in *The Responsive Body. A Language of Contemporary Dance*, ed. Brian Webb (Banff: The Banff Centre Press, 2002), 96-108.

[2] Friedrich Nietzche, *The Gay Science: With A Prelude in Rhymes And An Appendix of Songs* (New York: Random House, [1882] 1974), 375.

[3] Giorgio Agamben, *The Coming Community*, trans. Michael Hardt (Minneapolis: Minnesota University Press, 1993), 1–3.

[4] Ibid., 64.

[5] Giorgio Agamben, "Le geste et la danse," *Revue d'esthétique* 22 (1992): 12.

[6] Gene Youngblood, *Expanded Cinema* (New York: Dutton, 1970), 41.

[7] Alain Badiou, *Handbook of Inaesthetic* (Stanford University Press, 2004), 66.

[8] Youngblood, *Expanded Cinema*, 42.

[9] Alain Badiou, *Handbook of Inaesthetic*, 66-67.

[10] See Jean-Luc Nancy, *Being Singular Plural* (Stanford: Stanford University Press, 2000); and his *L'Intrus* (Paris: Galilée, 2000).

[11] From John Cage to La Monte Young, and Alvin Lucier to, more recently, Carsten Nicolai and Ryoji Ikeda.

[12] Alain Badiou, *Handbook of Inaesthetic*, 66.

9 VARIATIONS ON THINGS AND PERFORMANCE[1]
André Lepecki

0.

The current investment in objects, and the incredible proliferation of stuff and things that we find in recent works of dance, performance, and installation art, characterizes the current performance and dance scene. In what follows, I propose that when displacing the prevalence of notions such as subject and object, performer and artwork, what emerges is the proposition for a deep link between performativity and thingliness. I offer nine preliminary theoretical variations on this phenomenon, which I believe to be less aesthetic than political.

1. The apparatus variation

In a recent essay, Giorgio Agamben made an intriguing proposition: that the world as we know it, and particularly the contemporary world, is divided into two major realms: living organisms on one side, and "apparatuses"(or *dispositifs*) on the other.[2] From the clash between these two realms a third element emerges: "subjectivity." However, in this trinity, apparatuses have the upper hand: "I shall call an apparatus literally anything that has in some way the capacity to capture, orient, determine, intercept, model, control, or secure the gestures, behaviors, opinions, or discourses of livingbeings."[3] Oddly powerful, this "anything" endowed with the capacity to capture, to model, and to control gestures and behaviors matches quite well the definition of that aesthetic-disciplinary invention of modernity, choreography, which can be understood precisely as an apparatus of capture of gestures, mobility, dispositions, body types, bodily intentions and inclinations for the sake of a spectacular display of a body's presence. But, as Agamben proceeds by listing a series of apparatuses, it becomes clear that his conception of the term goes beyond the notion of apparatus as a general system of control, and approaches instead a very concrete, and specific understanding of apparatus as a thing that commands. Indeed, Agamben's listing reveals a quasi-paranoid perception of the world, where what predominates is the omnipotence of things: "Not only therefore prisons, madhouses, the panopticon, schools, confession, factories, disciplines, juridical measures, and so forth (whose connection with power is in a certain sense evident), but also the pen, writing, literature, philosophy, agriculture, cigarettes, navigation, computers, cellular telephones..."[4]

2. Variation on the apparatus variation

It seems that Agamben's listing of commanding/controlling apparatuses could go on forever, since between pen and cigarettes, computers and cellular telephones the amount of objects that might be seen as controlling and commanding our gestures and habits, our desires and movements, is limited only by their availability in the world—particularly in "the extreme phase of capitalist development in which we live," characterized by "a massive accumulation and proliferation of apparatuses."[5] In other words: as we produce objects, we produce apparatuses that subjugate and diminish our own capacity to produce non-subjugated subjectivities. As we produce objects, we find ourselves being produced by objects. In the struggle between the living and the inorganic, it is not only as if objects are taking command—subjectivity itself is becoming a kind of objecthood: "today there is not even a single instant in which the life of individuals is not modeled, contaminated, or controlled by some apparatus."[6] It is in this sense that Agamben's definition of apparatus as a controlling thing becomes useful in order to probe the recent emergence and predominance of objects in some experimental dance. Firstly, because it uncovers a performativity in things, and secondly, because, since dance has an intimate relationship to the political and ethical question of obedience, of governing gestures, of determining movements, it is no wonder then that dance (but also performance art, thanks to its openly political verve, and particularly its concern about how objects elicit actions) must itself approach objects—since objects seem to be governing our subjectivity, seem to be subjecting us, under their apparatus-function. But perhaps, there is more to it than just control...

3. The commodity variation

Karl Marx noted that if human activity is capable of enacting corporeal transformations on matter by turning it into objects of usage (for instance, by turning a block of wood into a table), under capitalism, human activity makes objects endure a supplementary, "magical," or incorporeal transformation, where anything made for the use of humans turns into "a very strange thing" called a commodity. Guy Debord noted how in this peculiar mode of transformation, "we have the principle of commodity fetishism, the domination of society by things whose qualities are 'at the same time perceptible and imperceptible by the senses.'"[7] Debord took this principle of domination and used it to define our "society of the spectacle," which is not a society made of spectacles, but one where "the spectacle corresponds to the historical moment at which the commodity completes its colonization of social life. It is not just that the relationship to commodities is now plain to see; the world we see is the world of the commodity."[8] The political destiny of the commodity (very close, in a way, to Agamben's apparatus-thing) is, then, to complete its total dominance over social life, over the life of things, but also over somatic life, since its dominance inscribes itself deeply into bodies. Indeed, the commodity dominates not only the world of things, but also the realm of the perceptible, the imperceptible, the sensible and the infra-sensible, the domain of desiring, even the domain of dreams. The commodity governs, and so much so it even governs the very possibility of imagining governance. Moreover, the commodity governs not only subjects, but also the very life of objects, the life of matter—the life of life and the life of things. Under its domain, humans and things find their concrete openness for endless potentiality crushed or substantially diminished. Even if the commodity is a material object, its power is to make sure that things are not left in peace. The incorporeal transformation of a thing into a commodity corresponds to its entrapment within one single destiny: becoming a utilitarian object attached to an economy of excess, linked to a spectacular mode of appearing, firmly demanding "proper use," bound to capital, and aimed eventually at the trash-bin, preferably within less than six months, when it will become again a mere thing, i.e. valueless matter for capital. So perhaps, the counter-force of objects lies precisely in merely being a thing.

4. The dispossession variation

Let's propose that objects, when freed from utility, from use-value, from exchange-value, and from signification reveal their utter opaqueness, their total capacity to be fugitives from any apparatus of capture. When free, objects should gain another proper name: no longer object, no longer apparatus, no longer commodity, but simply thing. Fred Moten, theorizing on the "resistance of the object" that black radical performance always activates, remarks: "While subjectivity is defined by the subject's possession of itself and its objects, it is troubled by a dispossessive force objects exert such that the subject seems to be possessed – infused, deformed – by the object it possesses."[9] I call the dispossessive and deformative force always being exerted by any object: thing. Perhaps we need to draw from this force, learn how subjects and objects can become less like subjects and less objects and more thing.

5. The decolonizing variation

How can the performative power of things unleash vectors of subjectification away from Agamben's and Debord's generalized diagnosis of our contemporary subjectivity and objectivity as existing exclusively under the sign of subjugation and resignation before the imperial force of controlling objects, commodities, or apparatuses? How do we decolonize the violent suturing of objects and subjects under the rabid violence of colonialism, capitalism, and racism (understood as forces intrinsic to commodity-apparatuses)? Towards the end of his essay, Agamben proposes "profanation" as an act of resistance that would "restore the thing to the free use of men."[10] I find this solution objectionable, with "men" affirming their power over "things" by using them as they wish. The violence in this proposition forecloses the recognition of a radical alterity in things. I see some recent dance recognizing precisely the necessity to enact an ethics of things. Such an ethics implies being with things without forcing them into constant utilitarianism. This is why in much recent dance where objects are central, objects are not used as signifying elements, nor as proxies for the subject of enunciation or for the dancing body, but often objects appear simply to enact purely referential situations, where dancers and stuff remain within a kind of synchronous "along-sidedness" freed from utilitarianism, signification, and domination. Even freed from being "art."

6. The ethical variation

How does one engage with the ethics, poetics, and politics that a thing's radical alterity proposes? How to enact what Silvia Benso called "an ontological attitude whose implications border on ethics in its recognition of the multilayeredness of things, and in its intimation to an act of listening, caring, attention to their alterity"?[11] A possible answer is to say that perhaps a becoming-thing might not be such a bad destiny for subjectivity after all. As we look around us, it certainly seems a better option than continuing to carry on living and being under the name of the "human." A thing reminds us that living organisms, the inorganic as well as the organic, and that third produced by their clash called subjectivity, all need to be liberated from that subjugating force named the apparatus-commodity, a force that crushes them all into impoverished, or sad, or docile, or cowardly, or limited, or utilitarian modes of living. And a thing (the thingly element in any object and subject) may actually be that which offers us vectors and lines of flight away from the imperial sovereignty of colonizing apparatuses. In order to do so, things would have to be left in peace, allowed to become-thing once more—so as to actively counter their subjugation to a particularly detestable regime of the object (the commodity-apparatus regime) and a particularly detestable regime of the subject (the personhood regime) that imprisons both objects and subjects in mutual captivity. Perhaps some recent dance has been preoccupied precisely with this mutual liberation: of things and of bodies, of subjectivities and objects. In this mutual, necessary struggle, maybe we need to follow Mario Perniola's advice and "place our trust not in the divine or the human but in the mode of being of the thing."[12]

7. The anti-personhood variation

Mark Franko reminds us of the constitutive force of the "personal" in Renaissance dance, a force we can see traversing the whole history of Western theatrical dance: "The dancer's own person is the ultimate and single object of praise and dispraise in the dance." This is why "the dancing body must in turn display the admirable self for praise and index this display as praiseworthy, elicit praise."[13] Consequence of this foundational, constitutive element of personhood and self-centeredness in dance: is a blocking of the dancer's desire to become thing, to become animal, obfuscated as it is by the emphatic need to constantly affirm and reaffirm its personhood and its self. In the

1990s and early 2000s, some important experiments by Vera Mantero, Boris Charmatz, and Xavier Le Roy, among others, seem to have privileged a becoming-animal as a line of flight for dance. (Butoh had a similar political-performative impetus, becoming-animal as rejection of the human and of the person, Hijikata: "I adore rib cages but, again, it seems to me that a dog's rib cage is superior to mine.") It appears that now a line-of-flight can be found in dance's embracing of a becoming-thing. It is fundamental here to find other devices of visibility, where the object and the person does not occupy a center—thus other spaces must be invented, involving the viewer, dissolving the stage, scrambling distinctions. One of these new regimes of visibility is the installation in performance, where "the open horizon of the installations" leads exactly to this "spatial dissolution of the work of art,"[14] destroying the work as art to reveal the work as a "thing." Here, we can remind ourselves of Heidegger's formulation on the performativity of things: not to be, but to gather.

8. The lines-of-flight variation

Of course objects have always been present on dance stages. Rosalind Krauss once wrote: "a large number of postwar European and American sculptors became interested both in theater and in the extended experience of time which seemed part of the conventions of the stage. From this interest came some sculpture to be used as props in productions of dance and theater, some to function as surrogate performers, and some to act as the on-stage generators of scenic effects."[15] But now it is not sculpture created by visual artists that we see appearing on dance stages—but things, stuff that choreographers drag into the scene, precisely not to make a scene, but to create an environment. Moreover, things are used in ways totally different from how Krauss had described the use of sculptures in theatrical and dance events. Today, objects do appear, but not as "properties" (or "props" — as objects are significantly called in theater parlance), nor as generators of "scenic effects," or "surrogate performers" (i.e. as puppets). Rather, objects and bodies take place alongside each other and... and sometimes little else takes place. This simple act of just placing things in their quiet, still, and concrete thingliness alongside bodies, not necessarily together with the dancers, but just alongside, effects a substantial event: to underline the thin line simultaneously separating and joining bodies and things, to delineate a zone of indiscernibility between the corporeal, the subjectile and the thingly. This operation is not Duchampian, in the sense that it wants to affirm the everyday object as art, once the object is signed by an artist or brought into an art context. Instead, this operation wants to affirm the object as thing, to liberate the thing captured in the object that had been trapped by instrumental reasoning and artistic apparatuses.

To invest in things, not as proxies of the body, nor as signifying or representative elements of a narrative, but as co-partners in a sheer, co-determinant, co-presence—as co-extensive entities in the field of matter—is to activate a fundamental change in the relationship between objects and their aesthetic effects (in dance, theatre, performance art, and installation art). This change is the political activation of the thing so that it may do what it does best—to dispossess objects and subjects from their traps called apparatus, commodity, person and self. When this dispossession takes place within particularly involving environments, called installations, a reversibility takes place where "it is the installation that feels the visitor... penetrates him" (as Perniola would say), turning the visitor then also into a thing.

9. The final quote variation

"Therefore, when I give myself as thing, I do not mean at all to offer myself to the exploitation and benefit of others. I do not offer myself to the other but to the impersonal movement that at the same time displaces the other from himself and allows him in his turn to give himself as thing and to take me as thing."[16]

1 This text was commissioned by Lilia Mestre and Elke Van Campenhout and a first version was published in *IT, Thingly Variations in Space* (Brussels: MOKUM, 2011).

2 Giorgio Agamben, *What is an Apparatus? And Other Essays* (Stanford: Stanford University Press, 2009).

3 Agamben, *What is an Apparatus?*, 14.

4 Agamben, *What is an Apparatus?*, 14.

5 Agamben, *What is an Apparatus?*, 15.

6 Agamben, *What is an Apparatus?*, 15.

7 Guy Debord, *The Society of Spectacle* (New York: Zone Books, [1967] 1994), 26.

8 Debord, *The Society of Spectacle*, 29.

9 Fred Moten, *In the Break: The Aesthetic of the Black Radical Tradition* (Minneapolis: University of Minnesota Press, 2003), 1.

10 Agamben, *What is an Apparatus?*, 18.

11 Silvia Benso, *The Face of Things: A Different Side of Ethics* (Slbany: State University of New York, 2000), 146.

12 Mario Perniola, *The Sex Appeal of the Inorganic: Philosophies of Desire in Modern World* (London: Continuum, 2004), 110.

13 Mark Franko, *The Dancing Body in Renaissance Choreography* (Birmingham, AL.: Summa, 1986), 22.

14 Perniola, *The Sex Appeal of the Inorganic*, 103.

15 Rosalind Krauss, *Passages in Modern Sculpture* (Cambridge: The MIT Press, 1981), 204.

16 Perniola, *The Sex Appeal of the Inorganic*, 109.

COME HOME CHARLEY PATTON[1]
Ralph Lemon

An Incomplete Chronology

1863   Emancipation Proclamation

1865   Thirteenth Amendment formally abolishes slavery.

1933   Arne Bontemp's *A Summer Tragedy* is published.

1938   Blues artist Robert Johnson dies of poisoning in Three
        Forks, Mississippi.

1947   Under President Truman the phrase "civil rights" moves
        into common political parlance replacing the phrase
        "the Negro question."

1948   Gandhi is assassinated in Delhi, India. I am born in 1952.

1953   James Baldwin's *Go Tell It on the Mountain* is published.

1954   Supreme Court outlaws school segregation in *Brown v.*
        Board of Education.

1955   Fourteen-year-old Emmett Till is lynched in Money,
        Mississippi, for reportedly flirting with a white woman
        in a small-town grocery store. I take my first bus ride
        south in 1956.

1957   Congress passes first civil rights act since reconstruction.

1957   Jill Johnston, dance and art critic, writes her third critical
        essay on dance, titled "Abstractions in Dance."

1958   Merce Cunningham premieres *Summerspace*, music by
        Morton Feldman, set by Robert Rauschenberg.

1959   Bob Dylan moves to Minneapolis from Hibbing, Minnesota.

1960   Robert Dunn begins a composition course at the
        Cunningham Studio.

1961   Simone Forti makes *Huddle*, a community body-based
        work.

1961   Freedom Bus Rides begins, testing a recent Supreme Court ruling for the desegregation of interstate travel through the south.

1962   First Concert of Dance by the Judson Dance Theater.

1963   June. Medgar Evers, NAACP director in Mississippi, is shot and killed in his driveway in Jackson.

1963   August. March on Washington. Martin Luther King's "I Have a Dream" speech.

1963   September. Four teenage girls die in a church bombing at Sixteenth Street Baptist Church in Birmingham, Alabama.

1963   Nina Simone reaches No. 2 on the UK charts with a song from the hippie musical, Hair, "Ain't Got No/I Got Life."

1964   Lucinda Childs makes her *Carnation* solo. Steve Paxton creates solo *Flat*, Bruce Nauman has first performance of *Wall-Floor Positions*, and president LBJ signs Civil Rights Act of 1964.

1964   Also Freedom Summer. The voters' registration drive in the South. Chaney, Good man, Schwerner brutally murdered in Philadelphia, Mississippi.

1965   Trisha Brown makes *Homemade*, a solo with a camera on her back. In July of 1965 Congress passes Voting Rights   Act.

1966   Yvonne Rainer makes the seminal *Trio A*.

1966   (Little-known) Ben Chester White, who had worked most of his life as caretaker on a plantation, who had no involvement in civil rights work, is murdered by Klansman who thought they could divert attention from a civil rights march by killing a random black man.

1968   March. Merce Cunningham premieres *Rainforest*, music by David Tudor, silver clouds by Andy Warhol.

1968   April. Martin Luther King is assassinated in Memphis, Tennessee, while working with the embattled sanitation workers' strike.

1972   Steve Paxton instigates Contact Improvisation.

1975   I attend my first dance class with Nancy Hauser at the Guild of Performing Arts in Minneapolis, Minnesota.

1976   My daughter, Chelsea, is born.

January 2001

I travel to Cincinnati, Ohio, to take pictures of the place where I was born. The whole time I am thinking about the American South, well aware that Cincinnati is not the South, but across the Ohio River is.

February 2001

I travel to Sapelo Island, Georgia, to discover something authentic about the American South. "We are not Americans," they tell me. "We are Sapeloans." I discover that Sapelo Island is too far south (for my purposes; and in the ocean). I also discover boneyards there, whole trees falling where they stand, due to beach erosion, becoming skeletal. And I hear rumors of an existing Ring Shout dance called the Buzzard Lope tucked away in some old Geechee man's body. A very interesting place and also very abstract.

May 2001

My daughter and I reenact the Freedom Bus Ride of 1961. Thirteen original Riders, seven black and six white people, including John Lewis, left Washington DC, for New Orleans on two buses, a Trailways bus and a Greyhound bus, and traveled through the South testing a recent Supreme Court ruling on the desegregation of interstate travel, the stations' waiting rooms, restrooms, and restaurants. Our reenactment marks the fortieth anniversary. This research turns out not to be too far south, and not too abstract, and in fact, sits perfectly in the middle, geographically and in time. So it seems.

Overview

After a Chinese dinner on May 3, 2001, keeping to the historical map and research itinerary whenever possible, we left Washington DC for our first stop, Richmond, Virginia, arriving on May 4.

After a couple days in Richmond visiting friends and sightseeing, we took another bus to Danville, Virginia, the first place the original Riders were refused integrated service. From Danville to Charlotte, North Carolina, where there occurred the first arrest of one of the Riders due to, of all things, a shoeshine.

To Rock Hill, South Carolina, site of the first incident of physical violence. A mob of twenty attacked the group, and John Lewis was the first to be hit as he approached the white waiting room.

From Rock Hill to Atlanta, Georgia, where the Riders met with Martin Luther King on Mother's Day (and my daughter and I spent four days with my family).

From Atlanta to Anniston, Alabama, where forty years ago the Klan was waiting and one of the buses was fire-bombed. The group took another bus and continued the rides. Another group on another bus arrived in Anniston and were also brutally attacked.

To Birmingham where the first group of Riders was replaced because of the violence at Anniston. And another group of ten was arrested in Birmingham and spent the night in jail. They were literally driven out of town by Police Chief "Bull" O'Connor, who left the group stranded on the Tennessee border.

To Montgomery. Ah, Montgomery. Where, according to John Lewis: "Out of nowhere, from every direction, came people. White people. Men, women and children. Dozens of them. Hundreds of them. Out of alleys, out of side streets, around the corners of office buildings, they emerged from everywhere, all at once, as if they'd been let out of a gate. To this day, I don't know where all those people came from."

Where John Lewis almost died. Where James Zwerg, a young

white man, was beaten and never attempted to defend himself, even as his face was stomped into the ground. "Kill the niggerloving son of a bitch!" They sang.

To Jackson, Mississippi, where over the next several months wave after wave of Riders were eventually marched off to Parchman Penitentiary, three-hundred in total.

From Jackson my daughter and I continued to New Orleans, the original final destination of the Riders, where I bought a used trumpet before flying home, a Bach.

Throughout our modern and air-conditioned bus ride, we made side trips: to Greensboro, North Carolina, site of the cataclysmic Woolworth's sit-in of 1960, "the first sit-in," and to Durham, North Carolina, where there was an important but little publicized sit-in in 1957. There were side trips to visit family in North Carolina, South Carolina, and Georgia.

A side trip to Selma, Alabama, to ritually walk the Edmund Pettus Bridge, site of "Bloody Sunday," the beginning of a seminal civil rights march in 1965.

We had ritually structured events in all the mapped Greyhound bus stations and in the spot where the Greyhound bus stopped, burning on Route 21, outside Anniston, Alabama. At Kelly Ingram Park, in the rain, scene of protesting children, police dogs and fire hoses of 1963. And the Sixteenth Street Baptist Church in Birmingham. I bowed in the driveway of 2332 Margaret Walker Alexander Drive in Jackson where Medgar Evers was assassinated.

I found confused and fleeting ways to make my presence known in these highly charged spaces that are not the same spaces of forty years ago. That have elusive memories. But the civil rights movement did happen. There are photographs and books. Taxi drivers, white and black, are useful historians, "Where did this happen, where did that happen? Hell, I don't think I remember." "This used to be a thriving black neighborhood, commercial area." Or "This was Klan country, all back in the hills there, where everyone seemed to be named Adams."

Now, many of the Interstate motels, Days Inns, gas stations in Georgia, Alabama, and Mississippi are owned and operated by Indian émigrés.

Alabama is scenically one of the most beautiful places I've traveled.

Every event or structured activity was documented in order to contain the immediate moments. Capturing evidence that these personal events/actions did happen, and with some specificity. These events were not designed for an audience, at least not a conventional audience. The self-consciousness of these private acts created a radical pedestrian quality. Hyper-inconspicuous. I did not want to disrupt the communal ecology of these spaces. There were, however, installations created in all of our motel rooms for the very certain audience of housekeepers. I left stamped American-flag postcards for them to respond, with a promise to pay them fifty dollars if they did. I only heard back from one motel, from an Indian émigré housekeeper, named Neal.

Throughout the trip Chelsea made sure we ate at least twice a day. And most strangers assumed that she was my sister, my girlfriend, or maybe my wife.

———

Process Repetition II

More notes on the twentieth century

September 2002

I watch a pirated video of Bruce Nauman's 1964–65 *Wall-Floor Positions* for first time.

Letter to Bruce Nauman's Studio

There is much I could say about this request, there are many layers but I'll try to keep it simple.

I first saw *Wall-Floor Positions* at the Whitney Biennial, what, eight years ago? I was "floored." I've been experimenting with movement for most of my life and viewing this performance/body work/film/video stunned most of what thought I knew about moving. I did some research and discovered that Nauman did indeed make "dances," sort of.

Nauman's "dances" from the sixties are fascinating to me for their commitment and rigor to an "amateur" movement/art/dance perspective, the simplicity and obvious commitment to the task, and in how they differ from the work of the Judson Church dance canon, "postmodern dance," of the same period. That his "dances" surfaced to be more about being human (and untrained) than about anything else.

And there was/is the important time placement of these works. If my reading serves me correctly, Nauman created a version of *Wall-Floor Positions* in 1965(?), the same year Congress passed the Voting Rights Act and the same year Trisha Brown created *Homemade*, a seminal postmodern dance work. The 1968 film version of *Wall-Floor Positions* was made the year of Martin Luther King Jr.'s assassination. These seemingly disparate events are a defining and fraught part of my history as an artist and racial being.

What specifically interests me about *Wall-Floor Positions* beyond it's obvious relationship to art and the body, the beautifully ordinary and rigorous movement statement that it is, is the not so obvious parallel realities of a period in time, of "a white art freedom" and the black civil rights movement. Body as art material (I would posit that at the time Nauman embodied this concept/movement gloriously). And the body as invisible chattel. Where and how did these forces intersect beyond an inanimate sociology of walls and floors? Was that possible? Does it matter? The proximity of these things is of course precarious.

My partner in this potential venture is Djédjé Djédjé Gervais, a dance artist from Côte d'Ivoire, West Africa. I've been collaborating with Djédjé since 1997. Since our first meeting, our bodies have taken on some very interesting and useful ideas about American "modernity" as tradition, and West African "tradition" as something always modern. We are coming to separate but equal, simple terms. I could go on but won't.

My hope is that Nauman will send us detailed instructions to the original work, or new instructions that we would then follow. Our plan and participation in this "re-creation," is to place our physical history and body art politics in what I feel is a historically major movement work about a body negotiating a wall and a floor. In how that work is representative of now, and perhaps what it represented then. And it would be a "re-creation," not a "translation." Of course Djédjé and I bring different bodies, training, understandings, (unstable) cultures, and time elements to what Nauman originally intended—all the better. After all, it's 2002, not 1965/68. Nevertheless, it will essentially remain what Nauman structured. That is my hope.

My only request, beyond permission to recreate Wall-Floor Positions, is to have a free-standing wall so that Djédjé and I could perform the work simultaneous on either side of the wall, holding a conversation with Nauman's intended wall and floor, and with each other. Nauman, if it interests him, could also newly structure what this "simultaneity" is/should be.

As far as crediting the performance, we would be performing a "Nauman" work. Unless there's a more specific credit Nauman desires.

Let me know if I've left anything out. Thank you. R

What May Have Been Left Out Story
January 7, 2003
"She's not well but says she can't wait to meet you," Yolanda says over the phone, from an office in the basement of the Museum of Contemporary Art in Chicago. "She says you sound like an interesting man with an interesting project. Yes, an interview will be fine... She's still haunted by the story and still needs to repeat it, word for word. 'People need to be aware,' she's always saying. You know, she founded her own theater group called The Emmett Till Players, a youth theater

group that produces civil rights–themed plays here in Chicago."

Mamie Till-Mobley's father moved his family to Chicago from Webb, Mississippi, just after she was born, to get away from the cotton fields and the oak trees.

Mamie Till-Mobley died of heart failure in Chicago two hours after our Chicago contact had spoken with her about my interview request, two days after David Thomson and I arrive to begin a modest (research) workshop, one about migration and the stage (at the Museum of Contemporary Art).

We attend her wake on the same Friday we had planned to interview her, at the Apostolic Church of God on the city's south side, near Robert's Temple Church of God where Emmett Till's cathartic, battered body was famously viewed in September 1955.

On a freezing gray Chicago morning, Mamie Till-Mobley lay like a queen, silent, with a picture of her son pinned inside her coffin.

The next day, during a break in the empty theater of the museum, I visit the upstairs' permanent collection gallery and am struck by a work of David Hammons, titled "Praying for Safety." A mixed-media work consisting of two (found?) wooden statues of Thai monks kneeling in prayer pose, perhaps twenty feet apart, with a delicate piece of thread stretched between their praying hands. A safety pin delicately balanced in the middle of the taut thread. A spiritual art pun, I thought.

Back in the theater I tell David that I want to suspend what we had been working on earlier in the day. I don't know, I say, standing on the dimly lit stage, I'm kind of emotional today and I'd like to work on something new.

After a couple hours we come up with this physical script, memorial, and quote:

Two (black?) men with a forty-five(ish)-foot cotton string, the width of a proscenium stage. One man starts on stage, two feet out from the farthest downstage left wing; the other man is in the downstage right wing, not seen by audience. Each holds onto one end of the string, which lies loose along the length of floor.

At a given cue they simultaneously begin tying the string around their waists, pulling the string taunt. Delicate bowknots that can be loosened with a quick pull from one end of the string. Their timing must be immaculate. The audience sees only one man in tying action. Once they have finished tying the string around their waists the man onstage walks backwards, offstage, pulling the man offstage, two feet onstage. With the men now reversed, they untie the string and repeat the same delicate tying structure with the string around their necks, reversing, then their penises (the pants are pulled down at this point), reversing, and then their wrists. In that order. The whole action lasts about three minutes.

Of, course the neck and penis parts are more loaded, and potentially literal, especially in how the men are tying their own nooses or how the penis is pulled erect, but by the precise timing required and everydayness of the scripted approach, and with the last image/action of the bound wrists, where one man is led more humanly, tenderly, overtly, the string and meaning evaporate.

It will take hours and hours of practice, months. The two men need to be profoundly connected in responding to one other and to the string. The timing is the dance. The rest is immaterial. The point? Balance/imbalance. And then the few or many layers of human interaction explored: guidance, power, sex, death, race, love, partnership, and danger. (At one point in the process David tied the string around his testicles, instead of his penis, for safety reasons, he said, completely negating the point). A lot to be explored here. By fall 2004 I will have worked it so much that maybe it will no longer have an inkling of stage life. As it should be.

Opening Story

September 21, 2004

> Describe it. Whatever it is, describe it. If you can describe it,
> you may be able to control it. You may be able to answer the
> tyranny of what seems to be external.

—James Baldwin

And then Katherine who's been reading Baldwin, says, "He also said this: in order to write about a place you have to be able to 'sit down and turn your back to it.'"

Yes, James Baldwin, yes, I say.

"And he said this... 'I think all artists are religious.'"

Oh my Jesus! I say. (Borrowing a line from some person and or situation in almost every single trip I had ever taken down South.)

And then I quote Shakespeare, I can't help myself (although many years later Katherine informs me it's not Shakespeare, not at all, it's Wordsworth):

"... When the light of sense goes out, but with a flash that has revealed the invisible world."

The lights go down...

I imagine walking on stage, into a spotlight, holding a trumpet, my grandfather's trumpet, which I've borrowed from my uncle Trent, without getting shot. And Mattie was wrong; it was in his attic. (And Trent was once a boy full of innocence, would take a BB gun and shoot robins and sparrows out of the trees, the fat ones, would make a fire out in the field and feather, skin, and roast the little fat birds on sticks, eating the breasts.)

I begin by saying this: To dance about a place you have to...

And then I turn my back to the audience, ask a stagehand for a microphone and stand, and now amplified, continue (with little sense of humor).

Will it be useful talking about what's about to happen, or might we leave it to the wordless thought process of the body, my body? I ask.

I suppose we could talk about the theater of what's about to happen more easily than the rest. Because at this moment, right here, now, what else is there? I'm here on stage and you're out there, formally waiting for something to happen, a story. So let's start with theater, that kind of body.

I began with dance as biological physical theater, the theater of my body forming language. I now reside in my dance as a terrifically broad question of existence or a series of questions of existence. These impossible questions become my practice. (The sound of this last sentence comes off very pat.)

And then Katherine... Katherine as Mattie, as Mamie Till-Mobley, as Memphis Minnie, as Mrs. Helen Kent, as Frank Stokes, as Mississippi Fred Mcdowell, as one-hundred-year-old Walter Carter, as Bruce Nauman, as James Baldwin... planted, stands and calls out from the audience, "Questions? What are these impossible questions? Maybe you can't answer them, but do you have to obscure them? What would happen if you stopped right there where you are, turned around to face us, started over and articulated them in detail? Would that be so bad?"

That would be awful, I think to myself, pretending to be a little shocked that Katherine has interrupted me. No, I say, I won't stop, I can't stop, and I won't turn around; it is my passion. (And now I begin to raise my voice.) And in defense of my passions, I obscure. I obscure because my real life is spirited, yes, but also sloppy and mundane. I obscure from you most of what I eat, sleep, and shit... I share and show only what I find possible to construct, think, imagine, (mask?) outside of the prosaic dailiness of my existence. I share and show a bunch of deliberately different questions to the audiences outside of my own private thinking and questioning. These public questions, questions developed because of an audience, are questions I can direct, and articulate, fictively. I do my job, my work, and by working obscure my human fragility, showing only the fiction of my fears, if I so choose.

So maybe before there are questions, any questions, there is only discursive thinking. Life, unpackaged, unpresentable. Voiceless. And by obscuring I'm allowed to have a voice...

The audience applauds.

Now, may I continue? I say, quite moved by this response.

"Yes, please, go on; I'd like to hear the rest," Katherine, she, he, they say.

I begin with the body, no way around it. The body as place, memory, culture, and as a vehicle for a cultural language.

And so of course I'm in a current state of the wonderment of the politics of form. That I can feel both emotional outrageousness with my body as a memory map, an emotional geography of a particular American identity, and that I can reflect on empirical design. How mining a charged history can be in contradiction to a formalist art process and the separation that has to happen, transforming a culturally inherited abstract rage into art (play), a sharing. Changing the fundamental natures of race, art, and rage as I understand them.

My present American conflict becomes more internalized. Ludwig Wittgenstein, from a family of Christians, who considered himself a Jew, "my people," he called them, who no doubt had little practical use for jargon—words like race, culture, and rage—offered that there is no equivalent between what seems to be the case and what is the case. Only the tension prevails. What shape to give this tension interests me a great deal. An interest beyond race, cultural politics (art?), and maybe even rage, which seems very much aligned with love, in how they both have aspects of the divine. Although love is supposed to transcend empathic curiosity. Is supposed to.

What am I trying to say?

(At this point there is music, over the sound system, a theme song

317

from the epic western movie How the West Was Won, romantic American landscape music, soothing…)

OK, so let's say that art, as most of us like to consider it, is beyond the mire of a soul's unfiltered messiness. But art, as I appreciate it, is also not confined to transformation; it does not triumph over all. Sometimes, at its best, it sits in shit, nonfiction. And poor. Also possibly fake.

But then what is it?

Meaning is always constituted. Basically, whatever it is it should have a beginning and an ending that allow an audience, a witness like you, to come and to go, to walk away appreciating or not appreciating an experience clearly not your own, which is why you can love it or hate it or feel nothing at all.

Otherwise it's desk art, faultlessly private, or a luminous and barely seen "Living Room Dance," absolute and incontrovertible acts. Sub Rosa. Or audaciously bold and inversely defined:

After the September 11 attacks I told a friend I thought those jumping from the buildings were like dancers. She was outraged and I explained. Dancers, I said, that's how I identify with them. Bodies, unbounded, in space, giant space, and the unknown. For me, letting my body fall onto a stage has always been a brutal consideration… until now. And then I pause. And turn around facing them. Am speechless. How the West Was Won fades, to silence.

Silence. And more silence…

Beautiful and interminable.

I so wish I could blow this trumpet, I think to myself.

---

[1] These fragments are excerpted from Ralph Lemon, *Come home Charley Patton* (Middleton: Wesleyan University Press, 2013), the finale of his Geography Trilogy, after *Geography: Art, Race, Exile and Tree: Belief, Culture, Balance* published respectively in 2000 and 2004 at Wesleyan University Press.

BIOGRAPHIES

Alexandra Baudelot is an independent curator and art critic. She founded and directed the art space Rosascape in Paris, and, since 2012, is co-director of Les Laboratoires d'Aubervilliers. She is a frequent contributor and advisor to performances and dance festivals.

Michel Bernard, PhD in Philosophy, is Professor Emeritus in Theater and Choreographic Aesthetics, and founder of the dance program at Paris 8 University. He is author of numerous essays and books including *Le corps* (Seuil, 1972) and *Critique des fondements de l'éducation ou généalogie du pouvoir et ou de l'impouvoir d'un discours* (Chiron, 1988).

Jérôme Bel lives in Paris and works worldwide. Bel's works, from *Nom donné par l'auteur* (1994) to Disabled Theater (2012) with the company THEATRE HORA, have toured internationally. www.jeromebel.fr

Dominique Brun is a dancer, choreographer, and Laban notator. She co-founded the collective La Salamandre (1981-88) and the Quatuor Albrecht Knust (1993-2001). She created a partial reconstruction of Nijinsky's Rite of Spring for the film *Coco Chanel & Stravinsky* by Jan Kounen (2008). Her diptyque *Selon et d'après Le Sacre du printemps de Nijinski* will premiere in 2014.

Choreographer **Jonathan Burrows** is a former Royal Ballet dancer whose duets with composer Matteo Fargion have been invited widely internationally. Commissions include work for Sylvie Guillem, Ballett Frankfurt, and William Forsythe's Motionbank project. He has been Guest Professor at universities in London, Hamburg, Berlin,

Gent, and Giessen and his *A Choreographer's Handbook* is available from Routledge.

Boris Charmatz is a dancer, choreographer, and director of the Musée de la danse in Rennes. His pieces include *Aatt enen tionon* (1996) and *enfant* (2011), and he worked as a performer, most recently with A. Teresa De Keersmaeker and Tino Sehgal. He co-authored *undertraining* with Isabelle Launay and *Emails 2009-2010* with Jérôme Bel (Les presses du réel, 2002; 2013). www.museedeladanse.org – www.borischarmatz.org

Yvane Chapuis is an art historian and co-directed Les Laboratoires d'Aubervilliers (2001-2009) where she curated experimental projects in dance, theater, literature, visual arts, and edited the Journal des laboratoires. Her editing projects include *Le Musée Précaire Albinet de Thomas Hirschhorn* (2004-05) and *Le catalogue raisonné de Jérôme Bel* (2008). She is currently head of the research department at the Haute École de Théâtre, Switzerland.

Bojana Cvejić is a performance theorist and maker based in Brussels. She holds a PhD from the Centre for Research in Modern European Philosophy, London, and teaches at various dance and performance programs in Europe. Cvejić is a co-founding member of TkH editorial collective (http://www.tkh-generator.net) and most recently published *En Attendant & Cesena: A Choreographer's Score*, co-written with A.T. De Keersmaeker (Brussels: Mercator, 2013).

Anne Collod is a French dancer and choreographer. Co-founder of the Quatuor Albrecht Knust, she pursues her own work since 2004, focusing on issues of reinterpretation and the utopias of the collective. She received a Bessie Award in 2009 for her reinterpretation of Halprin's major work *Parades & Changes* (1965).

Franz Anton Cramer is Senior Researcher with the Inter-University Centre for Dance Berlin. From 2007 to 2013 he was directeur de programme at the Collège international de philosophie in Paris. Collaborative projects include the online journal *Media – Archive – Performance* (www.performap.de) and *Dialogue franco-allemand sur le spectacle théâtral* (www.transfabrik.com).

Mark Franko (Temple University) is editor of *Dance Research Journal* (Cambridge University Press) and the Oxford Studies in Dance Theory book series. Franko received the 2011 Award for Outstanding Dance Scholarship from the Congress on Research in Dance. His most recent book is: *Martha Graham in Love and War* (2012).

Isabelle Ginot is professor in the dance department at Paris 8 University, and a Feldenkreis practitioner. Her early works focused on the analysis of contemporary dance. She now works on somatic practices in a political and social environment.

Laurent Goumarre is a journalist, critic, producer of the weekday program RenDez-Vous-Journal de la Culture on Radio France Culture, and the host of the TV broadcast Entrée Libre on France 5. He is also the deputy programming director of Lyon Dance Biennal, and a dance writer for *Art Press*. He has written on the work of the choreographer La Ribot and theater director Pascal Rambert.

Miguel Gutierrez, a dance and music artist based in Brooklyn, has been making solo and group pieces since 2000, with a variety of artists under the moniker Miguel Gutierrez and the Powerful People. His work, characterized by the immersive quality of the attentive state that it imposes on the audience, centers around enduring philosophical questions about desire, longing, and the search for meaning. www.miguelgutierrez.org

Simon Hecquet is a dancer and a founding member of the Quatuor Knust. With Sabine Prokhoris, he directed the film *Ceci n'est pas une danse chorale* (2004), published *Fabriques de la danse* (2008; syndicat de la critique award), and created *"Elle m'avait pas dit tout ça..."* (2013, Montpellier Danse festival).

Jenn Joy, PhD, teaches at Rhode Island School of Design and is scholar-in-residence at Danspace Project. Recent writing appears in *DANCE* (Whitechapel/MIT Press, 2012), *BOMB, BLEED, Movement Research Performance Journal*, and her book, *The Choreographic*, is forthcoming from MIT Press

Bojana Kunst is a philosopher, dramaturge, and performance theoretician. She is a professor at the Institute for Applied Theatre Studies in Justus Liebig University Giessen, where she is directing an international master program in Choreography and Performance. Her most recent publication is *Artist at Work, Closeness of Art and Capitalism* (Ljubljana: Maska, 2013).

Isabelle Launay is professor in the dance department at Paris 8 University. She frequently collaborates with artists in the field of contemporary dance. Launay co-wrote *undertraining – on a contemporary dance* with Boris Charmatz (Les Presses du réel, 2002).

Ralph Lemon is a dancer, choreographer, writer, and visual artist. He currently serves as the Artistic Director of Cross Performance, a company dedicated to the creation of cross-cultural and cross-disciplinary performance.

André Lepecki is associate professor in the department of Performance Studies at New York University. His is the author of *Exhausting Dance: Performance and the Politics of Movement*

(Routledge, 2006) and editor of *DANCE* (Whitechapel; MIT, 2012).

Xavier Le Roy has worked as a dancer and choreographer since 1991. Through his solo works such as *Self Unfinished* (1998) and *Product of Circumstances*(1999), he has opened new perspectives in the field of choreographic art. More recently, his group piece *low pieces* (2011) and *Retrospective* (2012) produce situations that explore the relationship between audience/performers, and the production of subjectivities.

Laurence Louppe (1938-2012) was an influential author, critic, and dance historian working on the aesthetics of dance and visual arts. She taught in France and internationally, including the Université du Quebec, Montréal and P.A.R.T.S., Brussels.

Boyan Manchev is a philosopher, Professor at the New Bulgarian University, guest Professor at the Sofia University, and at the HZT (UdK Berlin) and former Vice-President of the International College of Philosophy in Paris. His recent publications include *Logic of the Political* (Sofia, 2012), *Miracolo* (Milano, 2011), and *L'altération du monde: Pour une esthétique radicale* (Paris, 2009).

Erin Manning is a philosopher, visual artist, and dancer. She holds a University Research Chair in Relational Art and Philosophy at the Faculty of Fine Arts, Concordia University, Montréal, and is the director of the SenseLab (www.senselab.ca). She is the author of many publications on movement and philosophy and frequently collaborates with Brian Massumi. http://www.erinmovement.com

Julie Perrin teaches in the dance department at Paris 8 University. She published *Projet de la matière – Odile Duboc: Mémoire(s) d'une œuvre chorégraphique* (Centre national de la danse;

Les presses du réel, 2007) and *Figures de l'attention. Cinq essais sur la spatialité en danse* (Les presses du réel, 2012).

Chantal Pontbriand is a contemporary art curator and critic. She founded and edited *PARACHUTE* magazine, and directed the Festival International de Nouvelle Danse, Montréal. Pontbriand is currently associate professor at the Sorbonne-Paris IV. Her book, *The Contemporary, the Common: Art in a Globalizing World* was recently published at Sternberg Press.

Céline Roux holds a PhD in Art History and is an independent researcher working on performative practices in the French choreographic field. She is the author of *Danse(s) performative(s)* (L'Harmattan, 2007). Next to her academic work, she initiates workshops in various contexts.

Noémie Solomon holds a PhD from New York University and is currently a Mellon Postdoctoral Fellow at McGill University where she teaches dance and performance theory. Her writing and translations have been published in *Dance Research Journal*, *TDR*, *Planes of Composition*, and *Perform Repeat Record*.

Mårten Spångberg is a performance related artist living and working in Stockholm. He has been active as performer and creator since 1994, and has since 1999 created his own choreographies, from solos to larger scale works, which have toured internationally. He directed the MA program in choreography at the University of Dance in Stockholm from 2008 to 2012. In 2011, he published *Spangbergianism*.

Myriam Van Imschoot is a Brussels-based artist. Her interest lies in the performative potential of archives, documents, and landscapes, and the construction of alternative historiographies through them in performance, video, or installation. Currently she works on a cycle of works that deal with yodeling, crying, and waving. myriamvanimschoot.wordpress.com

Christophe Wavelet co-founded the Quatuor Knust (1993-2001). He collaborated on numerous international exhibitions, conferences, and publications, as a curator, scholar, and critic. He was the artistic director of LiFE, a cross-disciplinary and transnational contemporary art venue (2005-2010). As a fellow of the Akademie Schloss Solitude in 2011-2013, he is working on the French translation of essays written by Brazilian artist Helio Oiticica.

ACKNOWLEDGMENTS

This book is published in conjunction with
DANSE: A French-American Festival of Performance and Ideas
Presented in New York from May 1st to May 18, 2014.

Major sponsors:
Institut français, Ministère de la Culture et Communication, Société des auteurs et compositeurs dramatiques (SACD), and Cultural Services of the French Embassy in the United States in partnership with FACE (French American Cultural Exchange)

Thanks to Antonin Baudry, Cultural Counselor and the team of the Cultural Services in New York.

With gratitude to the authors and to the translators Timothy Stroud, Patricia Chen, Simon Pleasance, and Helen Boulac.

Special thanks to Béatrice Arnaud, Carolyn Bailey, Gelsey Bell, Nicole Birmann Bloom, Suzanne Buracas, Thomas Michelon, Toni Pape.

Graphic design:
Franck Gautherot

Cover by M/M Paris

Printed in France
in January 2014
by Présence graphique, Monts